US FOREIGN POLICY IN WORLD HISTORY

Has the United States contributed to the promotion of liberty and justice through its foreign policy?

US Foreign Policy in World History is a survey of US foreign relations and its perceived crusade to spread liberty and democracy in the two hundred years since the American Revolution. This book explores whether consciousness and 'spirit' has been the main motivating force in US foreign affairs or whether in reality it has been driven by materialism. David Ryan undertakes a systemic and material analysis of US foreign policy, whilst also explaining the policy makers' grand ideas, ideologies and constructs that have shaped US diplomacy.

US Foreign Policy explores these arguments by taking a thematic approach structured around central episodes and ideas in the history of US foreign relations and policy making, including:

- The Monroe Doctrine, its philosophical goals and its impact
- Imperialism and expansionism
- Decolonization and self-determination
- The Cold War
- Third World development
- The Soviet 'evil empire', the Sandinistas and the 'rogue' regime of Saddam Hussein
- The process of economic integration in US foreign affairs

David Ryan is Principal Lecturer in History at De Montfort University, Leicester.

THE NEW INTERNATIONAL HISTORY SERIES
Edited by Gordon Martel
Professor of History at the University of Northern British Columbia, and Senior Research Fellow at De Montfort University

EXPLAINING AUSCHWITZ AND HIROSHIMA
History writing and the Second World War, 1945–1990
R. J. B. Bosworth

IDEOLOGY AND INTERNATIONAL RELATIONS IN THE
MODERN WORLD
Alan Cassels

GLOBAL COMMUNICATIONS, INTERNATIONAL AFFAIRS AND
THE MEDIA SINCE 1945
Philip M. Taylor

THE CARIBBEAN BASIN
An international history
Stephen J. Randall and Graeme S. Mount

REVOLUTIONARY ARMIES IN THE MODERN ERA
J. P. MacKenzie

US FOREIGN POLICY IN WORLD HISTORY

David Ryan

London and New York

First published 2000
by Routledge
11 New Fetter Lane, London EC4P 4EE

Simultaneously published in the USA and Canada
by Routledge
29 West 35th Street, New York, NY 10001

Routledge is an imprint of the Taylor & Francis Group

© 2000 David Ryan

Typeset in Times by
BC Typesetting, Bristol
Printed and bound in Great Britain by
Biddles Ltd, Guildford and King's Lynn

British Library Cataloguing in Publication Data
A catalogue record for this book is available from the British Library

Library of Congress Cataloging in Publication Data
Ryan, David, 1965–
US foreign policy in world history/David Ryan.
p.   cm. – (New international history series)
Includes bibliographical references and index.
1. United States–Foreign relations.   I. Title.   II. Series.
E183.7 R9645 2000
327.73–dc21   00-036888

ISBN 0–415–12344–5 (hbk)
ISBN 0–415–12345–3 (pbk)

For Daniel Norman-Ryan,
Heidi Storeheier and Susan Ryan

. . . the richest development of human potentialities
can occur only in societies in which there is a wide spectrum of opinions
– the freedom for what J. S. Mill called 'experiments in living' –
in which there is liberty of thought and of expression,
views and opinions clash with each other,
. . . that subjection to a single ideology,
no matter how reasonable and imaginative,
robs men of freedom and vitality.

Isaiah Berlin
The Crooked Timber of Humanity, p. 46

CONTENTS

ACKNOWLEDGEMENTS

The academics that have supported and encouraged me in this project are too numerous to mention; though a special gratitude should be extended to Professor Gordon Martel who provided guidance and encouragement throughout. Thanks are also due to the librarians and archivists at the National Archives, The Library of Congress, The Nobel Institute, The London School of Economics and De Montfort University. In addition, I would like to thank De Montfort University, the Faculty of Humanities and Social Sciences and the Department of Historical and International Studies for providing the time to complete this book. My colleagues deserve thanks for providing a good atmosphere within which to work. At Routledge, special thanks to all who worked on the book, Heather McCallum, Victoria Peters, Gillian Oliver, Chris Hughes, Juliane Tschinkel and Margaret Deith.

Heidi Storeheier deserves special thanks for providing support throughout the process of research, writing and indexing. Daniel Norman-Ryan and Susan Ryan also provided constant support in their own idiosyncratic ways.

INTRODUCTION

Ideology and world system

Since Hegel and Marx historians have debated whether 'spirit' or materialism drove history. When Vaclav Havel, president of the former Czechoslovakia, addressed a joint session of Congress in 1990, he argued that Marx had got it wrong, that it was indeed consciousness that preceded being. The Hegelian dialectic gave precedent to the world of spirit and the realm of ideas.[1] Marx, on the other hand, argued that materialism drove history. At the end of the Cold War, in such august surroundings, President Havel was likely to celebrate the symbolic triumph of spirit over materialism. Democracy and self-determination were being restored to Eastern Europe. The people had asserted their sovereignty and liberty against the Soviet empire.[2] And given the western conceptual understanding of the Cold War, the United States stood for the victory of these ideas after its 'long-term' patient but firm containment of the Soviet Union. Such was the optimism of the period that one commentator revived the Hegelian method and argued that in fact History had come to an end. There was no better form of life, no higher consciousness for ideological development beyond liberal capitalist democracy.[3] These characteristics of governance were universally aspired to.

The strength of the idea of 'America', its ideals, democracy, liberty and self-determination, endure not only because these ideas and conditions of life are attractive, but because they were buttressed by a strong state that has also grown geographically, industrially, commercially and militarily for over two centuries. The 'national interest' became paramount in the construction of its foreign policies. The strength of its economy and its position within the world system was essential to its success, its identity, its influence and its hegemony. However, very particular ideological and economic national interests filled the history of US foreign policy with ideas and systems that undermined the liberty, democracy and self-determination of others.

1

The universalism and particularism that informed US policy can be captured in two recent debates. The End of History thesis posited that a set of values, ideas and institutions that was universal and progressive informed the meta-narrative of US foreign policy. But throughout its history the United States was also engaged in a 'clash of civilisations' that particularised US or later 'western' identity and animated its foreign policy against an ever-changing 'other' set of forces.

Coupled with this clash at the political and ideological levels there was the almost constant pursuit of economic integration, and once the United States had moved to the centre of the *world system*, an attempt to gain access to the economies, resources, labour and markets around the world. This systemic theory suggests that the world is divided into a hierarchy of zones from the *core* (the developed world) to the *periphery* (the Third World). The various economies exist in a symbiotic relationship. Third World poverty is functionally related to the wealth of the First World. Therefore, autarky or economic nationalism had to be overcome. Autonomous development or economic isolation retracted the nation-state from the world system that required 'that the market economy become global and integrated: a free world, one world'. McCormick explains:

> A single hegemonic power has a built-in incentive to force other nations to abandon their economic nationalism and protectionist controls and to accept a world of free trade, free capital flows, and free currency convertibility. As the world's dominant economic power, a hegemonic nation has the most to gain from such a free world, and the most to lose from nationalist efforts to limit the free movement of capital, goods, and currencies. So the predominant world power has an unequivocal self-interest in using its economic power as workshop and banker of the free world to create institutions and ground rules that foster the internationalization of capital. It finds it inherently advantageous to use its political power as ideologue of the world system to preach the universal virtues of freedom of the seas, free trade, Open Door policies, comparative advantage, and a specialized division of labor. It finds it necessary to use its military power as global policeman to protect the international system against external antagonists, internal rebellions, and internecine differences.[4]

The pursuit of an integrated economic system and universal prescriptions on the form of polity that best served the system again undermined national and individual sovereignty, self-determination and liberty.

Yet neither ideals nor materialism alone drove US foreign policy. Even though some world historians have attempted to eschew grand narratives or cosmic explanations, preferring to keep the zoo alive with real historical

animals to the exclusion of the 'mythical beasts', this book engages with
the metaphysical world of ideas and ideologies, with the material sphere of
the world system, and with the 'mythical beasts' constructions of the past.
The argument gives credence to systemic and material analyses, but it tries
to understand these by means of policy-makers' ideologies and the ideas
that shaped US diplomacy. But history was also driven by very influential
conceptual constructions on nationalism, identity and 'the West'.[5] For US
policy makers these may be accurate or not, but they were inspired by
various ideals, motivated by material interest and constrained or rewarded
by actual performance.

The United States emerged through what Eric Hobsbawm identified as
the twin revolutions of industrialisation and democratisation.[6] Americans
grappled with preserving their ideals while simultaneously engaging in and
integrating, philosophically and economically, wider and wider spheres of
influence. In the course of its history the US moved to the centre of a
world system that predated its existence by roughly 300 years. But participation in this system was coupled with the tendency to think and speak in
Manichaean terms, that is to create stark differences between new worlds
and old, the spheres of republicanism and monarchy, the 'free world' and
the totalitarian. Somewhat simplistic characterisations of the barbarians at
the gate motivated and galvanised US society. Diplomatic rhetoric 'orien-
talised' the 'other' and reduced a complex and often contentious past to
essential characteristics acceptable to the national consensus. Notions of
exceptionalism were preserved while the United States engaged with the
world. Ideologies conflate and reconcile the often contradictory material
and metaphysical forces that motivated policy. Reference to higher purposes, manifest destinies and nationalism facilitated the conceptual fusion.

Even though reconciliation occurred within US society, largely explained
by ideology, foreigners frequently looked on aghast at the apparent contradictions.[7] US hegemony extended over many parts of the continent or the
globe at various points, but there has always been resistance to their
expansion. When the threads of US diplomatic traditions find their way
into such seminal documents as the Declaration of Independence, the
Monroe message, the Open Door notes, the Fourteen Points, the Atlantic
Charter, the Truman Doctrine, on through to Clinton's *Strategy for
Engagement and Enlargement*, some people around the world are often
inspired and some look on with incredulity. It should also be stressed that
at most periods of US expansion, significant sectors of the 'domestic'
population, incredulous at the departure from assumed traditions, pro-
tested against the imperial agendas. Still, within the States there was an
eventual but powerful tendency towards reconciliation and national
consensus.

The evolution of US policy oscillated between the pursuit of power and
material opportunity on the one hand and the maintenance of its stated

ideals on the other. Ideologies, formal and informal, constantly adjust. So for instance when the limited sphere of traditional understanding on democracy was challenged, Madison invented a new expansive democracy that created a new synthesis in US thought. After considerable tension the new ideas were accepted and form the basis for ideologies that guide the nation towards its Manifest Destiny. Tensions are resolved through these values and later through the national collective memories. Reconciliation has remained a strong inclination. From new and expanded platforms the process began again. It played itself out in the debates on acquiring Texas and New Mexico again at the turn of the century, after the First and Second World Wars and after the Cold War. At each point the idea of America adjusted to include new opportunities. Beyond the contiguous borders the ability to extend hegemony was increasingly challenged, not only by opposing ideologies but also by various nationalists. Resistance to US hegemony was expressed least in areas where the population by and large benefited from the western system, that is, Western Europe. Hence the 'empire by invitation' thesis,[8] and the acceptance of the dominance of US power in NATO and elsewhere. Hegemony was also extended over areas that did not have the capacity to resist and pursue alternative visions. Propaganda was frequently used to extend the hegemonic vision and convince a sufficient array of forces that they would benefit from the system. The system for 'liberty', aligned as it was to free trade, was often not accepted willingly.

The tension between democracy and capitalism[9] is particularly noteworthy in this framework. In early US diplomacy expansion eased the problems of democracy. Madison's Tenth Federalist Paper is the seminal work in the modern period to invert the understanding that democracies could exist in only small constituencies. The fidelity to an economic equality of opportunity strengthened the notion that the system was more democratic. Still, 'democracy' depended on an expansive system. But the notion of 'the people', the citizens and the polity was quite exclusive.

The expanding spheres of influence and trade expansion are constants in the history of US foreign policy. In the liberal formula free trade enhanced prosperity and peace, which in turn enhanced democracy. These beliefs persisted through the twentieth century, through the writing of the modernisation theorists and their intellectual descendants, and found their ultimate expression in Francis Fukuyama's thesis on the 'End of History'.[10]

The actuality of the expansionist republic and then later the integrating centre of the world economy has undermined the prospects for democracy in many ways. The antithesis to the progressive, liberal and now neo-liberal formula suggests that the combination of the two seems to make a mockery of the vital elements of both. The combination of a global economy with a politically particular system designed around nation-states seems untenable. The power and influence of one erodes the constituency and the consent of individuals and nations in the other. States aid in the process of globalisation, but the effects of the global economy make nonsense of several fundamentals in democratic theory: consent, constituency, legitimacy. David Held argues that capitalism has never been a force bound by the nation-state for too long. Its tendency is to operate in pursuit of opportunity. For US citizens this may have enhanced their prospects for democracy and may have secured their way of life. But democracy '*in* nation-states has not been accompanied by democratic relations *among* states'.[11] Beyond these arguments the expansionist system has undermined concepts of self-determination, liberty, nationalism and democracy for others who do not agree with or succumb to the growth in US power and hegemony.

Liberty and the philosophy of history

A further contradiction arises in the combination of philosophies of history and polity based on progress within the nation-state, of political ideas essentially limited by jurisdictional boundaries and the perpetuation of an unbound economic system. That contradiction is between what Isaiah Berlin distinguished as negative and positive liberty. Negative liberty is essentially the idea of not being interfered with. Freedom extends to the point at which the limits of non-interference are guaranteed. By positive freedom Berlin means the ability to be one's own master, to determine one's own fate, to be a conscious agent of one's destiny.[12]

These distinctions are important when US foreign policy is being considered in conjunction with the broad conceptions that inform the basis of the US' identity and action. Liberty and the notion of progress in its prescriptive and exclusive form are not compatible. Within the United States, negative liberty was, to a certain extent, guaranteed to some. The Constitution ultimately provided for rights that could be exercised in theory at least. It is still well to remember, as Michael Foley indicates, that there is a darker side to the experience of freedom within the US. Recall the alternative narratives of the indentured system of servitude, the exclusion of women until recently, slavery, 'the genocidal clearance of Indian tribes', child labour, the 'intolerant nativism of the Ku-Klux-Klan', McCarthyite 'anti-communism', the internment of Japanese American citizens, and 'the continuing presence of ethnic and racial discrimination in the twentieth century'. Yet in foreign arenas the conception of freedom advanced by the United States is that of a nation that fought a civil war and two world wars to advance the cause of freedom; in the face of communism, Kennedy proclaimed that the United States would 'pay any price [and] bear any burden . . . to assure the survival and success of liberty'.[13]

When freedom replaced God in the narrative of historical progress, the United States found purpose for its foreign policy. The idea of freedom is still present in US historiography. For William McNeill, 'the core idea was simple enough: what mattered in history was the sporadic but ineluctable advance of Freedom'. Accordingly, other nations joined the historical narrative when they were 'discovered, settled, or conquered by Europeans'. Freedom may have been defined at the frontiers, but these peripheral locations, vital to conceptions of identity, were also sites of conquest and oppression. As space was conquered through colonialism, liberated and reincarnated as Manifest Destiny, time was conquered through exclusive narratives of progress.[14]

The crucial point to be made is provided by Anders Stephanson's distinction in Jefferson's thought and US foreign policy more generally, between the 'empire of liberty' and the 'empire for liberty'.[15] In the latter formulation and through the exertion of US power, influence, intervention, or hegemony, one not only sees a regular violation of the negative liberties of others but also, through the promulgation of universal conceptions of history and progress, the violation of their positive liberties. In the international sphere the pursuit of positive liberty, the search for recognition, for national self-determination has been denied through direct political interference and through the limitations on sovereignty brought on by the world system. The imposition of any system, even if benign, is a violation of the positive liberties of others. Action taken in the political or economic realm to insist on conformity to various political, intellectual, or economic systems has repeatedly violated the negative liberty, not just of sovereign states but also of the human rights of individuals.[16]

The 'American Century'

Throughout the twentieth century participants in the world system[17] have become increasingly conscious of US power and ideology. This has been actualised in many benign and brutal ways and is represented in the speeches of dignitaries, the cultural artefacts, commodities and symbols of the nation. In diplomatic terms one thinks of the profound impact of President Wilson's 'Fourteen Points', Franklin Roosevelt's 'Four Freedoms' and Reagan's rhetorical impact during periods of momentous change. Beyond the symbolic, the US economy grew enormously in both relative and absolute terms. And beyond the economic, US power was manifest in conflict throughout the century. Proclamations on New World Orders were released on three distinct occasions, during the First and Second World Wars, and after the Gulf War. Through each period, though not uncontested, the United States set the agenda and assumed 'world leadership'. Though each presidency brought its own identity to US foreign policy, reflecting the president's beliefs and ambitions, his party's traditions and inclinations, there have been some consistent elements that have run through US policy. At the end of the Cold War and with victory in the Gulf, US diplomats assumed their policies had been vindicated. Unleashed from various systems and mentalities of containment, once again, the Clinton administration could put US policy in a positive framework, presented as the *Strategy for Engagement and Enlargement*. Though the narrative has not been linear or unbroken, the contention here is that this strategy has been a constant in US foreign policy.

That famous and enduring article in *Life* magazine provided the apogee of a US[18] expression of its place in our world. In 1941 Henry Luce, editor of the magazine, identified the century as 'American'. Many of Luce's phrases or sentences could have been uttered by a number of the presidents mentioned above. For Luce thought of America

> as the dynamic center of ever-widening spheres of enterprise, America as the training center of the skillful servants of mankind, America as the Good Samaritan, really believing again that it is more blessed to give than to receive, and America as the power-house of the ideals of Freedom and Justice – out of these elements surely can be fashioned a vision of the 20th Century to which we can and will devote ourselves in joy and gladness and vigor and enthusiasm.

Practically, his argument was designed to overcome the isolationist sentiments that had gripped the national political imagination in the 1930s. He saw that 'The vision of America as the principal guarantor of the freedom of the seas, the vision of America as the dynamic leader of world trade, has within it the possibilities of such enormous human progress as to stagger the imagination'. Yet he asked the nation not to be staggered by the vision, but to rise to 'its tremendous possibilities'.[19]

This book is essentially a world history of US foreign policy during the 'American Century'. It will examine history as a narrative of progress, closely associated with the formal ideologies of US foreign policy in conjunction with an analysis of its integrative power and influence in the world system. At times it will naively assume that US politicians mean what they say. Whether this is the case or not would have to be examined on a case by case basis. The primary reason for according value to presidential speeches is that they capture or shape the mood of the nation through the prominent annual addresses, and they certainly speak to the constructions of US identity. In foreign policy these words, coupled with the sacred documents of the nation, provide meaning and identity in an otherwise bewildering world.

The constructions of the traditions of US diplomacy are examined in the first three chapters. The purpose of Part I is to set up three fundamental constructs that remain enduring influences in twentieth-century US diplomacy. These are the contradictory combination of empire with liberty, of universalism with particularism exemplified through the Monroe Doctrine and the search for Open Door economies. Chapter 1 is about the inherent contradiction that lies at the heart of US policy, its tendency to be at once aloof from and engaged in world affairs. A paradox emerged with the postulation that US culture was both exceptional and messianic. In Washington's attempt to extend its model to the world it contributed to the demise of its exceptionalism or its uniqueness. Insisting it was different, the US, through its foreign policy, sought to make others more like itself. And yet its views on the hierarchy of race and cultural exclusivity suggested that 'others' were unfit to adopt such a system. Serge Ricard argues that this

> brand of republican messianism that was to be invoked to justify later territorial aggrandizements was derived from the . . . postulate of American uniqueness; but rested on an irreducible contradiction that would forever vitiate U.S. foreign policy: the basic incompatibility of the exceptionalist claim with political messianism, of singularity with universalism. This fundamental ambiguity largely accounts for the incoherence and the inconsistencies of the American diplomatic tradition.[20]

A benevolent narrative on the promotion of self-determination centred on republican and democratic government remains influential. Yet from the outset the nascent states were expansionist. They created an empire, albeit republican, that eventually occupied the width of the continent by 1853, and by the close of the century incorporated Alaska and Hawaii. As with all the chapters in Part I, the idea is not to trace the intricacies of contemporary politics and history but to identify the origins of various traits that continue to exercise influence on the collective memories of society and policy makers in the twentieth century. The chapter therefore examines ideas associated with the collective memories of the revolution and the initiation of national identities. It examines the self-perception of the US as the 'project of mankind' and the messianic tendencies in US diplomacy, the belief that the United States should serve as an example to others.

Chapter 2 traces the constructs related to the evolution of the Monroe Doctrine. Even though the doctrine was written with specific political and imperial ambitions in mind, it was couched in the language of self-determination and republicanism. The United States suggested that it would consider it dangerous to its peace and safety if the Europeans attempted to recolonise the Western Hemisphere. The doctrine unleashed ideas that at once strengthened the anti-colonial sentiment and carved out a US sphere of influence. With the conceptual division of the world into the new and the old, Washington enhanced its Manichaean outlook on a complex and heterogeneous world; simultaneously it imbued US diplomacy with a moral tone and a crusading spirit.

Chapter 3 does not deal with the process of Manifest Destiny, the acquisition of the continent, former Mexican territories, or the consolidation of the political union following the Civil War. These events are undoubtedly of tremendous importance to US history, but the objective here is to set up the three predominant constructs that have influenced US diplomacy throughout the twentieth century. The one salient feature that needs to be identified, though, is the tremendous might of the United States and the potential, both economic and political, that it harnessed from creating a nation out of a continent. From that continental base the United States grew to a point where increasing competition with the other world powers for access to 'peripheral' areas meant that it engaged in formal colonialism with the acquisition of the Philippines and then rejected that option through the pursuit of Open Door expansionism.

These constructions are important because they form the assumed, sometimes invented traditions that have informed policy making throughout the twentieth century. How the 'collective past' is understood is important in coming to terms with how foreign policy is made. There are a number of tensions and contradictions that run through the traditions of US foreign policy, but these are assimilated and reconciled in the culture through various mental strategies, cognitive or not. Constructions of the past are extremely influential. To some extent, as Fernández-Armesto puts it, 'The course of history is influenced less by events as they happen than by the constructions – often fanciful, often false – which people put on them.'[21] Reference to these traditions and 'semi-sacred' documents buttress the advocacy of certain policies and mitigate potential dissent.[22]

Myths

The nearly deified traditions of US diplomacy over time serve the same function as cultural myths. Cultural stories stabilise and organise society around acceptable ideas; they 'insure solidarity [and] guard against lawlessness and chaos'. They are also morality tales that not only seek inspiration from the past, real, imagined, or half-imagined, but also look to the future. They inspire and mobilise. Like ideology, myths integrate the national experience and serve as vehicles to overcome internal contradictions.[23]

There are multiple representations of the past in most modern societies. Professional history, though important, does not necessarily have widespread impact except through the earlier years of education; and this is a simple narrative based around an orthodox interpretation. Other sites of collective memory[24] are more likely to assume the functions of myth. Though the process is never neat or complete in any sense, the analysis of

9

myth can help us to understand the popular acquisition of knowledge on foreign policy and therefore the parameters within which politicians necessarily operate. The analysis of myth and history is illuminating when one considers the desire for consensus in US policy circles. Constructing consensus has usually involved 'principled forgetfulness' of the past that cannot be culturally separated from 'its ethical meaning in the present'.[25]

Especially in foreign policy, where government is centralised and relatively exclusive, the ability to shape perceptions is strong. Moreover, when the US acts abroad, the nation has generally deferred to executive authority. Its legitimacy often rests on the 'manufacture of consent' through 'necessary illusions'.[26] The structures and the process through which information is both gathered and distributed have created a revolution in democratic theory. Free choice and consent on issues beyond the individual experience are increasingly reliant on centralised and commercially driven media; the construction and reporting of foreign policy are constrained by institutions and a national media with little ideological pluralism. Free choice is constrained by the operations of these narrow, and often nationalistic, frameworks. Hegemony is enhanced through this process of acquiring consent. There is a tendency to universalise the conception of identity. It provides an instrumentalist function, which ultimately permits those involved to naturalise the notions of identity.

Identity

Foreign relations were and are fundamental to US identity. Ultimately, identity relies on various forms of communication, description and representation. These processes are clearer in foreign policy than in the domestic US political sphere. Ideas that contribute to the national identity are generally formed from above, though those who formulate them must understand and feed the desires, the hopes and aspirations of the people within the Union. The diplomatic representation of the nation to others was essentially a centralised project. Documents such as the Declaration of Independence and the Monroe Doctrine have a lasting effect. In the American mind, they became the signifiers of United States identity to a wider world. In the absence of a shared past, the search for identity produced narratives of difference and exception. National identities focused on what the Americans were not, their practices and values were set apart from and above those of the Europeans of the 'old' world. The culture, which for present purposes is associated with the nation, necessarily had to forget the past which was shared with the Europeans. Collective memories had to be guided so that the Old World could be eradicated from the national narratives and then forgotten, to facilitate the process of nation building. History and democratic nationalism served each other. Some experiences (slavery and slaughter) that were incompatible with the righteous image of the nation were basically written out of the sites of collective memory. The diverse histories of the various colonial experiences were fused into a national narrative, taught for generations and to new immigrants. And ultimately these narratives, which fused individualism and democracy, 'acquired the force of uncontested truth'. The new 'cause of all mankind', as Paine put it, promised redemption from the vices of the Old World. New beginnings are always attractive after prolonged conflict. Lincoln's Gettysberg Address not only promised new departures but convinced the nation that they really did stand for a system of 'government of the people, by the people, for the people'.[27] New beginnings were offered after the most significant conflicts of the twentieth century too.

In many ways the national culture, through its interactions with others at the frontiers and the peripheries, where identity is usually more vigorous, makes a sharp distinction between 'us' and 'them'. The moral tone of US diplomacy, coupled with the need to maintain cohesion, has resulted in an often-combative xenophobia.[28]

In constructing identity, US culture and the various public pronouncements tended to reduce a heterogeneous and complex world to finite and comprehensible terms. The ideological imperatives that operate simultaneously with a reductionist understanding of the world ultimately suggest 'appropriate ways of dealing with . . . reality'.[29] In the history of US foreign policy there has been a tendency to regard opponents as threats, and homogeneous ones at that. Given the moral and exceptionalist inclinations, the tendency has been not to negotiate on equal terms, especially in the twentieth century, but to preach, admonish others and direct the supposed course of history. The consequences have often been tragic. Peoples and nations around the world have been characterised and then categorised according to this Manichaean outlook.[30]

A few instances will illustrate the point. Often, the discourses represent continuations of those that pitted civilisation against barbarism or, in a more subtle and recent formulation, the tendency towards what Said has identified as 'orientalism', that is, the tendency to regard others from afar and in some ways from above.[31] The discourse has existed through several periods. US civilisation was pitted against the 'savage' Native Americans or the 'backward' Latin Americans. Another bipolar conceptual division emerged through the Monroe Doctrine. Monroe warned the Old World against any intentions to colonise the Western Hemisphere. In an abstract sense the world had been conceptually divided somewhere in the Atlantic, somewhere between the States and the metropolitan centres of Europe. The United States was ostensibly out to protect the nascent democracies of the western world, to shore up republican government in the western sphere. Latin cultural and political diversity was ignored as the Latin countries were conceptually gathered into the New World of republican democracy. US policy suffered from the contradiction between universal and exceptional attitudes. Washington viewed its southern neighbours, from an orientalist outlook on 'otherness', as barbarians, but also included them in the first ambitious step towards western hegemony. Theodore Roosevelt's corollary to the Monroe Doctrine epitomised the division: they belonged to us, but they were the 'other'. The identities of both the United States and the 'other' were essentialised.

During the early years of the Cold War this division was extended to the Elbe, or to the imaginary Iron Curtain. One senator explicitly exhorted the White House to scare the hell out of the American people if the politicians intended to mobilise society to fight the new war, the Cold War against a new set of barbarians, the Russian communists. Again the 'enemy' was caricatured and essentialised. Further, various movements pushing for social or international change, whether socialist or nationalist, were subsumed within a single category and wherever possible identified as Soviet clients. A polycentric world was more difficult to deal with but, perhaps as importantly, it would be considerably more difficult to unify and solidify not just the 'West' but also internal US society, without a singular opponent. The reductionism of the Cold War mentality identified a homogeneous enemy, with disastrous consequences, especially in Vietnam. Expressions of social or economic change were filtered through the Cold War prism. Such categorisation assisted in the management of information overload and provided a clear direction to US policy. Complexity was shunned at the conceptual level and simplicity was rewarded in the political process. By the late 1950s, everyone knew that 'Egypt's Gamal Abdel Nasser is another Adolf Hitler. Guatemala's Jacobo Arbenz must be a Communist. If it looks like a duck and acts like a duck, it is a duck.'[32] It was assumed, axiomatically, that the duck was fed in Moscow. And when Moscow ran out of food Saddam Hussein became Hitler incarnate.

It is an irony that after the experience in Vietnam the US public was far less willing to accept Reagan's simplistic characterisations of the Sandinistas in the 1980s. But after the Cold War had been won, and methods devised to fight wars without soldiers, the society was again willing to swallow the simplistic yet potent characterisation of Hussein. Avoiding complexity facilitated the attempts to manufacture and maintain a consensus on US objectives. Maintaining the consensus required constant reference to essential identities filtered through ideology.

Such intellectual devices reduced the propensity of other powers to move off in centrifugal directions. Yet powers seek not just security but also respect and the ability to determine their own agenda. Polycentrism and pluralism, however, are inconvenient to the core of the world system. The prospects for pluralism, assertions of self-determination and the pursuit of localised democracy are diminished accordingly. Such essentialisation resulted in intolerance both towards other cultures and within the United States. This reductionist thought process, perhaps a systemic imperative, the desire for a clearly identifiable enemy, was a step towards illiberty in the domestic sphere and abroad.

Binary oppositions rarely exist before they are constructed conceptually. But then nationalists and the imperial powers cherish them. Simplicity polarises the debate between nations and serves the interests of those that maintain their power through confrontation. Diplomatic compromise in such contexts is rare. 'Throughout the exchange between Europeans and their "others" that began systematically half a millennium ago, the one idea that has scarcely varied is that there is an "us" and a "them", each quite settled, clear, unassailably self-evident.'[33]

The power to narrate is important. In US foreign relations an ongoing struggle has ensued in the historiography. These writings speak to the identity of the nation.

National meanings

'Nations themselves are narrations.' This was perhaps never more important in constructing the 'imagined community'[34] of the United States. Without uniform ethnicity, without shared religious beliefs, or without a 'common fund of stories, only a shared act of rebellion, America had to invent what Europeans inherited: a sense of solidarity, a repertoire of national symbols, a quickening of political passions'. The narratives created or invented in the decades after independence and continuously after that were powerful forces. Without shared experience, national meanings were often constructed in terms of oppositions. Ideologies, identities and national myths were constructed through the national narratives and the collective memories that were eventually formed. For instance, the Declaration of Independence and the Gettysberg Address were powerful symbols in the constructed narration of the community. The narratives of the nation induce a respect and subservience. They act as filters through which complex information can be processed. 'The power to narrate, or to block other narratives from forming and emerging, is very important to culture and imperialism, and constitutes one of the main connections between them.'[35]

The stories told and not told provide the foundations of national meaning. Understanding and knowledge about the nation and the sphere beyond the nation are acquired through nationalistic inclinations, with all their attendant values, ideologies and myths. Knowledge is constantly filtered to suit contemporary needs, whether this is a conscious process or not. Major national pronouncements engage thoroughly with the national symbols and the narratives of the nation. As suggested above, authorities need to genuflect in the direction of these stories, semi-sacred texts and doctrines, to maintain a congruence and cohesion within the nation. Such rhetoric is essential in the political process and in diplomatic discourse.

Historical narratives are as much constructions of the past as various theoretical or systemic approaches. They are stories told by historians or other cultural interlocutors, which generally organise material chronologically, focusing on a single coherent story. In the case of US foreign policy much of the story has focused on the march of democracy and liberty. But it is well to recognise that narratives are culturally bound, they exist within society and all the attendant intellectual, institutional and material forces compromise their objectivity. They are constructions that facilitate particular purposes. Nationalism is particularly susceptible to the shared narratives of the so-called 'imagined communities'. As Renan put it: 'Getting its history wrong is part of being a nation.'[36]

While recognising that national narratives are culturally bound, it is also important to understand that in constructing such stories the audience achieves closure and coherence to an otherwise disorganised and libertarian past. The process of organisation through narration 'imposes an unavoidable "continuity, wholeness, closure and individuality that every 'civilised' society wishes to see itself incarnating"'. It produces law-abiding citizens through the interaction with the imperatives of ideology.[37]

This analysis integrates the constructs, the material and national interests with ideology. An understanding of informal US ideology facilitates an understanding of, in particular, US nationalism. Yet material interests are often written out of public depictions of US foreign relations, except in the form that free trade and liberal democratic capitalism are major forces for progress in world history. Through this prism, democracy, liberty, justice and self-determination, for instance, are enhanced by free trade. Undoubtedly, these beliefs are held from time to time in some quarters and always in others.

The Enlightenment discourses were supposed to be integrative, inclusive and universal. These were values and ideas put forward for all 'mankind'. The crux of the problem was that such values and rights were at first only applied to certain white male citizens, only later widened to include others, and then but slowly. Still, Enlightenment discourses and world history were constrained by the institutional structures of the nation-state; and here they became exclusive, particular and partial. In the case of the United States, some say 'exceptional'. While democracy, liberty and self-determination were previously considered guarded by the state, the global economy grew to undermine notions of consent and constituency that are so vital to democratic theory. There is a lag in this instance between being and consciousness. The constructions of how things are, often produced through presidential rhetoric, all too often assumed that existing conditions are the product of a natural state of affairs. Moreover, as Said perceptively comments, the 'rhetoric of power all too easily produces an illusion of benevolence when deployed in an imperial setting'.[38]

14

Ideology, broadly understood to include cultural symbols and values, provides a nation and society with both purpose and a worldview.[39] Ideology explains our unconscious relationship with the world, and 'the ways in which we are pre-reflectively bound up in social reality'. Ideology reflects nostalgia and hope; an inaccurate past is projected into the future, and reality is often a casualty. This understanding of ideology is particularly important to US foreign policy because it engages with the narratives of the nation, posits a purpose for the United States in the world, and situates the nation within progressive discourses. Particularly pertinent for US diplomacy, ideology is a matter 'of fearing and denouncing, reverencing and reviling, all of which then sometimes gets coded into a discourse which looks as though it is describing the way things actually are'. Still, ideologies are more than 'imposed illusions'. There is enough reality in the ideological narratives to lend them social credibility. From such coherent understandings of the past and the present, ideology helps to form the basis of the national identity, through which individuals find motivation to translate ideas into action.[40] Ideological knowledge envelops contradictory concepts and gives them a coherent cultural meaning. For Clifford Geertz, 'ideology bridges the gap between things as they are and as one would have them be, thus insuring the performance of roles that might otherwise be abandoned in despair or apathy'.[41] In US foreign policy ideology locates the nation within the world, and its messianic tendencies induce moral action to 'shape a better future'.[42] For Hunt, the use of ideology in understanding US foreign policy induces us to 'focus on the consciousness of policymakers and the cultural values and patterns of privilege that shape that consciousness'.[43] This book combines a focus on ideology with the systemic economic expansion.

There is a basic incompatibility between democracy and self-determination and US expansion, both continental and global. US ideology, buffeted by the success and rise in world power of the States, has an intimate relationship to US nationalism. US history and foreign policies have been characterised by competing nationalisms. One relates to the territorial state and is located in the discourse of national security and defence procedures. The other was more closely associated with the ideals of the nation, the ideologies and the political beliefs that inspired generations.[44] US expansionism often violated the republican ideals, because the 'American way of life' was imposed on others without their consent. Simultaneously, nationalism was enhanced because the territorial aggrandisement further protected the nation, and therefore the institutions, ideas and the 'American way of life'. Throughout its history, various justifications for this evangelical foreign policy of conquest and hegemony have existed.[45]

All thinking is ideological; it takes place within 'webs of significance' that the culture has spun for itself. Thus, ideology derives from the 'socially established structures of meaning' associated with various systems of symbols, values and beliefs. It was an 'extraordinary ideological cocktail . . . concocted to assist an exceptional, and manifest, destiny'. The core ideas associated with the ideology helped the nation forge an identity, a sense of purpose and a character that were often forged in terms of opposition to other forces both real and imagined. Such opposition reinforces the coherence of the national narratives and the cohesion of the society. And the doctrines of national security limit the heterogeneity within the society. While a close symbolic relationship exists between US ideology and its concepts of nationalism, concurrently there has been an inclination to deny purely nationalistic motivations, as millennial tendencies, found throughout US history, have been influential.[46]

In the US the irony was that the nation was 'born into the modern world'. Its very particular narrative was simultaneously incorporated into the universal Enlightenment values and beliefs. Throughout there has been a dance of compromise, compliment and deceit. Nationalism worked as both a progressive and a regressive force in history. For instance, Wilsonian self-determination in the face of European empires was progressive. But the self-determination against European empires demanded by Ho Chi Minh in 1919 was problematic. Nationalism exercised against autarkic empires or US adversaries was encouraged, though nationalism that operated against the world system was rarely tolerated.

The second part of the book explores US policy in more depth, centred on the issues of self-determination, liberty, democracy, economic integration and dualistic political constructs. Chapter 4 traces the foundations of US power in the twentieth century. It examines US regional power, commercialism and the propagation of Wilsonian ideals. Even though the US advocated conditions of free trade and exchange, the state was at the centre of the system, promoting economic activity and preserving its centrality through preparations for war. War and the national security state have been central features of US policy throughout the twentieth century. The implications for democracy, liberty and self-determination have been profound.[47]

Chapter 5 traces the changes in the world system, the support for and retreats from decolonisation after the Second World War. The integrative economic system and the descent into Cold War compromised the attendant concepts of democracy and self-determination. The following chapter then focuses much more specifically on the structures and ideologies associated with the Cold War which influence the future struggles on development, revolution, democracy and self-determination. Chapter 6 is more concentrated in time and space than either chapter 5 or chapter 7. Its principal purpose is to identify the changes in ideology, economy and policy that the origins of the Cold War introduced. In many ways these changes were grafted onto the traditions of US diplomacy, which lent them even greater force and legitimacy. The Truman Doctrine, 'a defining choice in world history', extended the concept of two spheres and made essential the characteristics of both the West and the East. Differences within each bloc were played down. The Marshall Plan facilitated the integration of the western economies, but had more far-reaching consequences for the Third World and for issues of nationhood and self-determination. And finally the Manichaean world of NSC 68 activated US policy, galvanising the consensus within government and propelled containment to a global scale.

Chapter 7 continues the examination of liberty, self-determination and democracy in the Third World during the Cold War. By examining US responses to nationalism, revolution and development one can identify the areas in which the formal ideologies of the United States on democracy and national self-determination were frequently undermined by economic imperatives. The preponderance of the world system often necessitated the adoption of radical ideologies on the internal organisation of Third World societies.

Sandinista Nicaragua challenged the United States with very western conceptions of democracy and self-determination, just as Washington encouraged such values in Eastern Europe. Chapter 8 explores the increased militarisation of US society at the end of the Cold War and the destruction of democracy, the abuse of human rights, and the violation of sovereignty in Nicaragua. The Sandinistas' crime was that they were located on the wrong side of the conceptual construct that informed Reagan's foreign policy and that they challenged the neo-liberal economic order and regional politics sustained by repressive regimes backed by Washington. Chapter 9 closes with an examination of current trends. In recent foreign policy, economic integration has moved to the fore, especially in so far as Russia, Eastern Europe and China are concerned. The universal values were celebrated in the End of History thesis, and as that passed serious attention was given to the new potential 'clash of civilisations'.

'Sir Isaiah Berlin, following Hegel, has described the history of thought and culture as "a changing pattern of great liberating ideas which inevitably turn into suffocating straitjackets".'[48] The past accepted as singular, without questioning, with national purpose, with design, becomes a prison for the future and for 'others'; liberating for the peddlers of national purpose. For Berlin, pluralism has been central to the conception of history. It was a rejection of deterministic visions or systems which, with John Stuart Mill, he posits, 'robs men of freedom and vitality'. Concepts of liberty need pluralism, not only across space and cultures but also across time. History as a narrative on progress, without recognition of pluralism, with the constant and insistent rhetoric of US leadership, has in this sense denigrated the possible alternatives.

17

Enlightenment ideas, practised in an exclusive national sense and within the world system, have imposed structures of thought, economy and sovereignty the world over. During the 'American Century' US foreign policy has found expression and liberation through such straitjackets.[49]

Part I

CONSTRUCTIONS

1

THE EMPIRE FOR LIBERTY

The three initial chapters are not so much concerned with the intricacies of US policy in the eighteenth or nineteenth centuries. Their primary concern is to identify and to develop an understanding of three significant constructions that have remained potent forces throughout twentieth-century US policy making. The first concerns itself with the development of the collective memories and ideological assumptions that are frequent reference points in US diplomacy. The second examines the foundations of a 'spheres of influence' approach to policy making and the manner in which various universal ambitions are tempered by practical necessity or an inability to extend the sphere unchallenged. The third chapter examines questions of imperialism, both territorial and commercial. The traits of idealism, realism and the pursuit of economic opportunity or material interests have not only been reflected in the divisions of US historiography but continue to throw up contradictory forces in contemporary US foreign relations.

Despite the inherent contradictions, US foreign relations have been flexible and adaptable, evolving always to suit the needs of the US.[1] Aspiring to universal virtue in its public discourses, it is a foreign policy embedded in a type of nationalism not defined alone by territorial limits. US nationalism encompassed the formal ideologies associated with the beliefs in liberty and democracy, and a belief that free trade was symbiotic with these. The formal ideologies are frequently referred to in various presidential addresses: they have sometimes provided the motivation for policy and at others have disguised other intentions. The concepts associated with the formal ideologies ultimately became axiomatic, almost systemic. The foundations of these ideologies are found in the revolutionary era, through the enunciation of the Monroe Doctrine and subsequent Manifest Destiny, and through the political conflict centred on imperialism and Open Door economics in the late nineteenth century. Coupled with these, there were the informal ideologies, understood as 'a coherent, mutually reinforcing body of ideas that gives structure and meaning to the way policy makers and the broader public concerned with international affairs see the world and the American place in it'. Americans emerged with visions of national greatness, views on their racial superiority, and an aversion to immoderate revolution.[2]

Despite early and persistent messianic visions, the United States had to compete with other forces of progress and change in the world. Of course there were challenges, both internal and external, but even as the US was facing these, ideology provided policy makers with a reference point and an ability to adapt to their needs: 'they provided continuity when policy-makers shucked off the old doctrines and replaced them with new ones such as collective security, containment, and development theory'.[3]

The traditions of US diplomacy were crafted through the combination of beliefs, visions and interaction with the world outside. They were buttressed by the ongoing success of US diplomacy, which had a cumulative effect of reinforcement through experience. First there is the history and the more powerful collective memories of the American Revolution and the War of Independence, the idea that they were born into the modern world: they were children of the Enlightenment. The immediate implication of this construct was that they were different. They were separated from the Old World not only by the width of the Atlantic but also through their conceptions of exceptionalism. Second, strong messianic tendencies run through US diplomacy. Thomas Paine's pamphlet *Common Sense* is a symbolic example of the US's inclination to view itself, as he put it, as the 'project' for 'mankind'. The United States would provide the example, the political doctrines or the economic models for others to emulate, though there were frequent contradictions between the means and ends of US policy, and between what Washington expected from others and the history of the US's own experience. A contradiction was apparent from the beginning and Jefferson in particular was aware of it: how does one reconcile the promotion of liberty, democracy and self-determination with the constant expansion of first the United States and then its economic and cultural power? There was a recurrent tension between isolationism and engagement. Third, the Declaration of Independence set out goals that would for ever inform US policy. There were political liberties to be sought after and economic grievances to be addressed. The policies of Presidents George Washington and Thomas Jefferson and the writings of Jefferson and James Madison left profound legacies to the future, in both theory and practice. How ironic it was when Ho Chi Minh declared Vietnamese independence in 1945 along such similar lines as had Jefferson.

Born on the Fourth of July

Historical symbols are a far more important influence on twentieth-century ideologies than the actual histories of the US experience. The collective memories contributed to US identity and to the constructed images of itself that the US presented to the world. The identity of the nation portrayed through the significant state papers, the pronouncements each Fourth of July, influential speeches such as President Monroe's message, Lincoln's oration, the McKinley policies on the Open Door or Wilson's Fourteen Points, for example, often implicitly constructed an opposite through which the US character could be sharpened, brought more into focus.

The questions of whose history influences the ideological constructs of the twentieth century are always important. Policy makers and US diplomats are by and large representatives of a certain class in society: they are predominantly white, male, Protestant, harbouring the cultural baggage and material expectations associated with their previous success. For these people the symbols of the revolution invoke the grievances against British taxation, restrictions on their trade and on their movement west. They had no representation in the British Parliament. The Declaration of Independence symbolised the basis of separation, which was actualised through the War of Independence. While it was the first successful anti-colonial war in the modern period, it also represents one of the most advanced forms of white colonial expansion.[4] Unlike future wars for independence, the white colonials expelling the political authority of their former governors led the US revolution. Independence facilitated the process of future white expansion across the continent. Unlike the processes of decolonisation that characterised the rise of the nation-states in the late twentieth century, in which the indigenous populations rejected the foreign occupants, in America the foreign occupants were there to stay. The narratives associated with these experiences of colonialism and imperialism rarely entered the dominant ideologies held by the makers of US policy.

The literature on the revolution and the War of Independence is vast.[5] For the present purposes the most salient point is the construction of an identity of uniqueness, of exceptionalism. The thirteen states that unanimously proclaimed their independence from Britain were vast and disparate. The construction of a collective identity that united these different colonies was of paramount importance.[6] It made no sense to the colonial leaders that they should be governed without representation from three thousand miles away. The states had this in common. Beyond that there was little. They were treated differently by the British. The Southern states with complementary economies were permitted more freedom in trade that was not extended to the central and northern states. With their fleet of 1,500 boats, the British regulated their dealings, prohibiting direct contact with other colonies in the Caribbean or with the continental European powers.[7]

Despite the differences, a collective identity was important to cement the new unity against external hostility. It was found in the relatively unique experience of being born into the modern world. The social anthropologist Ernest Gellner indicates that the country has no 'collective memory' or even 'any haunting smell of' the Old World.[8] A tradition was invented that hung precariously between the creation of something new but retained the legitimacy that reference to the gravity of the past confers. Anders Stephanson writes:

> At the political level, this huge federation of states, with its potential for both growth and disintegration, had to confront the question of identity, what the national self might mean and how it might be projected. A set of simple symbols was required that would distil the past and at the same time proclaim the future. The extraordinary rapidity with which the Revolution was *monumentalized* actually showed the urgency: the revolutionary avant-garde turned into Founding Fathers, biblical patriarchs, Washington presiding as a near-deity, all evoked with ritual solemnity every July 4. In theory, there was otherwise nothing much one could put forth except subscription to the principles embodied in the Constitution, ultimately a purely political identity.[9]

Such practices provided the ideological legitimacy sought by the 'Fathers' of the new political entity. The revolution did not totally reject the past; it concurrently reaffirmed it, albeit a new past. The revolution did not reject the Lockean liberties associated with the Old World, but took place because they had been violated. The US revolutionary process is more accurately described as a war of independence. Though radical changes were to follow, the *Struggle for Power*, to use Draper's title, came first.[10] A part of this struggle was the construction of a separate identity.

As far as the subsequent US collective memory was concerned, the most famous passage in the preamble to the Declaration of Independence set the tone for the basis and future legitimacy of the government and of the existence of the United States. When Jefferson wrote the words: 'We hold these truths to be self evident, that all men are created equal, that they are endowed by their Creator with certain unalienable Rights, that among these are Life, Liberty, and the pursuit of Happiness', he was heavily influenced by the recent injection of political liberty, not only that of commercial freedom. Hitherto, Jefferson's writings had concentrated to a large degree on the commercial wrongs the colonies suffered. His first significant political contribution, two years before the Declaration, came with writings on the British prohibition on the American manufacture of fur hats, as 'an instance of despotism to which no parallel can be produced in the most arbitrary ages of British history'.[11] Between these two pieces, Paine's *Common Sense* appeared which separated the States and the Kingdom, not only in terms of commercial grievance but also on the issue of liberty.[12] This political element provided the crucial distinction between the two worlds, Old and New. Yet much of the grievance had been in actuality about commercial opportunities.

That pattern recurred throughout later US diplomacy. The political wrongs of US allies were frequently ignored when commercial opportunities were at stake. The political wrongs (despotism, tyranny, or the abuse of human rights) of opponents were constantly accentuated. In these instances the US liked to set itself apart: in the revolutionary period against the British, in President Monroe's diplomacy against the Old World, the Europeans, through the Open Door notes against colonialism, against fascism and then in Truman's Doctrine against communism. But working backwards through these examples, Washington saw little tyranny in Deng's 'communist' China, in the fascism of Pinochet's Chile, in the mandates or trusteeship territories that were open to US commerce and so forth. Crucially, political identity had to be constructed in terms of a binary opposition.

Yet the Old World powers were still very much a presence on the North American continent: the British in the north, the French to the west, and the Spanish to the south and west. With every ideological pronouncement against the Old World the nascent States invited a risk to their security, because tied to these announcements was a petulance and ambition that the Europeans perceived with some caution.

Politically, the United States promoted its difference around the manner in which political power was wielded. It would not be arbitrary, it would not be unaccountable, it would not be susceptible to capricious change by authoritarian dictate. Power would be checked and balanced through mutual scrutiny, it would be accountable to the representatives of the people, 'deriving their just powers from the consent of the governed'. And if 'any Form of Government becomes destructive to these ends, it is the Right of the People to alter or to abolish it' and form a new government most effective in ensuring security and happiness. Several grievances in the Declaration of Independence mention tyranny, consent, representation and arbitrary government. The collective intention among US leaders, the avant-garde revolutionaries, the conservative Founding Fathers, was to proclaim a difference. It was a self-conscious act of separation, of fragmentation from the world system that was dominated by European power and rivalry.[13]

The North American colonies had broken out of the system of empires and economic hegemony for reasons of both political dignity and economy just as Third World nations would attempt to do in the late twentieth century. The preamble to the Declaration struck the chord of fragmentation from the system that so sorely burdened it:

When in the course of human events, it becomes necessary for one people to dissolve the political bands which have connected them with another, and to assume among the Powers of the earth, the separate and equal station to which the Laws of Nature and of Nature's God entitle them, a decent respect to the opinions of mankind requires that they should declare the causes which impel them to the separation.[14]

How easily the Third World states of the late twentieth century could identify with these sentiments and the motivations to separate themselves from the prevailing world system in which their life, liberty and happiness were under constant threat! But by then the centre of global hegemony had passed across the Atlantic and the axis of Washington and New York was exercising much the same power as that against which their political forefathers had rebelled.

In the broader context of world history Americans were not that different from other people. But within a limited temporal context, and especially within the domestic context, their identity was deemed exceptional. The tendency towards absolutism caused Americans to believe that they had created something new, not relating to the Old World.[15] Questions on American exceptionalism (originally asked in pursuit of an understanding of why socialism was so limited) also suggested the country had no feudal past and therefore was almost entirely modern, middle class and liberal (at least comparatively speaking).[16] Prevailing thought suggested that this modern republic would become the new depository of civilisation. Given the beliefs that the course of civilisation moved ever westward and was extended by a single power, the idea was obviously attractive to colonies west of the original centres of Europe. Stephanson writes: 'To the American eye, it gave historical sanction to becoming the next great embodiment of civilisation. A series of "obvious" facts reinforced this view. . . . History could not conceivably evolve a better system of sustaining the liberty of man to permit the unfettered pursuit of his desires. Indeed, there could be nothing "higher," only more of the same.'[17] Similar thoughts resurfaced when Daniel Bell wrote of the end of ideology in the 1950s, and in the 1980s Francis Fukuyama suggested we had arrived at the End of History.[18]

The implications were immense for the future of US foreign relations. The 'exceptionalist syndrome' assumed that the New World was in part created by divine providence and therefore had 'a providential destiny and a universal mission'. The assertion of US power and rights was assumed to be natural. By the mid-nineteenth century they were justified through reference to manifest destinies, and later through discourses on progressivism, civilisation and modernisation.[19] In all cases the emphasis was on the modernist project of uplift and improvement. The moral tone of US diplomacy was cast from this mould. Morality was not the foundation but the cornerstone of US diplomacy. Propositions were put forward as self-evident, which made politics with the Old World and then with rival powers difficult, because compromise, traditionally a tool in diplomacy, was difficult without undermining the US's credibility and identity. Its diplomacy, engraved in principles of right, justice and liberty, was 'by and large non-negotiable'.[20]

Binary formulations often operate in the history of US diplomacy. Such conceptual divisions rarely accord with the more complex reality, but remain sufficiently attractive to impel their use. In another context Edward Said has explained that an 'orientalist' stance created a 'system of thought [that] approaches a heterogeneous, dynamic, and complex human reality from an uncritically essentialist standpoint; this suggests both an enduring Oriental reality and an opposing but no less enduring Western essence', which hides historical change and, in this case, hides US interests.[21] The past too is understood through ideological filters that have strengthened the benevolent narratives of US history. Ultimately these processes have affirmed the US's conceptions of itself in the world.[22]

Myths were (and are) potent forces. They tend to instruct, to codify beliefs; they act both to stabilise and to mobilise.[23] There is usually a threat from some 'other', real or imagined, that has affirmed the essential justice of US policy and mobilised the society towards confrontation, defence, or containment. Such threats have varied over time, but the simplistic binary characterisations would forever vitiate US policy, often removing the nuance from congressional oversight or the critical questioning from the media. At times the threat came from the 'merciless Indian Savages' as the Declaration identified the Native Americans, European empires, fascism, communism, Islam or President Clinton's bogeymen, the 'backlash states'. In the discourses that accompanied these engagements, the logic of civilisation and barbarism was never far away. There was a conscious sense in 1776 that the US was the locale for the new civilisation. Once independence had been secured, it remained to perfect the union and, as far as progressive history was concerned, to bring its project to an end.

The project of mankind

There is a messianic tendency that runs through US thought. In time the United States would provide the model for the world. The perfected Union would bring ideological development to an end; or, to go further still, according to Fukuyama's formulation, by the late 1980s History had ended. That self-conscious proposition was sparked off by the 1776 pamphlet *Common Sense*. Thomas Paine was largely written out of American memory even though John Adams considered him perhaps the most influential man of the age. *Common Sense* ignited the revolutionary spirit, and gave the revolution meaning; it injected freedom into the cause of the American colonies and that of 'mankind'. Paine was never considered a Founding Father, though he himself thought he could claim as much. When he died, the luminaries he had known were mostly 'embarrassed by the connection'. He was not eulogised, they 'wanted only to forget him. His papers were scattered and destroyed, and memory of him was allowed to fade.' He was an embarrassment, perhaps, because of his later attacks on organised Christianity (though from a deistic Quaker standpoint in the *Age of Reason* rather than that of the purported atheist) and because of his open letter against the government of George Washington, criticising it for its high-handedness.[24]

Yet Paine's influence was tremendous. *Common Sense* sold over 120,000 copies in three months in early 1776. Its publication had a tremendous impact on the momentum of the revolution, and was contemporaneously recognised by his friend Benjamin Rush, who indicated that 'its effects were sudden and extensive upon the American mind'.[25]

Critics, and there were many, pointed out that there was little original in his thinking and that he tended to reduce things to black and white. Nuance and the shades of grey were not a part of his analysis. Yet the force and popularity of his message were all the better served by such bluntness. The ability to speak truth to power served both to inspire and to mobilise a society. 'Paine's peroration strikes the universalist note of the Enlightenment; and what is remarkable about his political thought is not its originality, of which there is little, but the fact that it bounces back the truths of Enlightenment from the edge of the inhabited world to its centre.'[26] But when Third World nationalists bounced back similar truths in the twentieth century they were considered embarrassments, problems of public relations, or ignored in the face of larger strategic considerations. The centre of the world system had moved and such peripheral reminders of such truths became unwelcome.

Paine made the difference between the New and Old World more distinct. The material grievances pointed only to feelings of economic resentment. Freedom invoked an element of morality and improvement. America was to be the keeper of liberty for the people of the world, the guardian of Enlightenment values. But in this case, 'by serving themselves Americans would serve the world'.[27] The thinking had a contemporary basis. Even though aggressive nationalism was considered the enemy of Enlightenment thinking, the 'rights of man' were ultimately considered best guaranteed through the adoption of a social contract. 'The sovereignty of the nation-state was consonant with the sovereignty of the individual. Individual rights were microcosms of *raisons d'état*.' No higher form of freedom could be found beyond the nation-state. Decades later, Georg W. Hegel echoed this belief and it has generally remained within US diplomacy. Enlightenment values were simultaneously held with justifications for strong state action. Hegel's reflections illustrate the point:

The same consideration justifies civilized nations in regarding and treating as barbarians those who lag behind them in institutions which are the essential moments of the state. Thus a pastoral people may treat hunters as barbarians, and both of these are barbarians from the point of view of the agriculturists, &c. The civilized nation is conscious that the rights of barbarians are unequal to its own and treats their autonomy as only a formality. When wars and disputes arise in such circumstances, the trait which gives them a significance for world history is the fact that they are struggles for recognition in connection with something of specific intrinsic worth.[28]

The particular rights and interests of the state usually prevailed over the more universalist rights of the individual, especially human rights. The apotheosis of this tension was frequently evident during the Cold War, in which Washington often aligned itself with brutal dictatorships that violated human rights on the pretext that such alliances were vital to national security considerations.

For Paine the distinction between state and society was important. Society was generally considered as the productive classes: farmers, small merchants, artisans, labourers and manufacturers disconnected from the government. The state was made up of the 'plundering classes' that used their coercive power to live off society: government officials, aristocrats, established clergy and manufacturers with state monopolies and so forth. History was a reflection of the dynamism between these groups, of those who pay taxes and those who collect them. War 'was essentially this conflict writ large', promoting the dominance of the state over society. War was also 'an attempt by the plundering classes to distract their own productive classes from the abuses of government, for war served to "prevent people from looking into the defects and abuses of government"'.[29] Perpetual war, as in the 'Cold War', facilitated a process that Paine recognised. States benefited from a condition of crisis, they could 'fatten on the folly of one country and the spoils of another; and between their plunder and their prey, may go home rich'.[30]

Following Montesquieu and Adam Smith, commerce was seen as a stabilising force in international affairs. A mutual dependence was created and gentility grew through mutual interaction. Commerce would secure both peace and friendship with those who wished to trade. David Fitzsimons writes:

Commerce would not only strengthen liberal republics internally, it would also serve their interests by transforming the international milieu. International trade would "temper the human mind," help peoples "to know and understand each other," and have a "civilizing effect" on all who participated in it. Commerce would encourage peace by drawing the world together into mutual dependency; the greater the amount of international trade, the lesser the likelihood of war.[31]

US foreign policy was from the start an attempt to break out of the apparent vicissitudes of the regulation of commerce imposed by London. Capitalism was inherent in the American identity. It was considered a progressive force in world history because it was anti-feudal, anti-authoritarian, and it rewarded individual effort, irrespective of social position.

Despite the contradictions between progress and capitalism that emerged later, capitalism was much more than an economic system: it was a part of the identity of the nation, it was an ideology upon which values and assumptions were based. That it did not necessarily comport with the other traditional US assumptions about democracy and self-determination was not that important. In the abstract a clear contradiction resulted between the system of capitalism and the exercise of democratic rights, but in the culture, through its myths and ideological assumptions, such contradictions were overcome.[32] A strong consensus prevails to the point where the United States is one of the last to hold to the Enlightenment thesis of a universal civilisation based on 'democratic capitalism'. The vision and its attempt to impose the system of freedom in the market place have caused widespread misery, dislocation and instability.[33]

Declaring Independence

There was a tension in the philosophies of the Declaration of Independence and the writing of the Constitution with the elaboration on it contained in the *Federalist Papers*. An ongoing debate has occurred on whether the Constitution betrayed the democratic promise of the Declaration or enhanced it through erecting a more perfect Union. Both documents are a melting-pot of idealism and material considerations. Philosophers of political thought have long argued about the links between John Locke and Jefferson's Declaration. Why did Jefferson drop off the phrase on the pursuit of estate (or property) and insert the pursuit of happiness instead? The practical response suggests that it would have been an odd way to motivate the gathering armies against the British in a war of independence that was concerned with the issue of property. Who would be the wronged persons in the late British violations of their rights, the propertied people or 'all men'? Or was it the case that the Enlightenment had truly revolutionised the history of ideas by injecting 'the pursuit of happiness' into government's functions? Was there truly a new liberalism about the American Revolution?[34] The debate is too long to recount here. Suffice it to say that as far as US foreign relations in world history are concerned the two strands were and still are very much present. That both idealism and materialism were common motivators in US foreign policy is not surprising and yet it has been the locus of the chasm amongst the historians whose lot it is to interpret its past. It is not the intention here to explore the details of the actual policies, but to look at a set of contradictions that has had an enduring legacy in US foreign relations.

The tension is captured well by J. S. McClelland: 'Jefferson's *Declaration of Independence* is the foundation document of Americanness, just as the Constitution of 1787 is the foundation document of the United States.'[35] While the Declaration was aspirational in content, reflecting the rights of man, it was also a list of grievances. The idealistic content on the rights and the pursuit of life, liberty and happiness always had the much stronger appeal to the later collective memory. It was these words, if any, that would be recited by countless generations to come. The material interests and grievances were of course important, but they were also more particular and the benefits of obtaining and securing them were apparently not as democratic as the 'pursuit of happiness'. Material interests would always inform the making of US foreign policy, but they constantly changed and were usually more particular.

Fundamental to democratic theory is the idea that the legitimacy of a government is based on the consent of the governed. In practice this was not extended to all the governed, but to the citizens, to those who had a stake in society. The franchise was extended over time but it was not until comparatively recent times that the United States extended its franchise universally. After the revolution of 1791, Haiti was the first state to universalise the franchise. Within the United States the basis of consent needs to be considered within the appropriate historical context. But as far as the making of foreign policy was concerned, this base was even narrower.[36] The issue of consent also formed the basis for self-determination, which mingled the twin sovereignties of the state and the individual; of national interests and human rights. The former usually prevailed over the latter.

The gap between individual rights and the sovereignty of the state had to be reconciled, even though temporarily there seemed to be contradiction. Some of the Founding Fathers were not particularly enthusiastic about democracy, though this has necessarily been erased from the popular American consciousness. Democracy, they believed, could at best only be a transitional phase of government. As Richard Hofstadter has indicated, they believed 'it always evolves into either a tyranny (the rule of the rich demagogue who has patronized the mob) or an aristocracy (the original leaders of the democratic elements)'. He cited John Adams to capture the attitude: 'remember, democracy never lasts long. It soon wastes, exhausts, and murders itself. There never was a democracy yet that did not commit suicide.' The thinking suggested that if the democrats had the preponderance in the legislature then they would vote all property into their own hands, depriving the Founding Fathers and their associates of their possessions. Thus the citizen, requiring a stake in the society to conduct responsible affairs of state, had to be a property owner. Washington, Jefferson and Madison all shared these views. Madison recognised future threats that republican democracy might encounter from communism and fascism:

> In future times a great majority of the people will not only be without landed but any other sort of property. These will either combine, under the influence of their common situation – in which case the rights of property and the public liberty will not be secure in their hands – or, what is more probable, they will become the tools of opulence and ambition, in which case there will be equal danger on another side.[37]

The solution would come in giving sufficient people a stake in the society, making them property owners by giving them land. The relationship between strong government, immediately necessary to fight the British, and the democratic aspirations for the protection of individual rights could be worked out by increasing the participation of people in government, albeit through representatives, and giving the government sufficient power to protect the rights of the individual.[38]

Madison's solution that inverted traditional democratic theory had a pervasive influence on US foreign policy, because it soon resolved the problem of reconciling the differences in the powers of the state and those of the individual in foreign conquest, more commonly known as Manifest Destiny. Madison, in his most famous Tenth Federalist Paper, grappled with the problem of factions (interests) dominating the political situation. He understood faction as comprising 'a number of citizens, whether amounting to a majority or minority of the whole, who are united and actuated by some common impulse of passion, or of interest, adverse to the rights of other citizens, or to the permanent and aggregate interests of the community'. He continued: 'there are two methods of curing the mischiefs of faction: the one by removing its causes; the other by controlling its effects'. There were, again, two ways of removing the causes of faction, but both were antithetical to the American predicament. They would either destroy liberty or give to 'every citizen the same opinions, the same passions, and the same interests'. This too was anti-liberal and therefore rejected. It was folly to believe that enlightened statespeople would be able to control the effects of faction and subsume their power to the general will or public good. Madison warned that 'enlightened statesmen will not always be at the helm'. If the causes of faction could not be removed, it was therefore necessary to control the effects. Government would be so constituted that a system of checks and balances could be implemented and the citizens and factions could keep an eye on each other. Thus far in political thought it was considered necessary to limit the size of the state to maintain democratic practice. Madison's genius or temporal solution was to invert the process. Outlining the theory of checks and balances, he argued that the more factions within the Union, the less chance there was that any combination of them should get together and become tyrannical, or impose their will on a minority. 'The smaller the compass within which they are placed, the more easily will they concert and execute their plans of oppression. Extend the sphere and you take in a greater variety of parties and interests; you make it less probable that a majority of the whole will have a common motive to invade the rights of other citizens.'[39] The lasting effect it had on US diplomacy was the idea that national security and the pursuit of its citizens' happiness depended on expansion.

A few ironies arise. Though Madison intended to safeguard democracy and liberty through expansion, future technology reduced the sphere in terms of both transport and intellect. Authors of various opinions have noted the diminution of diversity. The option that Madison rejected was indeed revived. Ultimately, in the age of the 'global village' Madison's fear of people possessing the same opinions, passions and interests was not completely actualised, but moved in that direction, not through any conspiratorial act of either the publicists or the propaganda makers, but through a combination of cultural values and interests. The theorist Herbert Marcuse talked of the 'one-dimensional man', Francis Fukuyama about the homogenisation of society and ultimately the world. And Noam Chomsky warned society about the 'manufacture of consent' with its profound implications for democratic theory and practice. The homogenisation of the major media outlets, vital components in democracies, resulted from a subordination of the need to be informed (the basis of responsible consent) to commercial interests.[40]

A further irony was that future US policy would be un-American in the terms of Madison's solution. Who would check and balance US power in the future, once it had transcended the closing frontiers of the late nineteenth century? There may have been some formidable checks, but the balances were extremely unattractive if fascism or communism were representative of them. Other options were too weak to assert and protect people's rights. The theologian Reinhold Niebuhr articulated many of the pitfalls of US policy, and the manner in which they would undermine their own moral foundations in the twentieth century. Niebuhr thought that

> great disproportions of power are as certainly moral hazards to justice and community as they are foundations of minimal order. They are hazards to community both because they arouse resentments and fears among those who have less power; and because

they tempt the strong to wield their power without too much consideration of the interests and views of those upon whom it impinges. . . .

Genuine community is established only when the knowledge that we need one another is supplemented by the recognition that "the other," that other form of life, or that other unique community is the limit beyond which our ambitions must not run and the boundary beyond which our life must not expand. . . .

But it is easy to forget that even the most powerful nation or alliance of nations is merely one of many forces in the historical drama; and that the conflict of many wills and purposes, which constitute that drama, give it a bizarre pattern in which it is difficult to discern a real meaning.[41]

The constructions of both Jefferson and Madison go down as giants in the history of US foreign policy. Their ideas have had a pervasive influence and they have been manipulated and moulded to suit contemporary needs. The influence of these constructions is more important than the actual diplomacy of either Thomas Jefferson (Secretary of State, 1789–1793, and then President, 1801–1809) or James Madison (Secretary of State, 1801–1809, President, 1809–1817). Once, when John F. Kennedy was speaking at a White House dinner for sixteen Nobel Prize winners, he said: 'Surely this is the most intellectual gathering ever, except when Thomas Jefferson dined alone.' Such sycophancy is the norm when it comes to Jefferson. The myth of Jefferson is a difficult creature to get a hold of, though Petersen has gone a long way towards doing so. The myth is all the more valuable because it can be used in so many different ways.[42] Jefferson is remembered as the great author of the Declaration of Independence, the advocate of liberty and self-determination, the president who presided over the Louisiana Purchase of 1803, which almost doubled the size of the US. These memories are uncomfortable bedfellows. The Constitution did not provide for such expansion; and Jefferson's own ideals were flouted as far as the self-determination of Native American nations was concerned. Peterson argues that Jefferson went beyond the Constitution in the 'conviction that he was wrong'[43] Yet the acquisition of this vast territory in 1803 secured US trade in the region, giving access to the vital port of New Orleans and control of the Mississippi. The national interest was served through the promotion and facilitation of trade and the establishment of a more secure western frontier. Though considered morally wrong, it was deemed successful. The tension between the ideals, providence, Manifest Destiny and the rights of others could not be more apparent than in the conflict with and removal of the Native American nations that followed. Attitudes and ideologies relating to racial superiority may have provided the contemporary justification for such action, but 'Indian Affairs' was treated as a foreign not domestic policy issue. It was a matter that existed beyond the strictures of negative liberty imposed by the social contract or Constitution. The national interest and more ethnocentric considerations limited universal values. Attitudes towards racial superiority have been a consistent feature of US foreign policy and the early treatment of Native Americans may have set the context within which Washington would engage the Third World in the future.[44]

Jefferson and Madison remain giants despite their record. Bradford Perkins suggests that 'Jefferson expanded the national domain by acquiring the Louisiana country, a magnificent gain. Otherwise he and Madison were failures.' Generally, their diplomacy bordered on the inept. They brought the country into an inconclusive war with Britain that could have ended the Union. Despite espousing republican sentiments, Jefferson flouted their values in the purchase of the Louisiana territory, and his presidency witnessed a process of increasingly centralised power around the executive. In many ways the process of expansion necessitated increased centralisation, and the reference to national security issues often brought the legislative branch into submission.[45]

Jefferson's legacy left a strong belief that the best way for the United States to influence world events and promote democracy was by staying aloof and staying at home, though his ideas of 'home' changed from state to continental proportions, and later to hemispheric proportions, though this ambition was never realised. And here is also one of his seminal contributions to the constant paradoxes and contradictions in US foreign policy.[46] While Jefferson continually acted in an imperial way, he was fully aware of the contradictions. The revered Secretary of State John Quincy Adams later wrote about Jefferson: 'With the Declaration of Independence on their lips, and the merciless scourge of slavery in their hands, a more flagrant image of human inconsistency can scarcely be conceived than one of our Southern slave holding republicans.'[47]

US expansionism has been debated in US society and by historians of US foreign policy since its origins. The orthodox suggest that the expansion was related to a nation seeking security, that unless the continent was secure the other Great Powers still present could either alone or in unison, or with the Native Americans, pose a threat to the nascent republic. There was a psychological desire to feel safe.[48]

Another interpretation of the search for community, the expansion that was deemed essential for the survival of the democratic republic, involved looking west. Empire was a way of life. Jefferson may have had misgivings about the arguments of imperialism, with which his conscience grappled, but he was also a realist, a nationalist, looking to secure the American states. While perhaps haunted, if the interests of the state arose, Jefferson always took the imperial option. William Appleman Williams suggests that limits could have been introduced into the American culture if Americans had not considered themselves unique; 'if they were not well along to paranoid conceptions of security, and if they did not believe empire was the key to freedom and self-realization'. But there were few restraints on the individual in the interests of the community. Such ideas on community challenge ideals on the ownership of private property; hence 'community can only be realized through empire that provides a surplus of property'. Williams concludes that Jeffersonian democracy 'was a creature of imperial expansion'.[49]

The American character was not only formed by ideas from those associated with Crèvecœur's *Letters from an American Farmer* to the Frontier thesis; the identity of the nation was also forged in its interactions with the European powers around the Atlantic community. Jefferson had a clear idea of the US position in the world system, which within the contemporary context meant with the European powers. He articulated three foreign policy goals, which were: to secure the trade routes of the nation, that is, acquiring New Orleans and west Florida; to protect the right to trade with European belligerents; and to build a navy to protect these interests. Jefferson did not pursue trade because he believed it promoted pacific relations and understanding amongst nations; his understanding of trade was largely concerned with material interest. As he pointed out to Congress in 1793, his ideas of trade were very similar to those of the Europeans: 'As a branch of industry it is valuable, but as a resource of defense, essential.' The flag did not direct, but acted as guarantor for US commercial interests: 'The position and circumstances of the United States leave them nothing to fear on their land-board, and leave them nothing to desire beyond their present rights. But on their seaboard, they are open to injury, and they have there, too, a commerce which must be protected.' James Sofka indicates that Jefferson had lived through recurrent Anglo-French wars to control the resources of the North American continent. He knew the importance of the country within the world system. And while Jefferson strongly advocated the notion of neutrality and 'entangling alliances with none', in the political sphere, as far as commercial interests were concerned, he was aware that the southern states depended too much on trade with Europe and the Caribbean ever seriously to consider autarky.[50] The idea of the nation was formed both in the west and across the Atlantic.

The republican empire

That inversion of democratic theory, the injunction to expand the sphere, to move west, to engage in border colonisation,[51] to trammel the rights and liberties of Native Americans created an empire early on, though most historians use the term 'republican empire' to describe the latter part of the nineteenth century. There was an inherent contradiction in the US predicament. How could an imperial expansive state continue to reconcile these actions with the issues of democracy and consent? The workings of various ideologies formed a social consensus. But there was also considerable contemporary objection, either ignored, overcome or written out of history, as the narrative became more essential. Which of Jefferson's hands is more memorable? The one that held the Declaration of Independence or the one that held the title deeds to the Louisiana Purchase? In his *Mystic Chords of Memory* Michael Kammen identifies the numerous conflicts about tradition and the symbols, which form the identity of the nation. But

> ultimately there is a powerful tendency in the United States to depoliticize traditions for the sake of "reconciliation." Consequently the politics of culture in this country has everything to do with the process of contestation *and* with the subsequent quest for reconciliation. Memory is more likely to be activated by contestation, and amnesia is more likely to be induced by the desire for reconciliation.[52]

The contradictions never really get ironed out. They arise especially when the United States embarks on periods of expansion, and the society debates the fidelity of the statesmen to the social conscience of the imagined community. The normal reference points for the constructed identity run through Locke, Jefferson and Madison. Machiavelli earlier identified another salient trait. It was in the very nature of virtuous (read manly) republics to be expansive. The 'plundering' of state expansionism would dominate society, and in its militarism there was the propensity towards corruption. The Athenian model of democracy had been overturned in Madison's writings, and through the westward quest for plantations and land. Stephanson points out that 'the defensive insularity of the Spartan model was not an attractive alternative, for it offered no vision of greatness and would expose the republic to security risks'.[53]

Serge Ricard's predicament remains prescient. Throughout its history the US maintained identities that were both singular and universal. This fundamental ambiguity helps to explain the contradictions in US foreign policy. The US needed to preserve its sanctity, at the political and ideological level by avoiding 'entangling alliances' and maintaining a political isolation from Europe and the cast of Old World politics and power. And yet it needed to engage with the world at the commercial level; but US trade usually awaited the protection of the flag. The missionary spirit demanded engagement; millenarian visions implied that the US condition could be universalised, the conclusion of which would bring History to an end. US ideologies facilitated the combination of imperialism and anti-imperialism, the contradictory combination of expansionism and freedom.[54] The tension resurfaced often.

Dominant narratives of US foreign relations and history removed the word 'imperialism' precisely because of the constant reference to its specialness and exceptionalism.[55] Millenarian thinking and Enlightenment values meshed so completely, sometimes awkwardly, sometimes effortlessly, as to make the combination of nationalism and universalism quite normal. In US society and especially the culture of US diplomacy these conjunctions tended to promote memories of US principles rather than uses of their power.[56]

Conclusion

The birth of US diplomacy in the modern world made it a child of the Enlightenment with an exceptionalist self-perception. Messianic tendencies in its early visions imbued its subsequent diplomacy with a moral force. The goals of the nation were clearly articulated in the early writings on the States and the Republic. These writings ultimately formed the basis of a public identity. But there was the irreducible contradiction of singularity with universality, engagement and isolation. By the late twentieth century the isolationist tendencies re-emerged lamely, but the ideology was in part finally put to rest. Still, unlike any other empires, Washington tries to maintain its uniqueness through engagement. Clinton moved beyond the somewhat negative constructs associated with the Monroe Doctrine through to containment, and explicitly advocated a 'strategy of engagement and enlargement'.[57]

The popular provision of consent is a vital element of democratic theory. Within the Union, at least theoretically, the Constitution and the system of negative liberties associated with such social contracts did protect citizens. In practice, one cannot forget the exclusion, brutality or neglect suffered by Native Americans, African Americans, immigrants and women. These groups later increased their powers of representation within the system. Beyond the sphere, beyond the realm of the Constitution, there was little attempt to obtain the consent of those upon whom US foreign policy was enacted. 'Empire by invitation'[58] was a rare occurrence. More frequently Washington pursued unchecked positive liberties in the national interest.

Often US expansion did lead to contemporary debate; there was always considerable dissent within the society. This was later smoothed over in search of national consensus. Exceptionalism stressed the uniqueness of the US experience, 'that its history is to a large degree not comparable with that of other nations'. The American consensus maintains that 'in contrast to others, the American people overwhelmingly, nearly unanimously, agree on the fundamentals of government and policy'.[59] In the US collective memories, reconciliation is enhanced through collective amnesia.[60] Louis Hartz interestingly explains that there were two nationalisms operating in the United States of America: the nationalism of ideology – the ideas of Jefferson, the belief in democracy, individualism, liberty, republicanism and self-determination, for example; and the nationalism of state security based around territory and the 'national security state'. The nationalisms of state security vied with those of ideology. 'This ironic "Americanist" outburst against imperialism,' Hartz writes, 'a nationalism consuming nationalism which could only occur in America, led the partisans of the new imperialism to stress other concepts of American destiny' such as the eventual imposition of Lockean liberty. This both justifies and incriminates their case.[61]

2

SPHERES OF INFLUENCE
Monroeism in US policy

The formation of the Monroe Doctrine is symbolic in US policy of the combination of ideals and universals with more pragmatic particulars. Both the universal and particular derivatives of the Monroe Doctrine have remained influential in US diplomacy. Self-determination, anti-colonialism, spheres of influence, freedom and unilateralism are central characteristics of US diplomacy in the twentieth century. They are all tempered by the national interest and the pursuit of US opportunities, as was the formation of the initial doctrine. The Monroe Doctrine is of vital importance to understanding US foreign policy in World History. Wilsonianism was to a large extent predicated on the pervasive influences of Monroeism. President Wilson advocated the universal application of the doctrine. Its constituent elements appear frequently in twentieth-century diplomacy. They provided the foundations for the blend of universalism and 'spheres of influence' approach, they cloaked US opportunism and unilateralism in a benevolent framework and provided the basis of a Manichaean tendency towards essentialism, which enhanced the politics of identity.

The doctrine was a reflection of fundamental attitudes held at the time and a statement of future US intentions. It has been described as 'the most significant of all American State papers'.[1] It was used flexibly and frequently in US policy and yet for all its malleability it acquired almost religious dimensions within US culture. It was regarded and treated as an article of faith, diplomatically comparable with the importance accorded to the Constitution. Its invocation has often been assumed to produce 'miraculous results'.[2] It provided the justification for a diverse range of policies ever since President James Monroe delivered his message to Congress in December 1823. The doctrine passed through several incarnations, always closely associated with the American national purpose, whether it was to assert a republican identity, defend democracy, protect self-determination, oppose colonialism, impose progressivism or divide the world according to conceptual geography. The elements of the doctrine served divergent national purposes and served to legitimate and unite the nation around the prevailing temporal attitudes. Its flexibility enhanced its endurance, yet US opportunism provides a unifying factor throughout its history. It gave US foreign relations meaning; it gave the nation an identity. The central elements of the doctrine were closely associated with the principles of US diplomacy, whether adhered to or not. It created an epistemological myth closely associated with US beliefs. The 'New World', the Western Hemisphere, was the new agent of progress in World History. Nation building was in its heyday, and nationalism was an increasing point of reference. But with this message and its subsequent interpretations, the *raison d'état* was no longer sufficient to justify policy; higher purposes were required. World History was being swept along by the powers of democracy and republicanism, with the United States as the engine of progress. It was no longer sufficient to assume 'the people' would serve the state. The state had to work for the people, to assist them in their 'pursuit of happiness'. The effects of the French Revolution as a demonstration of a more radical alternative had to be contained. Would the eyes of the world necessarily look to the US 'city on the hill', or cast their gaze elsewhere?

Liberating straitjackets: self-determination

The enduring essence of the Monroe Doctrine has repeatedly contributed to US exceptionalism and the politics of identity. The essence of the speech of 2 December 1823 became fundamental to US policy and a force in World History. Among other things Monroe stated,

> as a principle in which the rights and interests of the United States are involved, that the American continents, by the free and independent condition which they have assumed and maintain, are henceforth not to be considered as subjects for future colonization by any European powers. . . . We owe it, therefore, to candor and to amicable relations existing between the United States and those powers to declare that we should consider any attempt on their part to extend their system to any portion of this hemisphere as dangerous to our peace and safety.[3]

The details are obviously relevant to the particularities of the day and the politics between the various powers: the US, the United Kingdom, Spain, Russia and the Holy Alliance. They are necessary for understanding the inter-American relationships and the domestic ambitions of the doctrine's main author, Monroe's Secretary of State John Quincy Adams (1817–1825). The details demonstrate that the United States was pursuing its particular national interests rather than primarily trying to promote the values that remained influential in US culture and ideology.

In 1823 the United States, though nearly fifty years old, did not cast long shadows. The collective memories of the revolution and the wars for independence were still existential realities for those who participated in the debates on US–European relations and on the wording of Monroe's message. From Washington and Jefferson there was the sentiment of isolationism. Washington's farewell (1796) expressed the sentiment of separation from the Old World: 'Our detached and distant situation invites and enables us to pursue a different course.' Jefferson's inaugural captured the intention in a much more quotable form: 'peace, commerce and honest friendship with all nations, entangling alliances with none'.[4] Yet there was the injunction to remake the world. Ironically, the United States separated its identity on the issues of colonialism and self-determination from that of the European powers, but proceeded with the process of border colonisation to the west that undermined Native American self-determination. In the context of US foreign policy the politics of identity was usually more referential to Great Power politics than to the manner in which it interacted with weaker powers.

Both the formal ideologies and the existential condition of the States shaped the Monroe Doctrine. The geographical reality and its links to a theory upon which the Constitution was based are fundamental to understanding the evolution of the doctrine. By 1823 the US had extended its sphere, but not to the limits of its ambition. In 1789 Madison's Tenth Federalist Paper invoked the people to 'extend the sphere' to protect democracy and further perfect the Union. Notions of expansion and liberty were thus introduced into a culture that would adapt this tense conceptual relationship to its contemporary opportunities. The experience of the Founding Fathers led them to understand the selfish motivations of the people. As Richard Hofstadter put it, 'they did not believe in man, [but in a] good political constitution to control him'.[5] Yet the language of US diplomacy too often discards this premise of inherent selfish motivation or later national interest in favour of the language of benevolence, of mission, of exceptionalism and of progress. This omission in the language has fuelled the momentum of various myths. There were US visions of empire, held by Adams in particular, which if limited might jeopardise the very existence of the States.

In 1823 this national mission was still incomplete. The search for opportunity, security and a more perfect Union encouraged continental expansion. Hunt's analysis of ideology[6] in US foreign policy yields important insights. The tendency to reduce complex realities to simple formulae both instructs policy makers and their culture, and facilitates the simultaneous adherence to many rational contradictions. Liberty and expansion went hand in hand because the 'rights' of others were denied for racial or strategic reasons. Ideology helped overcome the contradictions. The narrative of the nation and the nationalism that derived from it largely depend on the conflation of such contradictory ideas. The thought process ensured social cohesion, inspired and mobilised people.[7] These are the myths which assure Americans of their moral force in History, they legitimate and justify their position; they reassure them of their identity. The Hartzian observation again becomes apt. Two seemingly contradictory strands in their thought fuelled US nationalism: the nationalism associated with the political philosophy and the nationalism associated with state security. Through the integration of these tense conceptual relations the notions of expansion and liberty have commingled down to the present.

Traditionally interpreted, the doctrine is considered a defence of the nascent Latin American republics and US security. It created a world based on two spheres and asserted the principle of non-colonisation. The Western Hemisphere was not to be considered ripe territory for new European ventures. By way of reciprocity the United States would not interfere in matters that solely concerned Europe. The sense of isolationism was further enhanced through these statements. But philosophically Monroe's speech was intended to make an impact on World History, to assert 'a diplomatic declaration of independence'. The speech conceptually separated the New World from the Old, when the latter ostensibly held ambitions over territory in the former, and when democracy was being destroyed in France. Jefferson was enthusiastic about the Latin revolutions. He saw them as 'another example of man rising in his might and busting the chains of his oppressor'.[8]

The diplomatic declaration of independence

As a diplomatic declaration the United States created an independent identity that was strengthened over time. Crucially, though, it was constructed around both the positive aspects of US ideology and the negative characterisations of a Manichaean world. Much has been written about the influential message. There is wide agreement that the Secretary of State John Quincy Adams was its main author, but not all agree on the motivations. The British Minister to the US wrote to the British Secretary of State for Foreign Affairs George Canning, that the message 'seems to have been received with acclamation throughout the United States'. The US association with the territories that had emancipated themselves from European rule 'has evidently found in every bosom a chord which vibrates in strict union with the sentiments so conveyed'.[9] European powers either dismissed or treated the US announcement with contempt, thinking it unworthy of serious attention or further consideration. The European silence, however, should not be taken as a matter of flattery; 'it proceeded from a sense of American weakness, rather than American strength'.[10] US credibility was not yet associated with its power. Monroe, too, was nagged in part by that seeming weakness. Days after the announcement, Adams found the president 'singularly disturbed with these rumors of invasion by the Holy alliance'.[11] Adams of course did not share such concerns.

Jefferson wrote to Monroe that the issue 'is the most momentous which has ever been offered to my contemplation since that of Independence. That made us a nation, this sets our compass and points the course which we are to steer through the ocean of time opening on us.'[12] Though this influential doctrine galvanised the principles of US diplomacy, by the late twentieth century it had undergone several mutations. At the time the message divided the world into two spheres. Monarchy, absolutism and other sorts of authoritarianism generally characterised the Old World, while the New World, whatever the realities in Latin America, was characterised as republican and at times democratic. Jefferson wrote to Monroe of the differences of the continents: 'America, North, and South, has a set of interests distinct from those of Europe, and peculiarly her own. She should therefore have a system of her own, separate and apart from that of Europe. While the last is laboring to become the domicile of despotism, our endeavor should surely be, to make our hemisphere that of freedom.'[13] The separation of spheres and intention was an important conceptual difference for those in the US cabinet and the wider public. The United States, composed of such diverse peoples, had to express its sense of nationalism through statements of opposition, of what it was not. It created its identity against an 'other'. Nationalistic sentiments that sprang from the positive domestic cultures were much more precarious, whereas its foreign policy was a great arena for social cohesion and national galvanisation. The 'two spheres' principle asserted differences and affirmed US nationalism. It enhanced security and identified the US as a progressive force in history.

The conceptual division of the world along lines that in actuality characterised neither portion of the globe had a tremendous impact on the history of US foreign policy. It enhanced the discourse centred on civilisation and barbarism, or of 'orientalism'. It reappeared at many subsequent junctures, setting the West aside from and above, at least on the ideological level, the rest. Simple divisions were potent forces at the beginning of the twentieth century in Theodore Roosevelt's rhetoric on Latin America, at mid-century in the Truman Doctrine and then in the 1990s in the popular thesis on the 'clash of civilizations'. The potent and simple concept of the 'West' continually expanded.[14] It worked well, especially when invoked concurrently with an apparent security threat; it provided justification for what could be presented as essentially defensive policies. It appealed to public opinion and so became a powerful tool in political campaigns. It fed the various national myths and the meta-narrative of US history. It fuelled the sense of purpose.

The second great principle of the message was that of US opposition to colonialism. The issue was repeatedly returned to in the cabinet meetings and in the correspondence between the US representatives and their European counterparts. The United States would not view without disquiet the reimposition of the colonial system by any European power to the Latin American states that had gained their independence. The statement was fundamentally aimed at recolonisation by European powers, but not the type of border colonisation exercised through Manifest Destiny and the acquisition of Texas or Mexican territory. It is an irony that westward expansion was not considered to harm 'the spirit' or identity of the nation.

Adams's injunction of 1821 remained vitally important. The United States was a relatively weak power, and therefore went 'not abroad, in search of monsters to destroy. She is the well wisher to the freedom and independence of all. She is the champion and vindicator only of her own.' To do so might jeopardise the Union itself. It would provide the example and avoid the wars of 'interest and intrigue'. To become involved carried risks, the 'fundamental maxims of her policy would insensibly change from liberty to force. . . . She might become the dictatress of the world. She would be no longer the ruler of her own spirit.'[15] Without comparable force the United States did little when the British took the Falkland Islands in 1833, or later, preoccupied by the Civil War, when France briefly extended its empire to Mexico.[16]

Third, perceived security threats were vital to the message. Europeans were warned to stay out of the Western Hemisphere. Their removal from the continent was an initial aspiration. There was much deliberation on this issue prior to the delivery of the message, both in cabinet meetings and in correspondence with the British. The possibility that the Spanish, the Holy Alliance, or the Russians might extend their influence, or even the British acquisition of Cuba, could not be accepted. These powers, acting singly or in concert, could threaten the security of the United States as it then stood. The Spanish occupied Cuba and Puerto Rico, seen as commanding points for controlling the Gulf of Mexico. The Holy Alliance was vehemently anti-republican and might have facilitated the return of the Spanish empire. The Russians maintained a presence on the west coast, and the British commanded the seas. Monroe stated 'any attempt on their part to extend their system to any portion of this hemisphere [would be considered] as dangerous to our peace and safety'.[17] In the twentieth century US concerns for security were linked to financial and commercial interests by the Taft and Wilson administrations, and to ideological differences throughout the Cold War.

In correspondence and conversation with Stratford Canning, British Minister to the United States in 1821, Adams had made it clear that the US coveted the entire continent below the border with the Northern Provinces (Canada). Adams indicated that they would not encroach on that British territory, 'but leave the rest of this continent to us.'[18] He thought it an absurdity that Britain in the north and the Spanish in the south should hold such 'fragments of territory' and remain permanently attached to the rapidly growing nation. Adams's vision of empire encompassed the entire continent; to pretend otherwise, he wrote, would only 'add to our ambition hypocrisy'.[19] Adams's vision, no doubt, shaped the eventual speech.

Exceptional diplomacy

A key feature of twentieth-century US diplomacy, that of unilateralism or 'independent internationalism',[20] perhaps also derived from early US diplomacy. The perceived threats to US security, the concerns for Latin independence and self-determination could better have been served through a joint application of the doctrine with the British. But there were pressing reasons why the United States acted alone: it sought free passage for its own expansion across the continent. It was not that long since the British had been openly hostile, encouraging Native Americans to attack the United States. The problem would obviously be compounded if the Spanish or the Holy Alliance moved to restore absolutist power in the Western Hemisphere, or if the Russians insisted on their economic claims to trade on the west coast. Or if these powers moved to recolonise these areas, Washington thought that this would surely bring the British into the 'scramble' for Latin America and the Caribbean, perhaps taking Cuba from the Spanish. As it was, the British had taken advantage of the Spanish decolonisation by increasing their trade in the area. Likewise, US trade had also increased during the period of European war. Once the boundary treaties with Spain (1821) that ceded east Florida to the United States had been completed, recognition of Latin independence could be mentioned openly. With recognition of the southern borders of the Louisiana Purchase and the northern and westward limit of the United States secured as far as the Spanish were concerned, Adams could put his case more forthrightly. He had earlier supported the 1811 'No Transfer Principle', a sort of secret precursor to the Monroe Doctrine, but now he sought to remove the limits on US expansion: 'Who shall dare to set limits to the commerce and naval power of this country?'[21] It was this vision of empire that fuelled Adams's ambition and ability to persuade a reluctant cabinet to make the Monroe declaration unilaterally in the form it took. The liberty, independence and self-determination of the Latin states were a by-product of US ambition. The alternative scenarios were far worse. The commerce in the south would be restricted and the west would be insecure.

Adams was the prime author for the most enduring, because most malleable, doctrine in US foreign policy, though there were significant other contributors. The No Transfer Principle shaped early US attitudes towards its southern neighbours. There were Latin American antecedents too. But most immediately and most powerfully the British Foreign Secretary, George Canning, had made a similar offer in the summer of 1823. Canning proposed that Britain and the US make joint cause in their policy on Latin America. He thought the Spanish recovery of the lost colonies was hopeless; that recognition of their independence was a question of time; that it did not aim to possess any portion of the colonies, but 'that she could not see the transfer of any portion of them to any other Power, with indifference'. Declared together, with the commanding British navy, US stated interests and Latin independence would have been more secure.[22]

Flattered by the offer, Monroe was inclined to accept Canning's proposal. Seeking advice, he sent the correspondence to former presidents Madison and Jefferson. Both urged acceptance of a joint declaration. Jefferson thought it would be a momentous opportunity to bring the British 'mighty weight into the scale of free government'. Without British power Latin independence would be insecure, but with it the United States could remove one power which 'can do us the most harm of any one, of all on earth; and with her on our side we need not fear the whole world'. Madison too urged acceptance, even though Britain's objectives were not identical. Within days, Madison also wrote to Jefferson: 'With the British power and navy combined with our own we have nothing to fear from the rest of the World; and in the great struggle of the Epoch between liberty and despotism, we owe it to ourselves to sustain the former in this hemisphere at least.' Despite the assurance British power would provide to Latin independence, Adams calculated that they would exercise that power in any case and therefore there was no need for a joint Anglo-American compact. Adams laid out his geo-strategic calculations to the cabinet on 15 November 1823. He did not share the Secretary of War John Calhoun's concerns that the Holy Alliance would restore the lands to Spain. Adams considered the Alliance's years numbered and that it was therefore unwise to tie the US down to a matter of principle. He doubted Europe's ability or ambition to restore its authority over Latin America. Moreover, even without the joint declaration British commercial interests would still check moves by Spain or the Alliance in the Western Hemisphere. Even though Adams based his reasoning on a realistic calculation of interests, he was reluctant to join the British because they had not recognised Latin independence and could alter their policy according to changes in the European balance of power. He proposed that the issue should be returned to the British as a test of a principle, 'a test of right and wrong'. He wrote in his diary: 'considering the South Americans as independent nations, they themselves, and no other nation, had the right to dispose of their condition. We have no right to dispose of them, either alone or in conjunction with other nations. Neither have any other nations the right of disposing of them without their consent.'[23] The British representative in Washington informed Canning that British recognition was absolutely necessary for the joint declaration to proceed.[24] Monroe delivered his message the following day.

Despite the proposed test of British principles and Adams's concerns about gaining the consent of Latin nations, self-determination was not the principal motivating factor in US policy. Self-determination coincided with US interests in the early nineteenth century but later that century and early in the twentieth century self-determination in Latin and Central America frequently inhibited the pursuit of US commercial or political interests. Reviewing the doctrine ninety years later the soon-to-be Secretary of State, Robert Lansing, argued that it was motivated by selfishness not altruism. Self-determination accorded with US policy, but was not a motivating factor. The declaration in 1823 was based on national interest, excluding possibilities of European expansion and precluding the self-determination of Native American nations 'at home'.[25]

Adams's strategy was based on realism. Cuba's position, not just westward expansion, informed US policy. Madison wanted to know whether Britain's proposals disclaimed any possibilities of acquiring the island. Jefferson confessed 'that I have ever looked on Cuba as the most interesting addition which could ever be made to our system of States. The control which, with Florida Point, this island would give us over the Gulf of Mexico, and the countries and isthmus bordering on it, as well as all those waters flowing into it, would fill up the measure of our political well-being.' Even though acquiring the island by force was ruled out, the common belief was that because of its geographical proximity it would gravitate towards the Union. But there were political reasons why Cuba could not be admitted to the Union. The nation was not yet psychologically attuned to the idea of extending its empire overseas and inclusion of Cuba would add another slave state to the balance. In April 1823 Adams wrote to Hugh Nelson:

> Such indeed are, between the interests of that island and of this country, the geographical, moral, and political relations, formed by nature, gathering in the process of time, and even now verging to maturity, that in looking forward to the probable course of events for the short period of half a century, it is scarcely possible to resist the conviction that the annexation of Cuba to our federal republic will be indispensable to the continuance and integrity of the Union itself. . . . There are laws of political as well as of physical gravitation; and if an apple severed by the tempest from its native tree cannot choose but fall to the ground, Cuba, forcibly disjoined from its own unnatural connection with Spain, and incapable of self-support, can gravitate only towards the North American Union, which by the same law of nature cannot cast her off from its bosom.

By November, Adams still denied any intention of seizing either Cuba or Mexican territory, but argued that, should they solicit to join, the Union and Washington should not preclude the possibilities of such additions by tying itself to Canning's limitations. As Adams put it to the cabinet: 'Without entering now into the enquiry of the expediency of our annexing Texas or Cuba to our Union, we should at least keep ourselves free to act as emergencies may arise, and not tie ourselves down to any principle which might immediately afterwards be brought to bear against ourselves.'[26]

When Dexter Perkins wrote *Hands Off* in the late 1940s, he argued that the average American saw the doctrine as a noble attempt to save the New World from the vicissitudes of European despotism. The construct of a certain benevolence in the western sphere has usually been opposed to a threat to US principles from some 'other'. Throughout, the perception or the construct of the threat was usually more important. By the 1950s the Eisenhower administration sought to preclude alien ideologies from Guatemala, and the 1980s reinvigorated the Monroe Doctrine around a much-exaggerated Soviet conspiracy in Nicaragua. The perception of a threat, rather than an actual threat was often pertinent. Perkins writes: 'we must admit that the message of 1823 was directed against an imaginary menace. Not one of the Continental powers cherished designs of reconquest in November or December of 1823.'[27] Within years most had recognised Latin American independence.

While unilateral opportunity motivated the content and the form of the message, it was important to rest the case on principle to distance US identity from that of Europe. Shunning the options of quiet diplomacy with Russia and Britain, Monroe's message was put forth through a form of open diplomacy via the annual congressional message. The Europeans learnt of the message through their ambassadors' assessments and the US public reaction to it. The message enhanced the national identity and ideologically separated the New and the Old Worlds. In practice the US did not pledge to stay out of European affairs, but only out of their internal affairs; thus assistance towards Greek independence was not considered interference in European affairs. Westward expansion was not considered a violation of the principles of self-determination; expansion enhanced liberty. Indeed, Monroe echoed Madison's Tenth Federalist Paper on the increasing benefits of cohesion brought about through expansion. He told Congress:

> Over this territory our population has expanded in every direction, and new States have been established almost equal in number to those which formed the first bond of our Union. This expansion of our population and accession of new States to our Union have had the happiest effect on all its highest interests. That it has eminently augmented our resources and added to our strength and

respectability as a power is admitted by all. But it is not in these important circumstances only that this happy effect is felt. It is manifest that by enlarging the basis of our system and increasing the number of States the system itself has been greatly strengthened in both branches. Consolidation and disunion have thereby been rendered equally impractical.[28]

Despite the particularities of the message, the constructs associated with self-determination, republicanism and liberty remained potent forces in subsequent US diplomacy. It is around these concerns that the traditional narratives of US history and diplomacy were formed, not Adams's more realistic considerations. Perkins contends that 'they were to have an ecumenical significance for several generations of men. The liberty, which Monroe desired and defended for the republics of Latin America, was, in the course of the century, to be diffused throughout no small part of Europe as well. The President of the United States spoke not only for his people, but also for his age. He spoke, indeed, for more than his age.'[29] President Wilson reinvigorated the messages of self-determination and liberty, and indeed suggested a worldwide application of the Monroe Doctrine at the close of the First World War.

Opportunities and Manifest Destinies

The message remained strong through the collective memories associated with the meta-narrative of liberty, democracy and self-determination. It contributed to a type of 'orientalist' discourse in US rhetoric and diplomacy, a tendency to portray conflicts in Manichaean terms. Complexity was shunned in favour of a crusading spirit against some almost monolithic 'other'. In the immediate term, the genius of the speech freed the US to conquer territory to the west. At each point of expansion the tension between liberty and expansion resurfaced; the nationalisms of state security and of ideological constructs vied with each other. Madison's injunction to extend the sphere provided a limited justification, but the Missouri Compromise on the balance of slave and free states became unbearable within four decades.

The passage was clear for US colonisation of the west. Even though the anti-colonial sentiment remained a pervasive influence, no guarantees were given or unions formed with the Latin Americans even when they tried to instigate the process. Proposals for Pan-American unions were ignored, rebuffed or modified for 100 years until in the 1930s Roosevelt's Good Neighbor policy moved in that direction. The primary concern of US diplomats was to gain access to the markets. Interests were still limited in the early nineteenth century, but ministers of state were expected to seek equal access to the markets, secure religious freedoms for US citizens, and encourage republican sentiments. Territorial questions or those concerning the rights and liberties of Latin Americans were, again, incidental. US diplomacy intended to extend its sphere of power. To Adams, colonialism implied commercial monopoly and US exclusion. Though the Latin markets were not vital as yet, the message was also aimed at the Russians in the northwest. Such exclusion, as Adams saw it, was unthinkable, unnatural to US ambition and centrifugal force within the world system.[30]

European reaction was largely indifferent. George Canning dismissed the US rhetoric, referring to the strategy as the politics of the 'bazaar', seeing the pursuit of commercial opportunity as its primary motivation. Had it been otherwise, why would Washington have rejected his offer? Prince Metternich found the message 'indecent' and scornful of European institutions. The US was accused of commercialism. Adams was suspected of playing politics for his own electoral advantage. No power dignified the United States with protest. It was not considered necessary.[31]

In the region the message was taken seriously for a time. In 1826 the Latin American nations sought consultation with Washington at the Bolivarian Conference held in Panama. They invited Washington to attend, though the two US diplomats never made it, to consider 'the means of making effectual the principles announced by President Monroe'. The danger of reconquest had passed and President Adams wanted to keep his hands free. He did not want to place the United States under obligation, forced to respond to situations in which its interests might not be involved, and such agreement would also have caused problems for US expansion in the south and west.[32] Washington did not commit itself to a pact of mutual security until the 1947 Rio Pact.

While Bolivar's dream was of a Pan-American union, Washington wanted no such formal ties. Latin nations were searching for such links even before Washington had passed the No Transfer Principle, or Canning had penned his proposal, or Adams and Monroe had finally shaped their message. The message was primarily concerned with European exclusion, to make way for US opportunity. Latin America was the object of the document, but the subject was Transatlantic relations; the New World versus the Old World. In 1810 as Chile sought independence, its Declaration included a passage suggesting: 'the States of America must unite for their external security against the aims of Europe, and to avoid wars between themselves which would annihilate these new born States'. Several contemporary statements preceded Monroe's message. Perhaps the most proximate to the US message was made by Don Manuel Torres, the Colombian chargé d'affaires in Washington in 1821 who wrote to Adams, outlining the monarchical ambitions of the Holy Alliance in Mexico. He urged Monroe 'no longer to delay a measure which will naturally establish an American alliance, capable of counteracting the projects of the European Powers, and of protecting our republican institutions'.[33]

Adams was not interested in such compacts on independence or self-determination. Latin statesmen were made aware in 1826 that they would have to fend for themselves should any threat arise. Washington sought unilateral freedom, while Latin America sought mutual security arrangements. While Bolivar, like the Wilsonian League of Nations later, sought entanglement for mutual benefit, for Pan-American solidarity, Secretary of State Clay warned against such collusion. Bolivar wanted to promote republicanism. The Congress of Panama wanted to assist Cuba and Puerto Rico achieve independence from Spain, but the US did not want to see change at that time. Clay indicated that 'for ourselves we desire no change in the possession or political condition of that island, and . . . we could not, with indifference, see it transferred from Spain to any other European power. We are unwilling to see its transfer or annexation to either of the new American States.' Washington's unilateral ambitions meant a rejection of collective security in Panama in 1826; how ironic that Woodrow Wilson should later propose the universal application of the Monroe Doctrine! It was assumed that the United States would be the commanding power, and that Latin nations would be the subjects of their decisions. It was not a Pan-Americanism of mutual respect and the equality of nations; it was not a doctrine that sought to secure and advance the cause of republicanism. The primary US ambition was to consolidate power and to leave the way open for further annexation, conquest and settlement of the continental empire. It was essentially fuelled by nationalism. Writing in 1934, Nerval regretted the outcome:

> For if Pan Americanism had been born then, in Panamá, it would not have been the Pan Americanism of Blaine – the Pan Americanism of the *Pan American Union*, of non-committal, diplomatic flirting, of flowery speeches and forgotten "recommendations" – which is still the Pan Americanism of today, and which, from time to time, has permitted the Pan Americanism of Theodore Roosevelt's *Big stick,* of Taft's *dollar diplomacy,* of Wilson's *paternalism,* of Coolidge's *big brother* rôle.[34]

That sort of paternalism and the US sense of superiority lasted beyond Nerval's time. By the 1980s President Reagan still sought Nicaraguan subservience: 'Say, Uncle,' he demanded, between an onslaught of rhetoric on the principles of US foreign policy. In the 1820s US officials had little contact with Latin Americans. Their attitudes were formed through collisions with Mexicans. Both Mexico and the United States were born out of the system of British and Spanish decolonisation and the systemic rivalry that existed between the colonial powers continued into the nineteenth century. By the end of the US–Mexican war of 1846 to 1848 Mexico had lost half its territory. John Quincy Adams died of a stroke in 1848 resulting from a vigorous damnation of the use of power to acquire that territory. He expected such places to gravitate of their own accord towards the Union. Still, the prevailing attitude, fuelled by much domestic propaganda, was that Latin Americans were both economically and politically backward, oppressed by Catholicism, ignorant, racially inferior, and insufficiently republican. Latin Americans were imagined and depicted as infantile, often feminised or needing some form of tutelage in US-style civilisation. These attitudes facilitated the US justification to 'educate', police, or generally assume the 'leadership' of the Western Hemisphere.[35] Manifest destinies opened new horizons for US expansionists and simultaneously removed the individual agency or culpability for undermining self-determination across the continent through references to higher, more noble purposes.

Conclusion

The 'empire for liberty' in the north was free to colonise the continent while stressing its belief in self-determination in the south.[36] But self-determination was asserted against the European colonial powers and not for the nascent Latin nations. Their struggles for independence were used by Washington to demonstrate that there existed a changing world and that Europe should not seek to deny such progress. The hard-won liberty, born out of Napoleon's victories in Spain, were incidental to US diplomacy, the preservation of which was not necessarily an end. Indeed, in the name of the Monroe Doctrine, Latin American nations were often denied their self-determination through US intervention, especially from the 1890s to the 1920s, and again during the Cold War period. Democracy was often secondary to other US interests: order, stability, opportunity, the exercise of hegemony, access to resources, the denial of alternatives, whether nationalist or socialist.

To Europeans the message began with the assertion against colonisation. But Washington could do little when the Malvinas were occupied and said little during the 'scramble for Africa'. Colonialism was opposed to the extent that it limited US opportunity and interests. To that extent the message of 1823 anticipated the Open Door notes of 1899 and 1900 in which self-determination was concurrently promoted with US economic access. Advocating an open and international system, Washington often pursued a 'spheres of influence' approach, at each point reinventing the West, securing its existence, against external pressures and alternative philosophies.

That the United States led by their example on the issues of decolonisation, self-determination and democracy needs to be seriously questioned. At once US officials were aware that democracy depended on popular consent and yet they did not consider a Catholic-ridden continent fit for the virtues of democratic government. The irreducible contradiction between messianism and exceptionalism was not resolved, unless one assumes that its primary aim was to galvanise US society and enhance its identity.

The Monroe Doctrine survived as a cornerstone of US diplomacy into the late twentieth century. But in the late nineteenth and early twentieth centuries, especially epitomised by Roosevelt's corollaries, it was used to justify US intervention in Central American and Caribbean affairs. President Wilson used both elements of the doctrine. In search of monsters to destroy, he put it forth to begin the dismantling process of European colonisation after the First World War. And he frequently used the 'big stick' in the Caribbean and Central America. Franklin Roosevelt, to some extent, revived Bolivar's understanding of state to state Pan Americanism. 'Defending the West', Truman, Eisenhower, Kennedy, Johnson, Nixon and Reagan used the doctrine to preserve the hemisphere from the 'Soviet menace'. The doctrine was used frequently in the history of US diplomacy and in such a diverse set of circumstances that it could usually be used to gain approval for US policy and ambition. Given the deference of the US public to presidential rhetoric, especially when directed against an external threat, the doctrine was an effective political tool. LaFeber contends that in 'US diplomacy the Doctrine has become the equivalent of the Emperor's new clothes'.[37]

3

IMPERIALISMS

Old and new

The third construct that remained potent throughout the twentieth century derived from long traditions of US imperialism. From soon after the Declaration of Independence, the former colonies, by then states, expanded westward. Territories were acquired and incorporated into the Union. Texas, an independent state, was added in 1845. Mexico lost half of its territory in the wars of 1846 to 1848. And then Americans settled the west, fulfilling their 'manifest destinies' through processes of border colonisation. Even though 1853 completed the contiguous territorial expansion, Alaska and Hawaii were added in 1867 and 1898. The Civil War fought in the 1860s prevented the Confederate states' secession. Colonisation and imperialism were central to the US experience even though those characteristics are not normally associated with their identity or collective memories. The foundations of US power derive from the historical reality that by the late nineteenth century they had acquired a vast continental empire rich in land and resources. The Civil War intensified the process of industrialisation and over subsequent decades US manufacturers, business and government realised that the domestic sphere was insufficient to sustain the growth of the economy and the industrial boom. US imperialism turned outward. Washington acquired a string of colonies across the Pacific, protectorate status over other islands and ultimately when the old-style European colonialism proved divisive and inefficient, when the Anti-Imperial movement rejected the option of continued colonialism, US expansionism returned to the more informal, less obvious, more efficient economic expansionism. The policies associated with the Open Door were ushered in. With the combination of both forms of colonialism, Washington constructed a new empire.[1]

At each juncture of expansion the society was divided on the true nature of US identity. Each time expansion took place there were groups that objected on the basis that expansion betrayed US traditions, undermined the notion of consent and the self-determination of others. These issues were even more acute with overseas US expansionism because these areas and peoples would not ultimately be included in the Union and therefore would not benefit from the negative liberties afforded by the Constitution. The rejection of formal colonialism coupled with the pursuit of economic expansionism resolved the dilemma on the government of others and reinforced the accepted traditions of US diplomacy.

Imperialism

Imperialism lies at the heart of US foreign relations. Distinction needs to be made between the formal 'European' style of imperialism (normally colonialism) and that of the so-called informal 'American' imperialism.[2] Traditional interpretations characterise the United States as an imperial power between 1898 and 1946, the period of colonial government of the Philippines. The more informal methods of control were downplayed. Such constructions best suited the US identity and were often reflected in the historiography as an aberration, the worst chapter in US history. However, wider definitions of imperialism facilitate a better understanding of US policy. The periods of formal expansion, 'domestic' and 'overseas', and the exercise of hegemony beyond the political sphere must be included. Motivations are important, as are the economic structures that propel the world system. Said suggests a more inclusive term beyond 'colonialism' or the settling of territory to include the practice, theory and 'attitudes of a dominating metropolitan centre ruling a distant territory'. Hence control or a dominating influence that moves beyond mere political authority needs to be acknowledged and identified. Far from being an aberration, US expansionism has been a consistent feature of its history and this has always involved power over others. Apart from intentions, one must incorporate outcome. Manifest Destiny and Progressivism may have been the justifications, and provided ideological legitimacy, but the conduct of westward conquest and then overseas imperialism had devastating effects on the Native Americans and the Filipinos which cannot be written out as aberrations. Joseph Fry contends that, 'only by ignoring such outcomes and the coercion involved or by attempting to narrowly define US imperialism out of existence can the image of American innocence and the fundamental uniqueness of imperialism, American style be sustained'. Wider definitions of imperialism incorporate the US experience more effectively. Osterhammel suggests,

> 'Imperialism' is the concept that comprises all forces and activities contributing to the construction and the maintenance of *trans-colonial empires*. Imperialism presupposes the will and the ability of an imperial centre to *define* as imperial its own national interests and enforce them worldwide in the anarchy of the international system.[3]

In addition to the wider definitions, one has to include the systemic and ideological basis for expansion. By the turn of the century economic access and integration were considered increasingly important to relieve domestic tensions. The theological explanations for expansion gave way to secular justifications. The discourse of Manifest Destiny remained pertinent, but the movement overseas was a much more conscious act that involved central organisation, of a military type, rather than the widespread westward migrations and settlement (though the military was also used to secure that process). The destiny to expand beyond the borders was not manifest to a wide range of people in the culture of the 1890s. The widespread controversy on imperialism forced Americans to rethink their identity and their place in the world, which had become smaller and more proximate through technological advance and European imperialism. Stephanson writes, 'the outside world of the 1890s was far closer both in time and space, appeared in fact ominously crowded and competitive. The setting was now different, and so, ultimately, was the framing of destiny.' Theological explanations gave way to language based on modernisation and civilisation, and 'as geographical destiny ceased to be continental and "American," its spatial character became clear, less manifest'.[4]

While there were specific antagonisms, there was considerable Anglo-American collaboration and shared attitudes.[5] US imperial attitudes shared the British values, especially under Theodore Roosevelt. The rhetoric of 'civilisation' was tremendously important during this period for justifications of both US empire and British imperialism. US justifications rested on 'civilisational imperialism under Anglo-Saxon impress'.[6] The 'special relationship' derived in part from the passing of power from one hegemony to the next during the transition in the world system. The sheer size and growth of the US economy propelled it into the imperial 'game' with the European Great Powers and Japan. As the US imperial economy followed that of Britain's, the British, so the Americans liked to think, became more American. Further democratisation in Britain made the ideological partnership based on Anglo-Saxon civilisation more acceptable. For Perkins, 'England no longer symbolized monarchical opposition to the ideals of the American republic. . . . [Whereas] Americans never took French republicanism seriously, bewailing the evident lack of cohesion and balance. Russian czarism alienated them.' Washington was also wary of Germany because they 'never seemed nearly as convinced of the wisdom of the American lesson as England'.[7]

Washington was now in an increasingly competitive world in which the dominant narratives of US history were closely linked to their ideals and formal ideologies, though realism and the 'search for opportunity' were central to their experience. 'Henry Cabot Lodge . . . sought to awaken Americans to their place "as one of the great nations of the world." With "a record of conquest, colonisation, and territorial expansion unequalled by any people in the nineteenth century."' As Hunt cites him, they should join the race for 'the waste places of the earth'.[8] It was only after the experience in the Philippines with the continued cost, guerrilla warfare, the casualties and domestic opposition that the United States returned to its anti-colonial identity. It was not that colonialism was un-American, it had simply become too expensive.[9]

The driving force of the new empire was economic. Foreign policy had been somewhat dormant after the Civil War. The process of economic integration and reconstruction occupied the nation. The 'west' was further settled and later rapid industrialisation provided the foundations for the power and might of the United States throughout the twentieth century. Rapid industrial expansion, 'hyper-productivity' coupled with under-consumption led many to search for solutions abroad. Domestic labour unrest and increasing immigration coincided with closing economies abroad through European colonialism. The perceived limits placed on US exports had a significant influence on US attitudes, which were further affected by the perceived closing of the domestic frontier. At the end of the nineteenth century overwhelming domestic economic success impelled Washington to adopt a more active foreign policy.[10]

There was little doubt on the growth of the United States. Britain, partly in deference to the changing relative power, was more amenable to rapprochement. Expansionism presaged domestic controversy, echoed since by historians. The arguments were fundamentally about US identity. How could claims of exceptionalism be reconciled with charges of imperialism?

Colonialism

President William McKinley's (1896–1901) administration was the first significantly to engage US power across the globe. The Philippines was formally colonised and the Open Door notes facilitated continued US expansionism despite the social rejection of formal colonialism. Both pro-cesses had a profound impact on US identity. Despite the rejection of colonialism, Washington had entered the world of imperial powers; it engaged an old European power in war and defeated it easily, it acquired a string of colonies, it projected its power outside the Western Hemisphere, and engaged with the European powers in China.

On one level US imperialism spread through the pursuit of 'interests' similar to those the British had experienced earlier. Ronald Steel reflected back on the British imperial experience, though one could as easily relate a similar narrative on the US pursuit of 'national interests'. Steel explained that having established commercial interests in India, London was com-pelled to protect the northern border in Central Asia and the shipping lines through the Suez Canal. This required a police power in the region and the interests grew ever wider as the population grew ever more disenchanted with their rule. Welfare benefits, infrastructure and police powers were required to maintain an order in these territories. 'Soon they were engaged in tribal conflicts in the heart of Africa – ostensibly to protect their position in India. Since each link was considered vital, the chain got longer and longer until they were running an African empire.'[12] Washington followed a similar pattern although apart from the Philippines it did not administer any other *major* overseas territory as a direct colonial possession. The federal government both promoted and secured US trade and commercial interests.[13] Colonies, territory and naval bases were gathered to secure trade.

However, domestic resistance soon threw up impediments to the initial course. The Anti-Imperial movement made colonialism politically costly and embarrassing, and the suppression of the Filipino resistance led by Aguinaldo imposed unacceptable costs on the US system. Colonialism had suddenly become costly. The treaties with the Native American 'internal colonies' turned into domestic issues.[14] If the anti-imperial sentiments primarily springing from the northeast raised the political costs, the business community and influential intellectuals continued to insist on access to foreign markets and a global US role. The Open Door notes provided a much more cost-effective solution. Economic imperialism was more efficient and much more difficult to associate with US identity.

The McKinley administration is also associated with two features that remain central characteristics of the US experience in the twentieth century: militarisation and centralisation. The McKinley administration was the first to act abroad with the power of the newly created US fleet, which by 1908, when it sailed around the world, was the second largest in the world. Such military strength combined with the domestic pressures to expand gave McKinley the will and the opportunity to engage the Spanish empire in both Cuba and the Philippines. With the increasing propensity to act overseas, there was a concurrent tendency to centralise power around the executive branch relative to that of Congress. The term 'imperial presidency' thus characterises the predominant influence of the executive over the other branches, diminishing the democratic accountability and the basis for the system of checks and balances on issues of foreign policy.[15] Military engagement necessitated increased executive power, which was linked to Brooks Adams's 'velocity' theory: that societies become more centralised and cohesive as power is extended.[16] The apotheosis of this trend was seen in the National Security Act in 1947, which extended executive powers earlier considered inimical.

The war with Spain came relatively quickly, though the causes of it had simmered for years in Cuban attempts to gain independence led by José Martí. In 1898 Washington wanted both to gain Cuban independence from Spain and to inhibit the Cubans from exercising it in any real sense; US opportunities could not be limited through a potential post-independence assertion of Cuban nationalism. The issues of self-determination ran counter to the interests of US business. Martí had earlier warned that the United States posed a threat to what he called 'our America' to distinguish the Latin Americans from the predominantly Anglo-Saxon states. Martí thought it would be necessary for the Cubans to assert a second independence from US expansionism. Laurie Johnston writes:

> Martí did not fear anything so crude as invasion and conquest. Rather, he recognised the dangers posed by an unequal economic relationship. "The nation that buys, commands," he cautioned. "The nation that sells, serves. It is necessary to balance trade in order to guarantee liberty. The nation eager to die sells to a single nation, and the one eager to save itself sells to more than one. A country's excessive influence over the commerce of another becomes political influence."[17]

Despite the assistance against the Spanish, Cuban aspirations for independence were ultimately undermined through US control. The progressive ideologies of the period, the desire to uplift, to educate and to civilise the Cubans provided the ideological justifications in Washington. Cuba's self-determination was considered in terms of national independence from European colonialism, but was not promoted in terms of enhancing democratic participation within the state. To have addressed such popular desires would have run counter to US hegemonic interests.

When the *Maine* was sunk on 15 February 1898, media competition and US jingoism pushed the country towards war in the belief that the Spanish were responsible. Congress supported the cause of Cuban independence and the protection of US interests and property. McKinley obtained $50 million to mobilise for war.[18] A barrage of ultimatums was put to Spain, though McKinley chose to ignore some diplomatic options. The Teller Amendment, attached to the war message of 1 April 1898, served both an ideological and economic purpose. The assertion 'that the United States hereby disclaims any disposition to exercise sovereignty, jurisdiction, or control over said Island except for the pacification thereof, and asserts its determination, when that is accomplished, to leave the government and control of the island to its people' enhanced Washington's reputation as a new type of Great Power, but prevented equal economic exchange between Cuba and the US.

Though Washington wanted to see the Spanish out of the island, its earlier policies in part caused the economic misery on the island. LaFeber contends that in this (and other) instances initial disorder created more long-term US opportunities. Washington triggered the revolts through economic tariffs that exacerbated the Cuban situation. The 1894 Wilson–Gorman tariff inhibited Cuban economic access to the United States and brought on a decline in Cuban living standards. Cuban nationalists directed their anger first at the Spanish authorities, but soon identified the US as part of the cause of their condition and destroyed US property. The dangers of Cuban nationalism had loomed in the anti-US stance of Martí's followers.[19] Thus Washington was content to promote national independence that would enhance its opportunities in the world system, but was cautious about enhancing Cuban self-determination that might harm US interests.

The 'splendid little war' was brought to a quick end when the Spanish sued for peace in July 1898. Independence was immediately controversial. On the surrender, no Cuban signed the document. The island was soon declared a protectorate, to be tutored in democracy, which formally lasted until 1902 and more informally until 1959. The constitutional convention gathered under General Leonard Wood in 1900. Though Cubans were given responsibility for domestic laws, Washington maintained considerable control. It could intervene to protect Cuban 'independence'. Foreign debt could be limited to prevent European powers returning in search of repayment, and Washington obtained a lease on Guantanamo, which remains a US military base. The phraseology in the Platt Amendment of 1901 to the Cuban Constitution is more reminiscent of Locke than of Jefferson: the US had the right 'to intervene for the preservation of Cuban independence, the maintenance of a government adequate for the protection of life, property, and individual liberty'. Despite the progressive meddling the United States was not responsible for Cuban 'happiness'. Cuban consent to the Constitution was only provided following economic duress. General Wood told Roosevelt there was 'little or no independence left' for Cuba.[20] In the longer run the Platt Amendment became a symbolic focus for Cuban resistance, resentment and anti-Americanism. The following decades of US intervention and client regimes fermented the subsequent revolutionary movements more than any 'alien' or 'Soviet'-inspired ideologies. The Philippines was acquired after a relatively brief war. But Filipino resistance to US occupation, the domestic US opposition and the 'pacification' programme quickly turned the public against the formal colonial experience. Democratisation had not been the intention of the war, but progressive intellectuals and politicians used it as a justification for their occupation. The prevalent US perception was that the Filipinos were an inferior, ignorant and superstitious people, to paraphrase William Howard Taft, the US governor and later president. McKinley further justified US power through reference to Christianity, even though the Spanish had largely converted the islands. McKinley thought 'there was nothing left for us to do but take them all, and to educate the Filipinos, and uplift and Christianize them. . . . I went to bed . . . and slept soundly.' The reasoning, coupled with progressive ideals, appeased sectors of US society, even though in 1900 Taft indicated that they would need training for about 50 to 100 years to learn 'what Anglo-Saxon liberty is'. After 'pacifying' Aguinaldo's forces resulting in 220,000 deaths, and 4,000 US fatalities, Washington introduced political and social reforms and institutionalised democracy on the islands, which remained a colony until 1946.[21] But democratisation was the second best option. Statehood had been considered and rejected on the grounds of ethnic difference. The inclusion of the Philippines would have made it the largest state in the Union.[22]

The nationalist forces were armed and resisted US intended sovereignty until it was imposed. 'Democratisation' came at the expense of Filipino self-determination. Instead Washington relied on a 'nationalized client class' to carry out the US programme. When, in the 1930s, it was decided to grant independence, it was largely a result of congressional concerns to limit Filipino imports. Moreover, there is little evidence to suggest that either Britain, in granting India independence (1947), or France, in resisting Indochinese independence (till 1954), paid the slightest attention to Washington's leadership on decolonisation in 1946.[23] The idea that the Philippines provided a model for decolonisation is a misconception. Throughout, US actions were predicated on its contemporary needs rather than concerns for liberty, democracy or self-determination.

Anti-imperialism

The imperial experience brought back the old tension between liberty and expansion in US society and with it the struggle over national identity. The century that had opened with Jefferson questioning whether man could 'be trusted with the government of others' ended with the colonisation of the Philippines and elsewhere. The colonisation of these territories could be justified on the assumption that they would eventually be granted statehood and enjoy the benefits of negative liberty and representation. The competing groups in the debates on imperialism could harness the two experiences and characteristics of US history. The tension between self-determination and expansionism returned, but both groups could invoke the same source to legitimate their argument. Republican Senator George Hoar put it succinctly: 'The mighty figure of Thomas Jefferson comes down in history with the Declaration of Independence in one hand, and the title deed of Louisiana in the other. . . . Do you think his left hand knew what his right hand did?' The anti-imperialists George Hoar, William Jennings Bryan, William James, Carl Schurz could claim the true identity of the nation by pointing to the Jefferson of 1776 or 1801. With as plausible validity the imperialists Theodore Roosevelt, Henry Cabot Lodge, McKinley and Alfred Thayer Mahan, for example, could point to the

Jefferson who in 1803 doubled the size of the United States. The nationalisms of state security and formal ideology clashed.[24]

The anti-imperialists were a diverse group of congressmen, ex-presidents and state officials, authors, industrialists and educators. Their diversity diminished their effectiveness. They considered the imperial venture un-American. Moreover, it could draw the United States into imperial competition, and impose burdens on its resources and corrupt the democratic foundations of the state. These morally inclined arguments had already assimilated the experience of the internal colonies that had just been incorporated under domestic law. The imperialists, however, invigorated by the arguments of social Darwinism and racist attitudes, saw in the struggle for the Philippines a test of their worth, strength and identity. The associations of militarism, struggle and progress in history were closely associated with Theodore Roosevelt's ideas and remain potent connections in the identity of US foreign policy.[25]

The anti-imperialists objected on several grounds. The Constitution and US traditions were violated because the foundations of representative government were undermined. US forces did not protect individual liberties and did not gain the consent of those governed. After three years of imperialism, in 1901, Congress argued that 'extra-constitutional powers' could be exercised as an 'insular case'. Diplomatic arguments suggested that the exclusive US possession of the islands would draw them into an imperial conflict with the Old World through which they would lose their political exceptionalism. Racist objections suggested that the Union could not tolerate such a large and different ethnic group. Moral and political objections were raised to assert that liberty, democracy and republican government were the right of all peoples and should be universally applicable. And finally, echoing John Quincy Adams, the United States should 'go not abroad in search of monsters to destroy', but lead the world through its example. The historical basis of the movement suggested that 'imperialism destroyed the unquestioned belief in American innocence and uniqueness'.[26]

By the turn of the century Washington increasingly resorted to militarism to obtain concessions and pursue interests abroad. Since expansionism was no longer continental, its justifications had to change; Manifest Destiny required readjustment. Imperialism in its colonial guise was rejected but there was considerable consensus on continued expansionism. The conflation of various contradictory ideas may have placated the domestic population, but foreigners were often incredulous. LaFeber writes that the fact that the US had 'competed with Europeans for world power was true. That they ultimately proved to be as vulnerable to the demands, even corruptions, of world power as the Europeans and Japanese also was true. That they appeared, with good reason, to Filipinos, Cubans,

Chinese, and Central Americans as little different than other imperialists was true as well.'[27]

Even if there was a strong reaction to colonialism in the Philippines, the culture had little propensity to resist the much more ameliorative term 'expansionism'. US traditions and ideologies had always been closely associated with expansion, but these visions of national greatness[28] were often contradictory to the negative liberties that informed so much of its formal ideologies and principled pronouncements. Notwithstanding this contradiction, the US needed to continue expansionism and link it to the promotion of liberty and democracy. Free trade, an issue at the heart of the American Revolution and one cause of the war for independence, could therefore be closely associated with US traditions and identity. Economic power, unlike political power, was far less likely to attract the same opposition in a culture that assumed that capitalism enhanced freedom. Moreover, issues central to democratic theory, negative liberty, human rights and consent are rarely addressed in US economic policy even though the impact on human welfare was and is profound.[29]

Opening doors

Frederick Jackson Turner's thesis brought together comfortable explanations for the unrest, the strikes, the labour violence and the depressions of the 1890s. US culture was ready to accept arguments that new frontiers would provide solutions to these problems. The Turner thesis pointed out that many American characteristics – individualism, nationalism, democracy and the political makeup of the nation – depended on the ability to expand west into the free land. But this period of history was over. Centuries of success and expansion had been checked by the closing frontier and Americans had to come to terms with the implications: their living space was limited. They either had to adjust their institutions and worldview, revise their methods or expand in a different manner. Turner's words introduced a new era: 'And now, four centuries from the discovery of America, at the end of a hundred years of life under the Constitution, the frontier has gone, and with its going has closed the first period of American history.' Expansion into the west could no longer resolve US dilemmas; and yet liberty required adherence to Madison's injunction to 'expand the sphere'. The new 'West' into which the US could pursue expansionism would ultimately be found in the 'East'. Civilisation would be represented in its highest form under systems of capitalism. Liberal thought assumed that the pacific elements of free trade would reduce international tensions and promote the American vision of an increasingly homogeneous world.[30] The rather influential phrase, 'the business of America is business', epitomises the cultural conflation of often-contradictory concepts.

But just in case US business was not competitive or effective, or if others chose not to share the vision predicated on more than a century of conquest, other intellectual and strategic formulations were necessary. Alfred Thayer Mahan's thesis on the *Influence of Sea Power on History* postulated that domestic production and the search for colonies drove the competition amongst the great sea powers. Though colonies were politically unattractive, expansion was at the heart of great power status. With Brooks Adams's thesis in *The Law of Civilisation and Decay* expansion was deemed necessary to sustain US power. The boundaries of international trade provided new frontiers. Where previously the oceans had been regarded as a moat for US protection, they were transformed into highways of commercial activity and exchange, supported by a large navy developed during the 1890s.[31]

The federal government was heavily involved in assisting US 'free trade'. Emily Rosenberg uses the term 'promotional state' to describe the connections between government and business during the period. Even though the US market could have been expanded through domestic innovations such as more intense advertising, policy makers of the 1890s assumed that expansion of foreign trade was required to relieve domestic tensions. The government both promoted US trade and goods and ensured a conducive environment for trade abroad. Fuelled by the belief that spheres of influence and closed economies lead to militarism, Washington became active in opening up closed economies and maintaining access. The State Department opined in 1898 that 'enlargement of foreign consumption of the products of our mills and workshops has, therefore, become a serious problem of statesmanship as well as of commerce . . . and we can no longer afford to disregard international rivalries now that we ourselves have become a competitor in the world-wide struggle for trade'. The idea of 'struggle' complemented prevalent Darwinist theories and the associated cultural values. But even as Washington endeavoured to open the trade of the East through the Open Door notes of 1899 and 1900, Europeans were quick to notice that the Western Hemisphere was increasingly closed to outsiders through Washington's negotiations on special tariff measures. 'Fair field and no favor' had only limited applicability.[32]

Not all countries would prosper from an open system, or their national interests were better served through closed or colonial economic arrangements. Europeans did point out that Washington only implemented their ideas on the Open Door approach in areas where the other powers had the political advantage. Charles Conant, a State Department adviser, made the link between commerce and the military. 'The United States have actually reached, or are approaching, the economic state where . . . outlets are required outside their own boundaries, in order to prevent business depression, idleness, and suffering at home.' He explained that in these circumstances markets and access were crucial and the government had to enter international politics 'reluctantly', but was 'compelled by the instinct of self-preservation'. The world had shrunk through modern technology and the domestic sphere was no longer large enough to contain the US expansionist drive. Rosenberg writes succinctly:

> Lurking in Conant's analysis was a proposition that Woodrow Wilson would elevate into a national article of faith: that creation of a liberal international order would ultimately foster the conditions for world peace. As long as restrictionism and spheres of influence prevailed, however, militarism – particularly the construction of a larger navy – would seem a necessary part of the promotional state.

Even though Americans did not agree on the form of expansion there was a considerable consensus that it was vital, through dissemination of superior American ideas and goods.[33] Sea power and later air power were frequently the guarantors of such ideas and an international order was predicated on Open Door economies.

Empire had become a way of life in American culture. Expansion had been a continuous trend since independence, even if the methods and the justifications had changed.[34] Understanding US ideologies is central to explaining policy makers' attitudes, yet these attitudes need to be coupled with their material interests and their unwillingness to engage seriously with local protest and voices of dissent. Ideologies associated with progressive policies may explain the basis for US domination over other societies, but often progress in the economic sphere was assumed to represent progress in the human condition. The distinction between economic growth and human progress needs to be made. Dependency theorists posit a crucial difference between 'growth' and 'development'. The former reflects the performance of investment and capital, while the latter deals more with the human condition.[35] In arguments on whether free trade promotes growth it is crucial to distinguish between the growth of the national economies and human development, based on criteria involving living standards, liberty and justice.

The conflict between the imperialists and the anti-imperialists was not just a two-sided affair. US expansionism, to which no major domestic constituency objected, continued without the need to acquire colonies. Howard Zinn refers to this third way as 'a more sophisticated approach to imperialism than the traditional empire building of Europe'. Washington wanted to convince the European powers and Japan that the exclusive colonial system was confrontational, dangerous and inefficient. Commerce, on the other hand, was a catalyst leading to pacific relations. Washington tried to secure access to the China market through Secretary of State John Hay's Open Door notes in 1899 and 1900.[36]

The new frontiers of US diplomacy, the site of individualism, character building and initiative, could be forged through business. The psychological stress of conceptually closing frontiers could be overcome through an invigorated foreign trade. Interests rapidly moved beyond the continent, secure in ideological consensus, governmental support, and a strong navy. US exports increased seven-fold during the decades around the turn of the century, while imports did not keep pace. Though not formal colonies, the nations that we now refer to as Third World were subject to decisions made thousands of miles away at the metropolitan centres of the world system. Chinese self-determination was incidental to the second set of notes sent in 1900. Washington did not apply the objective of self-determination consistently over time or space. The Caribbean and Central American countries were frequently subject to US intervention. In China the Open Door notes accounted for US interests first. Self-determination was a legitimating tool that accorded with the assumed traditions of US diplomacy, and could be used to inhibit Chinese colonisation by the other Great Powers. But the Chinese were permitted little latitude to determine their fate or regulate the decisions affecting their economic relations. Their views were rarely considered and Washington rarely consulted them.

The word 'imperialism' can be used to describe situations in which the ability of local power to exercise self-determination was undermined through economic decisions taken in distant metropolitan centres. The characteristic is not immediately apparent when Washington primarily conducts its relationship with the national élite, who also benefit from the world system, even if the national interest or human development is not served through such connections. Promoting democracy in such cases would hinder US interests. Where the national élite did not benefit from reciprocal trade arrangements, or intended to assert their self-determination through the rejection of US conditions, however, Washington frequently sought their removal or tried to promote a form of democracy. The 'big stick' imposed a form of economic and with it cultural imperialism, which undermined self-determination just as effectively as older forms of colonial rule. The 'peripheral' regions were required to maintain systems ameliorative to the global economic system; they were increasingly subjected to pressures to open their economies in an increasingly competitive world system. Despite these injunctions to the European and Japanese governments, Washington closed doors in the Western Hemisphere. The 'big stick', dollar diplomacy, and an extension of the Monroe Doctrine to cover commercial issues under President Wilson ensured that the sphere remained relatively closed. The decline of rival powers, the globalising economic system and the advances of technology and communications that increasingly penetrated the sovereignty of nation-states ensured that there were few who could check US power to revive its profitability and pacify domestic industrial strife.[38]

The notes delivered in 1900 added to the issue of equal access that of self-determination. US policy was to 'seek a solution to bring about permanent safety and peace to China, preserve Chinese territorial and administrative entity, protect all rights guaranteed to friendly powers by treaty and international law, and safeguard for the world the principle of equal and impartial trade with all parts of the Chinese Empire'. The conjunction of equal access with self-determination made the link between US commercial interests and its foreign policy stance. It established the basis for a principled defence of freedom on the seas while the United States was still building its navy, and could be linked to the ideological values of promoting freedom. Its widespread applicability later meant that it lost the coherence of a formal doctrine in US policy. Ultimately, it had a profound effect on US attitudes to trade and to the history of US foreign relations. The growing US trade with China and the aspect of self-determination included in the notes strengthened the idea that impartial trade avoided the need for European-style colonialism and enhanced peaceful relations between states.[39]

Hay's basic description of the Open Door notes was 'fair field and no favor'. But in this case the assertion of fairness was clearly in the US interest. Washington, to the incredulity of others, was selective about the application of these principles. Spain was granted a ten-year access to the markets of the Philippines, but the other powers were not accorded such access to the archipelago or to the Western Hemisphere. In Europe, where US power was limited, it did not pursue an Open Door approach until after the Second World War. The Monroe Doctrine remained the central feature defining the two spheres. Yet Washington insisted on the freedom to traverse the oceans even in times of war. This demonstrated the importance of Europe to the United States, but the appeal to law demonstrated US weakness: 'when American naval strength grew to a point that it could not only effectively protect US maritime interests but advantageously command the trade of others, the doctrine of freedom of the seas was soon eclipsed'.[40]

McKinley was straightforward about his ambitions. Markets had to be obtained to secure US power, economy and the 'American way of life'. The Open Door notes had a profound impact on subsequent US diplomacy. The ideas advocating the notion of equal access of all powers, first specifically to the trade of China, and then more widely applied, formed the basis of US policy on trade into the future. The concept found its way into several subsequent statements of US policy: Wilson's Fourteen Points (1918), the Atlantic Charter (1941), the various GATT negotiations, and formed the basis of the World Trade Organisation (1995).

Conclusion

The Open Door relieved the domestic pressure associated with the closing frontier in the American mind. It took the 'fury out of the fight' between the imperialists and the anti-imperialists; it alleviated the concerns with colonialism, but enhanced economic expansion. The Open Door was 'conceived and designed to win the victories without the wars'. Though it differed considerably from traditional colonialism, it was a form of empire building none the less. 'When an advanced industrial nation plays, or tries to play, a controlling and one-sided role in the development of a weaker economy then the policy of the more powerful country can with accuracy and candor only be described as imperial.'[41] Whether benign or not, such restriction undermines national self-determination and democratic participation.

The spirit of Manifest Destiny had continued through the US industrial and overseas expansion. Those territories conquered from the Native Americans or from the Mexicans, and later the colony of Hawaii, could ultimately be justified through their inclusion within the system of negative liberty. After resistance, consent was derived through the electoral politics imposed on these territories (though in Hawaii there are still voices of dissent). Beyond the states there was little popular consent. And whatever ideological justification was used within the United States or to the recipients of US policy, Washington pursued more or less unchecked positive liberties. Though conflict and consensus are normal paradigms through which to view US history and policy, and though it would be ludicrous to suggest a homogeneity within the US after the Civil War, on foreign policy there was a predominant consensus on the needs for expansion, though not through further colonialism.[42]

With the increasing globalisation of US power through the Open Door policies, the political basis of liberty and democracy, bounded by the particular experience of the nation-state, was rarely questioned in US policy. Consent, legitimacy, constituency and representation were not considered problematic. The capitalist world system places a primacy on economic growth, the right to secure property, whereas the ideals of democracy and liberty, 'the pursuit of happiness', are more relevant to the human condition. The conjunction of the two has produced a lasting tension. US economic power, whether capitalist or a part of the promotional state, ignores political boundaries and undermines political rights. The fundamental notions of liberty, democracy and consent, beyond the sphere, have always been problematical. The imposition of US power through economic dominance relied constantly on 'words softly spoken, to adapt Roosevelt's use of the West African proverb, but its chosen instrument in foreign policy, where expansion was inhibited, was often the big stick'.[43]

Part II

THE AMERICAN CENTURY

4

CONSTRUCTING THE
AMERICAN CENTURY

Together, Theodore Roosevelt (1901–1909) and Woodrow Wilson (1913–1921) carved out several lasting patterns in twentieth-century US foreign relations. They have often been contrasted to each other in the traditional historiography in terms of hard-nosed realism and lofty idealism. And though more recently these characterisations have been broken down with more particular studies of the administrations, the cultural shadows these figures cast are more or less still wedded to their earlier images.[1] Roosevelt's policies ensured that the United States became one of the Great Powers alongside the European imperial powers. Where US power was not supreme, Roosevelt pursued realist balance-of-power relations in which spheres of influence were clearly understood. His attitude towards the Latin Americans, within the US sphere, was paternalistic. Their societies, economies and resources were there to complement that of the United States. Order and intervention in pursuit of US interests characterised the hemispheric policies of Roosevelt's administration. President William Howard Taft (1909–1913), less enthused by Roosevelt's wont to demonstrate supremacy through struggle, emphasised commercialism in US diplomacy, 'dollar diplomacy', as it became known. President Wilson injected a further dose of idealism in his ambition to promote democracy, self-determination for all nations and simultaneously to pursue US interests. The contradictions or the difficulties in reconciling these divergent aspirations in US diplomacy undermined Wilson's ability to conduct a coherent foreign policy. The Mexican Revolution undid many of his ideals, and he increasingly resorted to the use of power, frequently intervening in the Caribbean and Latin America. The First World War projected the United States into world affairs though Wilsonianism immediately suffered at the hands of the post-war settlement and senatorial rejection of his ambitions. Still, if one accepts the essentialist characteristics of these presidencies, the 'warrior', the banker and the 'priest' constructed identities that would inform and vitiate US policy throughout the twentieth century.

The irony of the Spanish–American–Cuban War was that in pursuit of Cuban self-determination it was anti-colonial but soon turned colonial with the US acquisition of the Philippines and hegemony over Cuba. US interests, commercial and colonial, now spanned the globe. In the first two decades of the twentieth century the United States adjusted its diplomacy to that of one of the 'Great Powers'. It was no longer viable to remain aloof from the world or sequestered in the Western Hemisphere. The maintenance of power, the pursuit of its destiny and missionary spirit propelled it to greater global involvement.

When Theodore Roosevelt became president after McKinley's assassination in September 1901, the United States was in a unique position. It had acquired a vast continental empire that was reluctantly united after the Civil War, it was increasingly settled and had undergone industrial boom. The foundations of US power rested in the size of the continent, the technological advances and industrialisation following the Civil War and the growth and consolidation of 'corporatism' by the 1890s. Overproduction stimulated the search for overseas markets in the East; whether these were absolutely necessary or not, they were certainly perceived by policy makers as indispensable.[2] Washington simultaneously became a colonial power and rejected a colonial future. But there was little dissent from the expansionist policies so long as they did not offend the assumed cultural traditions of liberty, progress and self-determination. The looser term 'imperialism' nevertheless still characterised the vigorous search for markets, the wielding of the 'big stick' in Central America and the Caribbean and the assertions of its parochial conceptions of civilisation and world order. The global circumnavigation of the Great White Fleet (1907–1909) symbolically announced the presence of the new regime, whose destiny, power and policies were increasingly recognised and influential. In the half-century to follow its power, commercialism and ideas were increasingly integrated into the world system that facilitated its post-Second World War hegemonic condition. US ideologies adapted to accommodate the opportunities presented by the tremendous growth and power. Theodore Roosevelt's conception of civilisation allowed him to construct a new foreign policy. Wilson grafted his ideas onto the power and vigour of his predecessors. Still, the irony remains, that just as Washington was entering the world of empires, revolution swept across world history, in China, Russia, Mexico and elsewhere in the Western Hemisphere, and challenged the assumed supremacy of the old orders.[3]

Reform was central to the period. And even though the achievements of the Americans fell short of their ambitions, their legacies remained influential. In the international sphere they opposed the extremes of the left and the right; they sought gradual reform between the revolutionary and reactionary options.[4] Yet imperialism of a kind was central to both presidents. In essence they began to lay the foundations of order in the American Century: the use of force, US unilateralism or 'independent internationalism',[5] the primacy of Anglo-Saxon values, and particular economic models of development that brooked little deviance where US power could control it.

Roosevelt's civilisation

Roosevelt's foreign policy was shaped in a world of empires. In the context of Great Power relations the globe was an increasingly crowded place. Europeans had consolidated their hold on Africa and much of Asia. The Open Door existed precariously and in limited places. In the Far East the primary US concern was to balance the powers and mediate the Great Power rivalries (especially those between Japan and Russia, for which Roosevelt received the Nobel Peace Prize in 1906). In Europe Roosevelt avoided involvement.[6] But the Western Hemisphere was crucial. Close to 50 per cent of US investments were in Latin America, primarily in mining and agriculture. Stability was essential to Roosevelt's order, in which US investments had to be protected, and instability or intervention was frequent to stem national movements that inhibited the vision of an integrated sphere. The Caribbean and Central America became especially important after 1904 with the acquisition of land in Panama to build a transoceanic canal.[7] The Roosevelt 'corollary' to the Monroe Doctrine was intended to preserve and promote US interests against encroachments by Europeans and the aspirations of Latin Americans.

A vigorous foreign policy required certainty in the exercise of power. Roosevelt's 'contribution to modernizing U.S. foreign policy consisted in traditionalizing it'. The institutional system of 'checks and balances' was increasingly tilted towards the executive and the White House. Momentum in foreign policy resulted in increasing centralisation. Democratic accountability suffered as a result of the process of traditionalising the making of policy. In time the growth of presidential power at the expense of congress was referred to as the 'imperial presidency'. Roosevelt admired Alexander Hamilton and neo-Federalism; the Jeffersonian ideals were sacrificed in the new world. Roosevelt was a masterly tactician and strategist, unlike Wilson, and had an acute interest in and awareness of the dynamics of international power. His policies still included the messianic traditions of US expansion. Roosevelt promoted his conception of civilisation through an active and strenuous exercise of power. Maintenance of virtue and the promotion of civilisation required exertion, conflict and competition. Decadence in civilisation was a constant threat. Hence, paradoxically, as he put it, 'unless we keep the barbarian virtues, gaining the civilized ones will be of little avail'. Struggle and engagement characterised his foreign policy. As Frank Ninkovich contends, these traits derived from his views on individual virtue and his perception of world politics. Its unity in space and time was crucial, for it obliterated the geographical, cultural, and temporal distinctions between old and new worlds. Should the United States fail to come to terms with this ecumenical trend and its implications, Roosevelt feared that "we shall become isolated from the struggles of the rest of the world, and so immersed in our material prosperity, so that we shall become genuinely effete." Given civilisation's global compass, the implication was unmistakable: henceforth integration into the mainstream of world history must be the guiding theme of American statesmanship.

Roosevelt, therefore, is seen as the statesman who laid the foundations of the subsequent decades of liberal internationalism.[8]

Though destiny was a central feature of Roosevelt's ambition, unlike various theories propagated in the post-Second World War period on the 'end of ideology' or the 'End of History', for Roosevelt the journey could not end. The fulfilment of destiny would mark the demise of the civilisation. The consumerism of the US citizen who inhabits the so-called 'post-historical' society would have appalled the president who advocated a 'strenuous life'.[9] The irony is that then as now the exercise of power was often in pursuit of commercial interests and an increased US comparative advantage. Such imperatives implied a vigorous engagement, primarily against 'disorder', and the universal application of parochial conceptions of civilisation and 'justice'. The sphere in which this was most possible was limited to Central America and the Caribbean.

Roosevelt's conception of civilisation was cosmopolitan but limited by his parochial worldview. His 'orientalist' perception of the world incorporated the discourse of barbarism and civilisation. Societies passed from one to the other with an interim period of armed despotism. The civilised powers were mainly Christian, Anglo-Saxon, western and primarily Anglophone, which facilitated the rapprochement with Britain after the Venezuela border dispute (1895). The barbarians were generally the 'rest' who occupied the underdeveloped spaces of the earth. Ideologies associated with the later writings on modernisation derive from these attitudes that the United States had an obligation to intervene in the name of progress, efficiency, or industry. As Stephanson writes: 'empire as civilized domination showed the historical necessity of establishing order by means of force in the unruly sphere and thus allowing "waste spaces" to be used in the interest of humanity'. Hence, subduing the Native Americans was equivalent of pacifying the Philippine insurrection.[10] And by extension, such sentiments might form the basis for the pacification of Vietnam in the 1960s and Nicaragua in the 1980s, and the isolation of the 'rogue' states of the 1990s. This conception of civilisation demanded integration and an adherence to a prescribed order.

Roosevelt's vision of history was progressive. It was informed by an ambitious nationalism that sought Great Power status. Yet his vision was not deterministic. Individual agency, action and responsibility were essential to his thought. Progress depended on activity, innovation and keeping fit for the purpose. The barbaric sentiment, expressed through conflict, was essential to maintain virtue and moral rectitude. As Stephanson points out, these 'sociobiological arguments could also be used to favor interventionism, [and] improvement'. Roosevelt held the belief that the civilised had both a duty and an obligation to uplift and develop the societies and the economies of the uncivilised. But his was no myopic humanitarianism; it was not characterised by uncritical missionary work. He had a clear eye on US power. He did not overextend US commitments at the expense of its power. His 'civilising' inclinations ended where US spheres or US advantage ended; primarily they were confined to the Western Hemisphere. Still, the ideologies were universal; they had to be. Inspiration and mobilisation would not result from the expression of parochial interests and ambitions. In accord with US tradition and Roosevelt's conception of progress in history, 'spatial stagnation meant regression. Destiny required constant, purposeful intervention in time and space.'[11] However, there was a problem. European powers were filling the globe with colonies and the living space abroad was fast diminishing. Washington had to maintain its sphere and intervention was frequently the method then and throughout the twentieth century.

The Roosevelt corollary

Like former empires, Washington's concern with regional order was related to the growth of its regional interests. In particular cases, where it served US interests, disorder was perfectly acceptable. For instance, rebellion was fomented in Panama to promote independence from Colombia so that the United States could gain access to the land necessary to build the transoceanic canal. The canal, completed in 1914, in turn created further interests inducing further US involvement. Disorder was largely ignored prior to the acquisition but for the rest of the century anything that smacked of regional instability caused apprehension.

Roosevelt's strategic genius is clearly demonstrated in his pronouncements (commonly known as his corollary) on the Monroe Doctrine in both 1904 and 1905. These statements served several interests. When his conception of civilisation and US mission appeared too cosmopolitan for those who adhered to isolationist sentiments, his use of the most enduring doctrine located him within the traditions of US diplomacy. When there were fears that he intended to annex Santo Domingo, the corollaries justified the continued exercise of US power without the acquisition of further territory. And the use of progressive language on improvement and efficiency undermined charges of imperialism. The 'corollary' served as a warning to the European powers to limit their activities in the Western Hemisphere at a time when this region was seen as one of the last opportunities for the United States after European colonisation of much of Africa and Asia. The intervention of the US facilitated its continued commercial opportunity and the protection of its regional interests.

While in 1823 the conceptual division in Monroe's message was between the East and the West, by 1904 that axis had changed to a division of the North from the South, adhering to Roosevelt's beliefs on civilisation and barbarism. He thought that 'in the long run civilized man finds he can keep the peace only by subduing his barbarian neighbour'. The spheres had been transposed but the traditions of orientalism and constructing identity in negative terms of opposition endured. Such binaries proved powerful motivating factors throughout US diplomacy.

Roosevelt's adaptation of the West African proverb to 'speak softly' and 'carry a big stick' is generally a good starting point for his corollary. The use of progressive language justified the transformation of the doctrine. Law and order were paramount while European powers threatened to collect their debts in the Western Hemisphere. Roosevelt's ambition was to keep European powers out of the hemisphere, to preclude them from collecting their debts as a result of regional disorder, and from pursuing potential colonial ambitions. Further 'threats' existed in the form of the nationalistic revolutionary movements most pertinently in Central America. Economic autarky could provoke Europeans to collect their investments and protect their citizens and exclude US interests. Considering such action a violation of the Monroe Doctrine, Washington ultimately decided to assume the role of debt collector and tutor to the region.[12]

Taking action in Santo Domingo, Roosevelt announced his corollary in December 1904. If the United States was limiting the scope of the extra-hemispherical powers, it had the responsibility to uphold obligations due to them. Thus, Roosevelt indicated, 'All this country desires is to see the neighbouring countries stable, orderly, and prosperous.' Development was essential to the justification. So,

> If a nation shows that it knows how to act with reasonable efficiency and decency in social and political matters, if it keeps order and pays its obligations, it need fear no interference from the United States. Chronic wrongdoing, or an impotence which results in general loosening of the ties of civilized society, may in America, as elsewhere, ultimately require intervention by some civilized nation, and in the Western Hemisphere the adherence of the United States to the Monroe Doctrine may force the United States, however reluctantly, in flagrant cases of wrongdoing or impotence, to the exercise of an international police power.[13]

The passage anticipated threads in US policy that constantly appeared throughout the twentieth century. Justice lay, not necessarily in development and socio-economic distribution, anathema to the US tradition, but in the efficient use of resources. Moreover, Washington was willing to exercise 'police power' to ensure that a particular order prevailed. Alternative options were not tolerated to any significant degree.

Ironically, Roosevelt then claimed that the interests of the Latin republics and the US were in fact identical. From his perspective and that of the later ideologies that informed the world economic system, these interests lay in the efficient use of resources: development implied economic growth. Yet dependency theorists have contrasted this with notions of development that concentrate on improving human rights and welfare.[14] Within his own framework, Roosevelt informed his audience that 'They have great riches, and if within their borders the reign of law and justice obtains, prosperity is sure to come with them. While they thus obey the primary laws of civilized society they may rest assured that they will be treated by us in a spirit of cordial and helpful sympathy.' However, if US 'rights' were violated through an 'unwillingness to do justice at home' which curtailed US 'freedom' and 'independence', then the nation 'must ultimately realize that the right of such independence can not be separated from the responsibility of making good use of it'.[15] The self-determination of the smaller powers was a corollary of US freedom not an end in itself.

Such formulations severely limited the sovereignty of other independent nations and set an intellectual precedent for continued intervention throughout the century, with a brief respite in the 1930s. The reasoning made nonsense out of the combination of a political system based on the Westphalia model of the primacy of the nation-state with the global economic system of integration and permeable borders. The sentiment and prescription of the Roosevelt corollary, though temporally limited to Central American and Caribbean, later undermined Third World sovereignty through US intervention, restricting the development of 'alien' political ideologies during the Cold War.

The prescribed economic order generated wealth for US corporations, for a local élite and, in absolute macroeconomic terms, sometimes for the state. However, growth rates were frequently unequal and the relative poverty of the states and especially of the majority of people also grew. Bradford Burns demonstrates that 'progress resulted in an increased concentration of lands in the hands of ever-fewer owners; falling per capita food production, with corollary rising food imports; greater impoverishment; less to eat; more vulnerability to the whims of an impersonal market; uneven growth; increased unemployment and underemployment; social, economic, and political marginalisation; and greater power in the hands of the privileged few'. Progress, growth and modernisation resulted in increased poverty and conflict for twentieth-century Latin Americas.[16]

As long as the region remained reasonably efficient, maintained a US preferred order, and paid its obligations, it had nothing to fear. Although the 'big stick' is generally associated with Roosevelt, Taft and Wilson were more prone to wield it. Even though the latter vociferously advocated the promotion of democracy and self-determination, the importance of the international economy frequently undermined political sovereignty. Self-determination, if pursued along unacceptable lines, was problematic. By 1918, the Wilson administration Inquiry Documents traced the changes:

> It was no longer a Monroe doctrine which merely shielded weaker neighbors and left them to their own devices. The world had greatly changed since the day when Monroe and Adams put forward their policy. The investments of Europe and the United States in all the countries south of the Rio Grande had become a vital matter. Underneath the diplomacy of all great countries was the question of economic interest greatly intensified. And the United States now had a stake in the economic life of each country concerned. These investments were increasing by leaps and bounds.[17]

The pursuit of US opportunity was at the centre of both messages. The first intended to inhibit European political power in the Western Hemisphere and facilitate US westward expansionism, the second inhibited European commercial power and facilitated US southward expansionism. In both cases the negative liberties and self-determination of Native Americans and Latin Americans were thoroughly undermined. Roosevelt's corollary adapted US opportunity to increase its international power under new circumstances.

The shifting world system

Roosevelt's adjustments to the Monroe Doctrine were a necessary part of its life. The doctrine could not be fossilised and inflexible, but had to be 'a living policy. It is to be justified not by precedent merely, but by the needs of the nation and the true interests of western civilization.'[18] The civilisation he had in mind existed merely amongst the Great Powers, Europe, Japan, and sometimes Russia. The 'corollary' suited US needs as never before. The centre of the world system shifted to the New York–Washington axis around the turn of the century. Latin America was a vital component of the US strategic and economic foundation, in part facilitating investments and US exports but also limiting the reach of European powers.

Two factors need to be considered here. Roosevelt recognised that the 'waste spaces' of the world were fast being occupied. Washington had attended the Berlin Conference in 1884 and witnessed the systematic division, specifically of West Africa and the Congo, and settlement far wider. The Open Door notes were issued to maintain US access to the mythical China market, though access was required by a minimal number of industries (oil and cotton). The key issue was that the 'civilised' powers had nearly completed their colonial acquisition of territory. Hence the British geopolitician Harold Mackinder indicated that Great Powers would endure in the future because of their efficiency and innovation, not just their territorial aggrandisement.[19] Such conditions suited the US well. Progressive ideologies stressed such virtues as efficiency and development. At a time when there was little more territory to acquire, Washington could stress its anti-colonial sentiments, and it could simultaneously capitalise on the vast territories that it had captured and integrated into its system over the previous century. Roosevelt's strategy thus consolidated the Western Hemisphere and limited the economic power of the European rivals, particularly Britain and Germany, in subsequent decades.

Territorial and economic power was vital to the period and the major wars of the twentieth century. Over the last decades of the nineteenth and first decades of the twentieth centuries the United States and Germany increasingly challenged Britain's hegemony. Both the United States and Britain combined their acquisition of territory with the development of capitalist systems, the British through colonialism and the US through continental conquest. Germany's challenge incorporated both strategies in the twentieth century. The number of its colonies was limited by its late arrival during the process of colonisation of the Third World and when these proved insufficient it sought its 'living space' through the continental conquest of Europe.[20] The resulting conflict in the First World War benefited the United States: its territory was sufficiently removed from the fighting for its economy to prosper through the war.

The United States was in a much stronger position than either Britain or Germany. Arrighi writes:

> Its continental dimension, its insularity, and its extremely favorable endowment of natural resources, as well as the policy consistently followed by its government of keeping the doors of the domestic market closed to foreign products but open to foreign capital, labor and enterprise, had made it the main beneficiary of British free-trade imperialism. By the time the struggle for world supremacy began, the US domestic economy was well on its way to being the new center of the world economy.[21]

The relative rise in US power over the period is astounding, assisted by its internal capacity and the reduction in European power through war. To Paul Kennedy it was one of the most decisive changes of the period.

Its absorption of capital, resources and millions of immigrants laid the basis for a strong internal economy and a vast industrial system. By the turn of the century, for instance, Carnegie was producing more steel than England, by 1914 US absolute and per capita income dwarfed European rivals. Hyper-productivity changed the pattern of the US economy to one based on export. Over the four and a half decades between 1860 to 1914 exports increased sevenfold, while protectionist measures ensured that imports did not keep pace. Industries demanded that the federal government gain access to or maintain open doors where possible. The state promoted US business abroad, belying notions of 'free trade' and the 'hidden hand'. The growth of the United States was so rapid that it rivalled the entire continent of Europe, not just any individual power. Short of natural disaster or civil war, the rise was inevitable. Its economic trajectory set it on course to overtake Europe in industrial output by 1925: 'what the First World War did, through the economic losses and dislocations suffered by the older Great Powers, was to bring that time forward, by six years, to 1919'.[22]

Latin America was a vital component in the US world system. The Roosevelt corollary basically ensured US access to Latin resources; imports doubled between 1880 and 1900 and then doubled again in a decade, so that by 1910, 33 per cent of US imports came from the region. By 1920, and for the next four decades, 20 per cent of US exports went there. Washington effectively closed the doors to the Western Hemisphere. Roosevelt and Taft ensured that US access was guaranteed and strategic European access was denied, while the Wilson administration further extended the Monroe Doctrine to the commercial system. Soon to be Secretary of State, Robert Lansing pointed out in June 1914 that the Monroe Doctrine was primarily about keeping Europeans out of the hemisphere and protecting US interests. He indicated that the immense growth in wealth over the past quarter century in both the United States and Europe had 'caused their people, in constantly increasing numbers, to seek investments in foreign lands'. The 'vast underdeveloped resources' of Latin America were extremely attractive. Echoing the past trend of imperialism in the 'scramble for Africa', Lansing argued that, 'with the present industrial activity, the scramble for markets, and the incessant search for new opportunities to produce wealth, commercial expansion and success are closely interwoven with political domination over the territory which is being exploited'. European access might therefore in time undermine US regional hegemony and consequently its economy and power. That is, a 'European power whose subjects own the public debt of an American state and have invested there large amounts of capital, may control the government of the state as completely as if it had acquired sovereign rights over the territory through occupation, conquest or cession'. Lansing enquired whether the doctrine should therefore be extended to include the limitation of European commercial interests, because ultimately these had a political impact on the Latin country and on the 'national safety of the United States'. Thus from early in the century concepts of 'national security' were closely linked to economic performance and potential. While the extension to the doctrine changed in form, its motivation remained largely traditional. Lansing wrote:

> In its advocacy of the Monroe Doctrine the United States considers its own interests. The integrity of other American nations is an incident, not an end. While this may seem based on selfishness alone, the author of the Doctrine had no higher or more generous motive in its declaration. To assert for it a nobler purpose is to proclaim a new doctrine.[23]

It was ironic that Lansing's arguments were largely an accurate assessment of how sovereignty could be undermined through an overburdening economic dominance on the part of the hegemonic power. It was also ironic that Wilson's close association with the promotion of democracy and self-determination had such limited applicability. His administration wielded the 'big stick' far more frequently than Roosevelt.[24] Moreover, the further irony was that Wilson's fame as the president who supported national self-determination and democracy was severely compromised by his ethnocentrism, racism and the imperative of US power in the world system.

Wilsonianism: 'liberal democratic internationalism'

Strange, given Wilson's record of intervention in Latin America, that he chose to globalise his conception of world order in terms of the Monroe Doctrine. Strange too, given his administration's assessment that the doctrine was inherently based on self-interest, that he expected others to adopt the proposition. Stranger still that, despite his immediate failures, his ideas, though compromised, were tremendously influential constructs in the twentieth century.

In January 1917 Wilson addressed the Senate on the terms of peace in Europe. The United States was not yet at war, but that was soon to change. He told the Senate that he was proposing 'that the nations should with one accord adopt the doctrine of President Monroe as the doctrine of the world: that no nation should seek to extend its polity over any other nation or people, but that every people should be left free to determine its own polity, its own way of development, unhindered, unthreatened, unafraid, the little along with the great and powerful'. But more famously, on 2 April 1917, convincing Congress that the US must accept war, Wilson said: 'the rights of nations great and small and the privilege of men everywhere to choose their way of life and of obedience. The world must be made safe for democracy.'[25] Wilson's respect for nationalism, however, was limited to the creation of European nation-states out of the collapse of the Austro-Hungarian and Ottoman empires. In the Middle East, a mandate system was imposed. Generally, Britain and France administered the area, but crucially Washington had obtained economic access. But in the colonial world of the victorious powers self-determination and democracy were postponed.

Wilson was the first US president to accept Paine's idea of 'America' as the project of mankind. His formula was basically an international system based on democratic nation-states in the political sphere, coupled with a world-wide liberal economy and an interdependent structure of collective security. The ideas were not completely original. They derived from the traditions of US diplomacy, but in his Fourteen Points of January 1918 he offered them to the world as the basis upon which peace could be negotiated. The results were severely compromised as Wilson was effectively outmanoeuvred and outwitted at the negotiating table particularly by British Prime Minister David Lloyd George and French premier Georges Clemenceau. Wilson sought open diplomacy and absolute freedom of the seas: 'The removal, so far as possible, of all economic barriers' and equal trade to consenting parties; 'A free, open-minded, and absolutely impartial adjustment of all colonial claims'; various specific adjustments; and his most treasured project, 'a general association of nations must be formed under specific covenants for the purpose of affording mutual guarantees of political independence and territorial integrity to great and small states alike'. The League of Nations, which ultimately Washington refused to join, had a short and sorry existence.[26] Wilson intended to produce a new world order based on collective security rather than the traditional balance of power. His genius, according to Tony Smith, was to combine the pursuit of national security with the promotion of democratic states that would be more likely to co-operate with the United States. Moreover, Washington would lead in integrating the 'three pillars of liberalism – economic openness, democratic government, and viable multilateral organisations' as central features of the world order.[27] These features increasingly found their way into the post-Second World War period.

For present purposes the more interesting aspect of Wilson's vision was the coupling of national self-determination with a liberal-capitalist economic order which was the formula most suited to US interests and security, and which was most conducive to the assumed traditions of the States. For Washington such a stance provided a model for the world order that avoided the extremes of European-style imperialism and Mexican or Russian-style revolution. For the victorious European powers it offered a route between social upheaval associated with revolution and an overburdening US dominance.

Wilson's nationalism was predicated on democratic legitimacy. But crucially this vision was an attempt to wed the liberal doctrines of trade with domestic self-determination. The inherent contradictions that arose when transnational economic interests undermined the sovereign rights of nation-states or the democratic rights of those within the boundaries were not considered extensively. Wilson's nationalism was animated by beliefs derived from the spirit of 1848, when demands for self-determination were made against the European empires. His ideas proposed political liberation from systems that compromised sovereignty in both Europe and Asia. In January 1918 he clearly echoed not only this sentiment but also the US Declaration of Independence, in which peace had to recognise the 'principle that governments derive all their just powers from the consent of the governed'. So, especially after the Russian Revolution in March 1917, Wilson celebrated the events by arguing that 'Russia was known by those who knew it best to have been always in fact democratic at heart'. Supposedly, the crumbling autocracy was not Russian in origin.[28] Victory in war and the conditions of peace could thus be put forward in terms of both democracy and self-determination: it was a war against autocracy.[29]

Within months the Bolsheviks had seized power and by the time the Great Powers met at Versailles, Wilsonian nationalism was accepted as the basis for discussion because of the collapse of the Central European empires and because the allies preferred to 'play the Wilsonian card against the Bolshevik card'. National self-determination, as long as the European colonies were exempt, animated the basis for agreement. At Versailles the nationalist sentiment spread rapidly throughout the colonial world, and even though the Europeans were lobbied extensively, the United States managed not to become embroiled in any commitments which might threaten its other agendas of securing the system of collective security and the open economy. Yet, in time, especially after the Second World War further weakened the European metropolitan centres, self-determination was exercised along the more radical lines adopted from the Soviet model of anti-imperial national liberation; that is, revolution combined with independence.[30]

Wilson's ambiguity about how far he would or could press for self-determination for the European colonies created uncertainty and doubt amongst those seeking independence and also amongst the Russians. His demands were offensive to the Europeans, who eventually did their best to whittle them down. Moreover, the Allies, especially the British, resented the changes in global power, status and the influence of US ideas in the post-war situation. The Allies were caught in a contradictory position. If the war persisted their national wealth would be depleted, to the advantage of the United States. Prolonging the war also threatened to intensify radicalism in Europe as the threat of revolution loomed. Thus the longer the war continued the more influential the United States became. While

European economies suffered, the US prospered through the process.[31] Despite the offensiveness of the injunction to adjust colonial claims, therefore, the termination of war was closely related to Wilson's demands.

The war had unleashed 'the most serious wave of popular protest and rebellion hitherto experienced by the capitalist world-economy'. The Russian Revolution became the focus of the wave of protest, and the attempt to redefine the relationship between the peoples and the state.[32] At the conceptual level, the Russian Revolution stood for political democracy against what the Bolsheviks considered industrial democracy; the rights of the individual were contrasted with those of property and business. Even though Wilson sought to 're-Americanise' an increasingly plutocratic United States, it was still regarded as an economically imperial power amongst revolutionary and nationalist movements, which were having tremendous impact in Europe and in the colonial worlds. Washington found itself philosophically on the defensive. Nationalists outside Europe did not perceive the United States as the champion of anti-colonial self-determination.

Wilson's Fourteen Points were released in part to offset the appeal of radical solutions and Bolshevism. Lenin and Trotsky promoted the idea of self-determination everywhere; yet the Allies were obviously willing to apply it only to the collapsed empires of Europe, to the vanquished but not to the victorious empires. Trotsky regarded the partial application of the idea as 'the most naked and the most cynical imperialism'. The Fourteen Points were intended to modify the Bolshevik ideological competition with Wilsonian internationalism, in Europe especially, but also worldwide.[33]

The Wilson administration regarded the Soviet crusade as an attack on civilisation, especially given the reforms Wilson had introduced within the United States and those he proposed for the entire world system. Lenin's writings on imperialism contradicted the Open Door thesis; he suggested that war resulted from the imperialism of industrial countries that expanded their markets in a finite world. Trade and commerce led to imperialism and then to war, not a more peaceful and integrated world. Trotsky's writings and pronouncements on popular democracy, too, alarmed Washington, and the implications for a system of self-determination based on democracy within the state. International proletarianism was anathema to the US tradition. Lansing, reviewing Trotsky's pronouncements, sent Wilson a memorandum: 'the document is an appeal to the proletariat of all countries, to the ignorant and mentally deficient, who by their numbers are urged to become masters. Here seems to me to lie a very real danger in view of the present social unrest throughout the world.' Indeed, the Soviet model of state capitalism struck at the heart of the Open Door vision of a liberal integrated economic world.[34]

Lenin's proposals were new, Wilson's were not. Lenin wanted to rearrange the entire national and international system, but Wilson sought only modification and reform. Regulation of international capitalism would suffice for Wilson, though for Lenin state capitalism was a primary objective in the short run. Wilson's ideas derived from the traditions of self-determination associated with the US and French Revolutions, the nationalism of the nineteenth century, and the traditions of US diplomacy, Monroeism and the Open Door. His departure from the conservative nationalism of the nineteenth century came in his attempt to wed national self-determination to individual liberty: he was 'trying to reclaim nationalism from the *Realpolitik* conservatives and return it to the liberal fold'. The move away from the old balance of power system to a more international liberal system was an attempt at introducing a form of social control over the international system. Collective security would place the responsibility of social control on all participants. Simultaneously, it allowed Washington to maintain its exceptionalism by avoiding the need to enter 'entangling alliances' in any 'balance of power' system. The League of Nations was supposed to fulfil this function. C. H. Cooley's *Social Control in International Relations* had influenced Wilson. With collective security Wilson could pursue his synthesis of 'control, universalism and unilateralism', which would continue that seemingly irreducible contradiction of desiring both unilateralism and engagement in a collective system.[35]

Despite his intentions, the Europeans at Versailles, especially Lloyd George and Clemenceau, ran rings around the US president and affirmed the primacy of *realpolitik*. John Maynard Keynes decried Wilson's negotiating abilities. His attention to detail was inadequate, his impatience to discuss the League was patent, and his delegation was partisan. Still, he believed he represented a moral force in the negotiations. The war had chastened the Old World and civilisation; a progressive history was about to rise from the embers of the European war. As Washington increasingly represented the force for progress, relativism and particularism increasingly attracted Europeans. The war was cast as a struggle for democracy and self-determination, with the United States the central point of civilisation in the world system, the 'new Israel' to Roosevelt's 'new Rome'. Wilson harboured a vision of progress in history in which the United States looked to the future and promoted universal rights, its eyes 'were lifted to the distances of history', it was lifting 'civilisation to new levels and new achievements'.[36] Yet for all this vision and moral force, the contradictory elements in his thought, and his ineptitude in Paris, and later the US Senate's rejection of membership of the League of Nations, doomed his policies in the short term.

One by one, the principles in his Fourteen Points were discarded, as he compromised with the Europeans to secure his League. Senators, both 'reservationists' and 'irreconcilable', soon undid the rest of his plans. They argued that the Monroe Doctrine was insufficiently protected and that Article 10 of the League mandated a US response should conflict break out in Europe or elsewhere. They did not want to get involved in wars that might defend European empires, and they feared the loss of congressional authority to declare war if Article 10 mandated automatic response.[37] International Wilsonianism came to nothing in his lifetime. Within years the world economy moved towards the practice of autarky, and the emphasis on national sovereignty was thoroughly undermined in the aggressive pursuit of 'German *Lebensraum,* Japanese *tairiku,* or Italian *mare nostrum*'.[38] Yet Wilson's vision did return after the Second World War. The Monroe Doctrine was protected by UN Article 51; collective security was a part of the UN Charter and more specifically a part of the various defence pacts such as NATO, into which Washington entered. Bretton Woods did set up a limited open world economy, and the process of national self-determination was unprecedented in the global process of decolonisation.

Wilson and the world system

Wilson's view of the US position in the world grew out of his understanding of the domestic sphere. Within the Union democratic freedoms and negative liberty animated Wilson's agenda. In theory it was to be applied to the world. His 'inner contradiction', as it has been referred to, was to combine systems that simultaneously promoted the positive freedoms of the United States with systems that undermined the negative freedoms of others. That is, national self-determination was, in some cases, thoroughly undermined by the pursuit of Open Door formulae. He thought the US system so worthy of emulation that it provided the model of democracy for others. If all developed along US lines there would be no 'inner contradiction' between 'the political formulas of nationalism and free trade'. Liberation for Wilson was represented by the essence of the Declaration of Independence, his vision was entirely American. Louis Hartz writes, 'The policy of Wilson in peace, so striking a contrast to the realpolitik of the Old World and ultimately so abject a victim before it, was shot through and through with absolute "Americanism" on the basis of which the war was fought.'[39] Wilson therefore did not see any contradiction in intervention in Russia, Mexico, on numerous occasions in Central America and the Caribbean, even if it undermined the notion of World History of self-determination, if such intervention was deemed to contribute to the US vision. Freedom was both animated by the people and compromised by an insistence on adherence to Progressive options. Wilson's was a system of liberal imperialism. Everyone was deemed fit for self-government, but liberties had to be protected by constitutional formulae. In this formulation intervention was acceptable if it was to secure progressive outcomes. Just as his 'New Freedom' facilitated government intervention in the domestic economy, so, applied to foreign relations, it sought to limit the abuse of powerful materialist monopolies.

Even though the progressives had played out the arguments between Roosevelt's New Nationalism and Wilson's New Freedom, both were still thoroughly within the American tradition. Differences between the New Nationalism and the New Freedom were subtle, yet real. Roosevelt, despite his reputation as a 'trust buster', believed that it was natural that trusts came into being. Thus the essence of his nationalism lay in controlling the abuse of trusts rather than destroying them. Wilson's New Freedom opposed monopolistic trusts though it still promoted big business. How exactly he proposed to control the wrongs committed by business was not clear. Despite these differences in approach, Wilson placed confidence in individual responsibility and free markets. Roosevelt's system of tariffs tended to restrict such free activity. Still, in the economic sphere Wilson's vision was imperial: 'If prosperity is not to be checked in this country we must broaden our borders and make conquest of the markets of the world.' But Wilson's New Freedom intended to advance the process through a reduction of tariffs, to 're-Americanize' the situation, or, as he put it, to secure a 'government devoted to the general interest and not to special interests'. Tariffs served particular interests, limited the scope of the US market, aped the methods of imperialism, 'stifled the growth of liberalism, and created the twin dangers of radicalism and reaction'. Even though Wilson promoted the Open Door, which originated partly in the promotion of a very limited number of business interests, he presented himself as anti-imperial. Gardner cites an essay Wilson wrote in 1907:

> Since trade ignores national boundaries, and the manufacturer insists on having the world as a market, the flag of his nation must follow him, and the doors of the nations which are closed against him must be battered down. Concessions obtained by financiers must be safeguarded by ministers of state, even if the sovereignty of unwilling nations be outraged in the process. Colonies must be obtained or planted, in order that no useful corner of the world may be overlooked or left unused.

Efficiency and liberal competition, however, were Wilson's watchwords against what he considered would be an imperialist system that would result from Roosevelt's tariff options. The implications for the domestic economy and US politics would be profound. Even though Wilson did initially reverse the post-Civil War tariffs through legislation in 1913, as soon as the war was over, the boom complete and recession reappeared, the return to tariffs and protectionism did not take long, and continued into the 1920s and 1930s.[40]

Moreover, with a shrinking world the government fell squarely behind US business to promote what Wilson insisted was the US national interest, not the interests of any particular corporation. Yet, he talked about a system of 'constitutional liberty' in the world, theoretically protective of national and individual negative liberties. Such a constitution would respect 'human rights, national integrity, and opportunity as against material interests'. In defining the US relationship with its southern neighbours in 1913, Wilson developed the theme of a family of nations under such constitutional protection.

> I want to take this occasion to say that the United States will never again seek one additional foot of territory by conquest. She will devote herself to showing that she knows how to make honorable and fruitful use of the territory she has, and she must regard it as one of the duties of friendship to see that from no quarter are material interests made superior to human liberty and national opportunity.[41]

Yet national sovereignty was compromised numerous times by Wilson's administration in pursuit of US national and material interests.[42]

Access to markets and raw materials was vitally important not just for the economic health of the nation but also for its internal social organisation and its national security. By 1916 Wilson had realised the Allies were resisting his proposals. He had to take seriously the French proposals to the British for a post-war economic alliance that would be directed against both the Central Powers and the United States. Germany too sought hegemony over Central Europe and was planning an economic war to follow the military war. Robert Lansing warned Wilson that such agreements would be critical for US trade and that such restrictions would necessitate a fundamental reordering of US institutions to organise the economy against the combinations and autarky of others. By 1916 it was not only a war between the European powers but a war for the future structure of the world order.[43]

The key contribution to the Allied war effort was the resources that the United States brought to the conflict, not just at the time of their entry to the war, but in the years before when the Allied powers had far greater access to US, Canadian and Australian resources. German attempts to limit this access through U-boat warfare were of course a part of the reason for US entry to the war. The overpopulated European continent had solved its resource problems in the past through its colonial territories, which provided a continuous supply of food. In war these demands became obviously much more acute. Clark points out that 'if access to the resources of an expansive global economy was the secret which won the war, there should be no surprise that such a project retained a powerful hold over the imagination of some who thought about survival in the post-war peace.'[44] Indeed, shortly after the Second World War, Kennan identi-fied US access to 'our' raw materials in Latin America as a key concern.[45] Kennedy indicates that the productive capacity of the Allied powers, coupled with the vast US resources, made the difference between victory and defeat in the war. Evidence of good and bad strategy exists on both sides, but ultimately, 'what was enjoyed by one side, particularly after 1917, was a marked superiority in productive forces. As in earlier, lengthy coalition wars, that factor eventually turned out to be decisive.'[46] Thus, material interests vitiated the ideals of US foreign policy, and frequently undermined the 'constitutional liberty', that is the self-determination and sovereignty of nation-states in the resource-rich South or later Third World.

The lessons drawn from the difference in productive capacity had impor-tant consequences for US society and its foreign relations from then on. In mobilising for war the Wilson administration initiated strong ties between government and the business community that endured. Unlike previous wars, the mechanisation introduced in the First World War brought about a symbiotic relationship with major corporations. Co-operation between the civilian and military sectors was enhanced, the war accelerated the Progressive economy, and 'introduced the idea and practice of industrial preparedness'. While some aspects of reform were enhanced by the alliance, others were distorted, compromised and reversed in the post-war years. The alliance between government and business, especially in terms of military preparedness, affected the US future. 'World War I made emphatically clear that in twentieth century America, war much more than reform would shape the nation's values, institutions, and ideology. During World War I, the nation had taken a major and seemingly irrevocable step in the direction of becoming a warfare or national security state.' After the Second World War the economic logic was so attractive that the National Security Act of 1947 institutionalised the system, which became increas-ingly prevalent after 1950 and the increased budgetary expenditures associated with NSC 68 and the Cold War constructs.[47]

The distinctions between the private and the public spheres were increasingly eroded during the Wilsonian period and after. Corporatist his-torians have traced the connections between 'foreign and economic policy' and 'the social basis of the state'. US power cannot be understood without these connections. US global power and the reach of its transnational corporations cannot be divorced from the state policies that assisted them. The 'promotional state' assisted with the expansion of and the US share of the global economy. In the minds of policy makers there was no contradiction between power and progress. It was assumed that the open liberal economy would benefit most, bringing prosperity and peace, by creating international environments conducive to business, albeit conducted by corporations. The government role in organising such environments through treaties granting 'most favored nation' status, regulating protectionism and tariffs for certain industries, regulating currency convertibility, deterring others from pursuing national economic solutions, applied conditions to other governments that not only undermined their sovereignty, left little in the way of political consent for foreign citizens, but also made nonsense of professions of a fidelity to 'free trade'. Other things apart, the magnitude of the US economy ensured their field was favourable and unfair.[48]

The war demonstrated the extent to which the regions of the world were connected, and the extent to which the relative strength of the Great Powers depended on access to the resource-rich areas of the South and the prosperous markets of the North. Isolationism, though practised at a superficial political level, was not considered desirable in terms of economic exchange. Arising out of this period economic growth was seen by Wilson and the subsequent Republican administrations as a tool to overcome autarky and promote processes of economic integration, which served US state and business power. Expansion was indeed a relief to several internal conditions; it ensured social stability within the state. Madison's injunction to 'extend the sphere' remained as relevant after the First World War as it had been in the late eighteenth century, though obviously it assumed different forms.

Attempts by other nations to limit the sphere, to practise economic autarky against US internationalism, punctuated the history of US foreign policy for the rest of the century, whether this was pursued by the conservative nationalism of Nazi Germany or the Cold War Soviet economy, or various Third World nationalists. Germany did not accept its defeat in the world system in 1918, and its attempts to 'extend its sphere' were reactivated in the 1930s, following the Japanese and Italian movements into Manchuria and Ethiopia.[49] Autarky not only limited the US sphere, it challenged the very conception of US ideologies, their visions of world order, and provided unwanted models of development for nation-states who thought they would fare better with closed economies. An economic system that passes as a natural expression of commerce and human interaction was and remains thoroughly supported by a hegemonic state at the centre of the world system. Even in the Wilsonian period, the process was well ingrained in US culture and ideology. Rosenberg concludes:

By helping American investment, products, and culture reach more people, they claimed to combat injustice, poverty, and ignorance. But they often offered ethnocentric solutions disguised as internationalist ones and subjective judgements dignified by the name of rationality and fact. Inspired yet blinded by faith in expertise. Most of the new professionals failed to see that a foreign policy based on the exportation of American-style liberalism might itself be illiberal.[50]

5

ARSENAL FOR DEMOCRACY AND SELF-DETERMINATION?

The burden and liberation of the past

Though Wilsonianism was repudiated for over a decade during the three Republican administrations of Warren Harding, Calvin Coolidge and Herbert Hoover (1921–1933), some of Wilson's goals, such as arms reduction and more open trade, were tentatively pursued during the 1920s. But with the election of Franklin Roosevelt (1933–1945) and New Deal diplomacy, US promotion of democracy and self-determination and the negative liberties associated with them were again prominent features of wartime diplomacy. However, Roosevelt first had to drag the United States out of depression, assisted by the Second World War, and then assert US power to temper the ideals and ensure the survival of the American-centred capitalist system. The onset of the Cold War solidified the transatlantic relationship, integrated the West politically and economically, which slowed US support for decolonisation.

This chapter traces the changes in the world system and the support for and retreats from decolonisation after the war. The conventional traditions of the Monroe Doctrine regarding self-determination were encouraged where Wilson failed. US concerns with economic access and security during the onset of the Cold War inhibited the outright promotion of democracy and self-determination. Nevertheless, ultimately, when the nations of the former colonial areas gained liberation, it was simultaneously an act against centuries of western colonialism and with the political systems that were created, the process also represented an extension of the western state system. The following chapter then concentrates much more specifically on the structures and ideologies associated with the Cold War which influenced the future struggles over development, revolution, democracy and self-determination.

The ideological baggage inherited through the traditions of US foreign relations weighed heavily on Franklin Roosevelt's administration. He was often castigated for his lack of a coherent foreign policy; but Warren Kimball makes a virtue of this trait, stressing that Roosevelt was 'a juggler', he often pursued policies that appeared contradictory. He was attracted to quick solutions and a good mix of tactics and strategies. For all the confusion, however, he is also regarded as a character of great political judgement, with an ability to read the mood of the moment and the era, his assumptions were constant, derived entirely from US culture and traditions. 'Never an ideologue, but always a believer in the "American way of life," he tried to combine humane reform with practical, workable politics. When asked to identify his greatest accomplishments, he said it was saving American capitalism, that combination of free enterprise and individual rights that . . . characterised society.'[1]

Though there are obvious contradictions between capitalism and democracy,[2] they were both central traditions in US diplomacy. Contradictions may be identified between the traditions of the Monroe Doctrine, the Open Door and Wilsonian internationalism, but the derivative ideologies have a very loose relationship to consistency and it should not be so surprising that all three of these political inclinations were advanced simultaneously. Each in its own way contributed to a pre-reflective understanding of social reality, providing the United States with a loosely coherent identity in the world and a basis upon which future action could be taken.[3] Still, the Monroe Doctrine, the Open Door and Wilsonianism exerted considerable influence on Franklin Roosevelt.

When policy makers borrow from the past their selection is utilitarian. When they use history to confirm a national identity they usually revive the benevolent aspects of the traditions. Franklin Roosevelt repudiated his distant cousin's corollary renouncing the US right to intervene in Latin America in 1933 at the Pan-American Conference in Montevideo. His reference to the Monroe Doctrine was more closely aligned to the traditional interpretations of safeguarding national self-determination. By the 1930s Latin economies were so securely linked to that of the US that intervention was unnecessary and counter-productive. In addition, such recognition of sovereignty eased the passage for authoritarian regimes to maintain control, inhibiting the development of democracy in their states. Even though the Good Neighbor policy promoted stability over democracy, it was the latter, coupled with self-determination, that found its way into the global application of the Monroe Doctrine. Democracy and self-determination were central features of Roosevelt's rhetoric on decolonisation. By the early 1940s FDR had his eye on the European colonial system; it undermined self-determination and excluded US commerce. Washington was in a unique position to use its enormous productive powers to take advantage of Europe's difficulties.

Roosevelt was well aware of the contradiction between the basis of US economic power and democracy. He pointed out in 1936 that the tendency to eliminate the 'small men, the average men in business and industry and agriculture . . . these dependable defenders of democratic institutions', to concentrate control in small exclusive and powerful groups was 'directly opposed to the stability of government and to democratic government itself'. Tony Smith has rightly argued that it would have been well for FDR to remember these words, because, with the implementation of the Good Neighbor policy and later the globalisation of the US-centred economy, increased productive output furthered the concentration of land and wealth, reducing democratic conditions.[4] Still, the inclination to globalise the Monroe Doctrine ignored the caveat on democratic enhancement.

Similarly, the traditions of the Open Door were taken at their most general level. The second set of notes ostensibly preserved China's self-determination against potential European colonisation. Wilson's third of the Fourteen Points furthered the momentum of the Open Door and was further conflated with his other political objectives. And most immediately, the lessons drawn from the depression – that closed economies reduce economic growth, that autarkic economic blocs first conduct economic warfare which degenerates into actual war – were powerful influences on US diplomacy during the war. Only open economies, whose trade barriers are lowered, contribute to the enhancement of peace, wealth and democracy. Lessons based on comfortable analogy were attractive in policy circles. Roosevelt and particularly his Secretary of State until 1944, Cordell Hull, and Under-Secretary of State Sumner Welles constantly repeated the message: free trade was a pacific agent in international relations.

In a limited sense capitalism was a progressive force in World History. It undermined the hierarchical and authoritarian forms of governance and 'liberal capitalism' ultimately made some contribution to weakening the European systems of colonialism. It was also a regressive force in that it broke up traditional lifestyles which practised forms of democracy quite different from the typical western variety.[5] It enhanced the growing inequality amongst states and within states that fuelled nationalist sentiments within the world system, and revolutionary sentiments within the state system. The combination pushed millions in search of national self-determination. It cannot be assumed that the world system, with the US economy at the centre, enhanced global democratic conditions, even if US economic power was a determinant factor in ending German and Japanese expansion and contributed to the disintegration of European colonialism. While negative liberty was promoted in the political realm, it was simultaneously eroded by the economic system. It was ironic that the economic leverage Washington had to pressure the British and the French to end colonialism, enhancing national self-determination, was later the economic system that undermined the autonomy of the new nations. They were often dramatically susceptible to the fluctuations of the global economy. The end of political colonialism had given way to economic neo-colonialism. President Kwame Nkrumah of Ghana posited in 1965 that 'the essence of neo-colonialism is that the state which is subject to it is, in theory, independent and has all the trappings of international sovereignty. In reality its economic system and thus its internal policy is directed from outside.'[6]

Last, Roosevelt was a Wilsonian, but a realistic Wilsonian. Roosevelt would not repeat the political mistakes Wilson made at Versailles and with the US Senate. Kimball relates that, whatever his initial intentions, 'once the United States entered the war his wartime policies and postwar goals shifted dramatically. Active participation meant a chance for active leadership, and that was an opportunity not to be lost.' The United States had gained a 'second chance' to provide world leadership, which necessitated the triumph of internationalism within the US over isolationist tendencies. This time the proposed liberal international order would include structures of power. Ideals were compromised to assuage domestic concerns. The League of Nations was given teeth in the United Nations through the power of the Security Council. The universalism of the League and the aspirations of the UN were tempered by regionalism and ideas of having four 'police' powers (US, USSR, Britain and China) envisaged for future world organisation. 'Liberal realism' supplanted 'the relative simplicity and the naïveté of Wilson's worldview'.[7]

Roosevelt's rhetoric was in part an attempt to galvanise domestic support for the emerging consensus of internationalism. Universal Wilsonian rhetoric sounded the cause of democracy. In the Second World War the United States became the 'arsenal for democracy'. This narrative was enhanced in the post-war period in which the war was retold as a morality play centred around the Nuremberg Consensus in which the Nazis were the sole aggressors in Europe and the Japanese in the Pacific. Consensus was formed around the stated war aims of the Grand Alliance, which masked the divisions between Washington and London, and between Washington and Moscow. The binary presentation of the war was one of anti-fascism conducted in the name of freedom and democracy. Roosevelt's Wilsonian rhetoric enhanced the dualistic consensus that emerged quickly, and largely still remains in the public imagination. He was later accused of betraying his ideals in the Baltic and of inaction on East European affairs. But the public had been duped by his rhetoric, while in actuality he had had a realistic, limited, 'spheres of influence' approach.[8]

Roosevelt's rhetoric fed the ideological foundations of US society. It clearly identified the national purpose in the world and enhanced the essentially democratic nature of US foreign relations with Europe. But others in colonial systems took note of the world's most powerful nation.

The world system: extending the sphere

The Nuremberg Consensus maintains a powerful grip on the public imagination and collective memories of the Second World War. The defeat of

Nazi Germany and Japan was of course an absolute necessity. The world had shrunk in time and space to the point where the United States could not remain aloof from the fight. Roosevelt had argued the case persistently, compromising the Neutrality Acts as the 1930s progressed. Affirming the Monroe Doctrine, he warned the Old World to keep its hands off the Western Hemisphere, but realised that isolation was impossible. US customs were inextricably entwined with those of Europe. His address on 14 April 1939 understood this: 'Beyond question, within a scant few years air fleets will cross the ocean as easily as today they cross the closed European seas. Economic functioning of the world becomes increasingly a unit; no interruption of it anywhere can fail, in the future, to disrupt economic life everywhere.' By January 1941 his State of the Union speech linked US security, democracy and business with 'events far beyond our borders'. The democratic cause would prevail and the most immediate task of the United States was to become the arsenal for that cause based around the Four Freedoms: of speech, of worship, from want and from fear. By August 1941 Roosevelt had outlined the common cause with British Prime Minister Churchill in the Atlantic Charter.[9]

But George Kennan rightly argues that the democracies were simply outgunned in the Second World War. The West had to take in one of the totalitarian powers, either the Soviet Union or Nazi Germany.[10] Pearl Harbor and the German declaration of war settled the issue. In the period leading up to the war the Japanese and then the Germans were increasingly identified as 'barbarians' and the war was soon characterised as a fight for democratic civilisation. The Axis powers were presented as anti-Enlightenment; theirs was an attempt to send the world back to the Dark Ages. The Wilsonian project was back on the agenda. The United States was once again a Great Power with a mission to lead the world. In Roosevelt's speeches the echo of Wilsonian internationalism was loud and clear. Hunt suggests that his 'October 1937 speech calling for a quarantine against an "epidemic of world lawlessness" set him on the road that led him to the Atlantic Charter of 1941. His route can be traced in his ever bolder public denunciations of the barbaric forces bent on world conquest and his ever more explicit calls for resistance in the name of civilisation.' By the end of 1941 the United States had become 'the arsenal for democracy'.[11]

The democratic project moved to centre stage in Roosevelt's opening and closing statements on the war: the Atlantic Charter (August 1941) and the Declaration on a Liberated Europe crafted at Yalta (February 1945). The United States was in a unique position to influence the content of any statement on war aims. Neither Britain nor Russia had that latitude. Later, at the Crimean Conference, the 'Big Three' affirmed the principles of the Atlantic Charter: 'the right of all peoples to choose the form of government under which they will live – the restoration of sovereign rights and self-government to those peoples who have been forcibly deprived of them by the aggressor nations'.[12] Yet Washington's allies in war were also undermining sovereignty and self-determination. However, the 'beautiful ideas' of the Charter had to wait until post-war stability prevailed.[13] The United States did not fight in the Second World War merely to defeat the Axis powers after Japan attacked at Pearl Harbor and Germany declared war within days. These were partly the results of the failure of US multi-lateral appeasement and the fragmentation of the world economy during the 1930s into more or less hardened trading blocs. Once in the war, Washington added both political and ideological agendas on self-determination and democracy, which were combined with economic con-siderations and the survival of 'civilisation' as they knew it. The war was cast as a struggle for progress in World History to gain every ideological and moral advantage.

Washington feared a closed world economy. The depression undermined confidence in the future of capitalist democracy; the collapse of the Latin American market as a result of the depression made the US economy even more vulnerable. The British exacerbated the problems by setting up the 1932 Imperial Preference System in Ottawa making trade with the colonies impractical. Fascism had risen dramatically in Italy and Germany. Their closed systems and that of the Japanese in East Asia extended the areas closed to the US economy. The Soviet Union, outside the system, was experiencing considerable economic growth.[14] The idea of Open Door capitalism was philosophically and structurally challenged.

Roosevelt knew that such philosophical and structural inhibitions would harm the prosperity of the nation and undermine US individualism. Economic contraction, the demands for scarce resources, would necessitate greater social organisation and more government intervention in domestic social and economic affairs, compromising the 'American way of life'. In the 1920s Washington rejected a greater international role so long as its economy was unfettered. By the 1930s it realised that maintaining order required government intervention. The fragmentation of the world system was inefficient. Economies duplicated activities, shunning the benefits of comparative advantage and reducing profits. More managed economies emerged in the form of Hitler's New Plan and Roosevelt's New Deal.[15] Within some internationalist and Republican circles this form of state planning was seen as anathema to business and individualism. Even former president Herbert Hoover enquired whether the New Deal was not 'an infection from the original stream of fascism'.[16]

Japan's expansion into Manchuria from 1931, its creation of the Greater East Asian Co-Prosperity sphere in 1938, and its move into Indochina in 1940 restricted both the sentiment and the potential for the Open Door in the Far East. In the West, Germany was on the move from 1936: remilitar-ising the Rhineland, intervening in the Spanish Civil War, moving into

Austria and Czechoslovakia in 1938, taking Poland in September 1939, attacking France, the Low Countries and Norway in 1940, Britain in late 1940 and Russia in June 1941. When Germany, Japan and Italy signed the Tripartite Pact in late 1940 it was quite clear that the US attempts at multilateral appeasement had failed. These powers could not be persuaded to adopt US economic preferences. Closed systems secured their 'living space'. *Lebensraum*, 'living space for Germany and Japan', McCormick writes 'was dying space for American private enterprise and for capitalism as an integrated world-system'. It was feared that the capitalist system could not function without these areas of free enterprise.[17]

These ideas became an article of faith amongst the policy makers interested in promoting an internationalist role and an Open Door policy. Under-Secretary of State, Sumner Welles, put the beliefs forward succinctly before the National Foreign Trade Convention in October 1941:

> The prosperity of our country, the level of employment, the best interests of labor and of the consumer, and the living standards of our people depend to a very great extent upon the condition of our trade. We are all of us concerned more deeply because the creation of conditions favourable to peaceful and profitable trade between nations is one of the cornerstones of the enduring peace which we so earnestly hope may be constructed in the place of the social wreckage and economic ruin which will inevitably result from the present war.

Welles, with some honesty, did not let the United States off the hook of responsibility, or at least deflected blame to the Republican administrations:

> Many foreign countries, which had not recovered from the shock of our tariff increases in 1921 and 1922 and were tottering on the brink of economic and financial collapse, were literally pushed into the abyss by our tariff action of 1930. Throughout the world this withering blast of trade destruction brought disaster and despair to countless people. The resultant misery, bewilderment, and resentment, together with other equally pernicious contributing causes, paved the way for the rise of those very dictatorships which have plunged almost the entire world into war. . . . We thus helped to set in motion a whirlpool of trade-restricting measures and devices, preferences, and discriminations, which quickly sucked world trade down to such low levels that standards of living everywhere were dangerously reduced. Faced with the disappearance of markets in the United States for so many of their exportable products, foreign countries were forced to cut their economic cloth accordingly. They erected high tariffs and established

restrictive quotas designed to keep their imports of American products within the limits of their reduced dollar purchasing power.
They sought desperately for other markets and other sources of
supply. In the process they entered into all sorts of preferential
arrangements, resorted to primitive barter, and adopted narrowly
bilateralistic trade-and-payments arrangements.[18]

Washington continually emphasised the importance of the global economy and the necessity for increasing integration. In a militaristic environment the market was no longer seen as a sufficient force to restore
individual liberty; the state, henceforth, became the guarantor. 'Military
Keynesianism' clawed the US out of the depression, not the New Deal, but
essentially the Second World War. The US corporations, which received
government contracts in a growing militarised economy, gained disproportionate power and influence in an increasingly centralised system.
According to Williams, the unwillingness to concede that marketplace
capitalism had failed enhanced the idea that Washington should be responsible for obtaining markets and controlling raw materials; 'alternatives
were anti-American because they were anti-imperial'. Since the rejection of
colonialism in the 1890s the 'American way of life' depended on economic
expansionism or, in Williams's framework, the imperialism of the
economic system. Given that such economic necessities were conflated with
the concepts of liberty and democracy, 'the imperial outlook had once
again become a vision of progress for everyone'. The sentiment was
universalised to gain increasing consent. Despite the US tariff systems, the
British Imperial Preference System of 1932 had to give way to US demands
for access because London depended on US assistance during the war.
Germany's trade controls of 1934 were similarly rebuffed. While Germany
had tried to negotiate bilateral deals, Hull refused to 'discuss the matter
unless there was "a fundamental acceptance by Germany of our trade
philosophy"'.[19]

Sumner Welles's mission to Europe in 1940, with the suggestion that the
colonial situation might be revised to redress some of the inequities of the
Versailles system, did not satisfy the British. In part it was determination
to avoid US pressure on both colonialism and the Open Door that pushed
Britain closer to appeasing Germany. Prime Minister Neville Chamberlain
was not about to give up the Imperial Preferential System or to concede to
transferring African colonies to Germany. To Chamberlain it appeared as
though Washington was meddling in essentially British affairs, and trying
to solve political grievances with economic solutions. Appeasement, however, might allow Britain to avoid the transatlantic pressure and avoid war
with Germany.[20]

These differences between the United States and Britain were downplayed during the war but are reflected in the titles of some of the histories

of the Anglo-American alliance: 'ambiguous partnership', 'competitive cooperation' and 'allies of a kind'. But the public image of solidarity, not only between the United States and Britain but also including the Soviet Union, contributed to the image that this was not only a war against German and Italian fascism and Japan, but also a war for democracy and self-determination. The disputes within the strange alliance would have to wait, at least in public perception, until after the war. There was a decisive shift in world power during the war that was reflected in the wartime tactics. Policy and strategy were often made with a close eye not only on the Axis powers but also on the Allies.[21]

Anti-colonialism: globalising the Monroe Doctrine

Slowly, the essence of the Monroe Doctrine would extend beyond the Western Hemisphere. The Old World system of colonialism wound down over the next few decades. Eventually, the West could not contain the democratic aspirations for independence, self-determination and democracy. The new US world order extended itself where it could, bringing republican government where possible. This is not to suggest that Washington was responsible for the third phase in the withdrawal of colonial rule in modern history, but merely to identify its aspirations under Roosevelt and the changes that occurred under President Harry Truman. The European empires, the British, the French and the Dutch primarily, did not collapse after the war. They were hit hard, but with the United States they returned to Asia to fill the political vacuum left by the retreat of Japanese imperialism. After the decolonisation of India in 1947, it took two more decades for the British to realise that their economic weakness, coupled with nationalist pressures, had ended their period of 'overseas orientation' towards a policy that looked more towards the European Economic Community. The French were driven much more through wars of national liberation from Vietnam to Algeria.[22] The United States was not central to these processes, but its policies before and during the Cold War shed light on its attitudes towards self-determination, democracy and the world economy.

Franklin Roosevelt's anti-colonialism, though perhaps personally sincere, had to account for competing interests. He was the president who finally timetabled US decolonisation of the Philippines; he was the president who put pressure on European powers through the language of Article VII of the Lend-Lease agreements and the Atlantic Charter. But he also shared the paternalistic attitudes and the assumed responsibilities of his position which tended to cast doubt on the abilities of the former colonies to govern themselves. Moreover, colonialism was good for short-term order. Finally, the colonial question was always linked to the economic and strategic health of his more important allies. Throughout, the war made him focus on these primary objectives.

Roosevelt repeatedly pushed the issue of decolonisation. Democracy and freedom were prominent themes in his rhetoric. The Four Freedoms enhanced the ideologies from which independence movements took succour. Though ironic in retrospect, considering 'the freedom from want – which, translated into world terms, means economic understandings which will secure to every nation a healthy peace time life for its inhabitants'.[23] Still, the Atlantic Charter provided a powerful symbolic statement of US intentions, especially the key point on which Roosevelt and Churchill agreed to 'respect the right of all peoples to choose the form of government under which they will live'.[24] The theme of self-determination was repeated constantly. Roosevelt clearly saw that the US was in a position to reshape World History. Democracy had gone into action to resist the forces of tyranny. 'We, the American people, are writing new history,' he declared at a dinner for White House correspondents. 'We believe that any nationality, no matter how small, has the inherent right to its own nationhood.'[25] The rhetoric created momentum. It gathered support through the US entry into war, it reduced Allied latitude on the issue if the Allies wanted materials from the US arsenal. Nationalist leaders now had powerful words to reflect back at Washington should its commitment to freedom waver. The colonial areas could use US rhetoric on decolonisation, from Jefferson, Monroe, and Wilson to FDR, to forge a link with Washington, to become 'allies of a kind too'.[26]

Despite the fact that Roosevelt dropped the topic on many occasions to preserve the harmony of the Grand Alliance, Kimball relates: 'He repeatedly sent his official and unofficial representatives around the globe to preach the gospel of independence. Everywhere he and his emissaries went, they discussed post-war self-government and freedom with nationalist leaders, emphasising American differences with the Europeans.'[27] India and Indochina were used as examples. Roosevelt wanted some progress in these areas, though he was quite willing to let other colonies wait. Washington intended to set the example through decolonisation of the Philippines in 1946, though there is scant evidence that other colonial powers were inspired by this.

Colonialism was an issue Roosevelt loved to loathe. His rhetoric was similar, no matter what colony he talked about. He had preferences that accorded with his paternalism. India and Indochina should be decolonised first, though his critical comments were often aimed elsewhere. British Gambia, he once stated, was 'the most horrible thing I have ever seen in my life. . . . The natives are five thousand years back of us. . . . The British have been there for two hundred years – for every dollar that the British have put into Gambia, they have taken out ten. It's just plain exploitation of those people. . . . Those people, of course, they are completely incapable of self-government. You have got to give them education first.'[28]

Washington supported decolonisation for ideological reasons. Responding to Indian criticism that Washington supported British imperialism, FDR argued that the war was a primary consideration, but that its objectives were to liberate the various colonial areas.[29] Washington supported decolonisation for political reasons to supplant the centrality of European power, which had prevailed for over four hundred years. It supported decolonisation for economic reasons, because of the recurring fears of a closed international economic order.

Wartime considerations inhibited Roosevelt from putting too much pressure on his allies, but he was not himself free of the paternalistic attitudes associated with the 'white man's burden', which insinuated that colonial peoples were untutored in the arts of self-government. He championed the idea of a trusteeship system under which former colonial areas would be governed by the international community as trusteeships of the United Nations, until such a time as they were deemed ready to steer their own ship of state. Washington expected imminent action on India and reacted negatively to the French desire to return to Indochina, but there was still no realistic sight of independence for sub-Saharan Africa. But it was assumed they would gain independence in time. Paul Orders argues:

> Roosevelt probably felt that concessions to the British and French over colonialism in the short term would not serve to derail decolonisation in the long-term. In effect, international economic and political circumstances served to alleviate tensions between his idealistic and realistic instincts. To this extent, those historians who have sought to emphasise the President's growing conservatism in relation to colonial issues in 1944 and 1945 are wide of the mark. Rooseveltian idealism was not eclipsed by Rooseveltian realism. FDR was a standard-bearer of anti-colonialism even as he sought to secure the future of the United States' relations with Britain and France. He was already looking towards a new period in world history in which colonialism was an historical anachronism.[30]

The attitudes echoed the paternalism of Theodore Roosevelt's period. Then it was 'Uncle Sam's' responsibility to tutor the Central Americans and the Caribbeans, and now in a less unilateral period the United Nations would administer a trusteeship over the former colonies. The attitudes are still evident in the strictures associated with accepting an IMF package today.

Washington also moderated its stance on decolonisation because colonialism was a useful system for controlling disorder. It contained volatile nationalism; it ordered pluralistic forces in the increasingly global system; it inhibited the centrifugal forces associated with the positive liberties of self-determination; and it also inhibited the ability of states to adopt the ideas of the major ideological competitor, the Soviet Union.

Since Washington intended to integrate the economies of the world in the post-war period, a process which had in fact begun during the war to secure the vital resources of oil, quartz and other vital materials, it realised that the European powers were in a good position to control the situation. Self-determination was one thing, but autarkic or pro-Soviet self-determination was quite another. The trusteeship system would provide both the mantle of legitimacy and the ability to maintain some order and access. The move towards complete independence could be graduated.[31] First, democracy had to be tamed. As in Wilson's period, the 'desire "to make the world safe for democracy" . . . came only after he unsuccessfully deployed U.S. military force "to teach the South American republics to elect good men"'.[32] The search for markets was not just related to economic prosperity but also to the attempt to contain radical ideas.[33]

Radical nationalism and Soviet models of development competed with the preferred US political and economic formulae in the emerging Third World. In the three decades after the Second World War independence was advanced according to western formulae, either left or right. Ideologies of universal progress and modernisation supplemented more traditional and particular forms of autonomy, democracy and development. The US example had been compromised by its own imperialism in Asia, its alliance with the colonial powers, and knowledge of Latin American reaction to the 'imperial' economy. Lloyd Gardner writes, 'How crushing, then, that so many Asians and Africans held up to America after World War II a new image in which Uncle Sam had become corroded and evil.' US exceptionalism could only be sustained as a cultural construct.[34] Moscow's planned economy and anti-imperial ideas provided an alternative model. Some nationalists combined the two: national self-determination derived from the writings of Jefferson and Paine, and social organisation based on socialist formulae. In 1945 Ho Chi Minh declared Vietnamese independence based on the US Declaration of Independence. The Jefferson of 1776 or 1801 was an inspiration and a useful political reference point.

The war offered the United States a unique opportunity to assert its hegemonic power.[35] Article VII of the Lend-Lease agreement and the Atlantic Charter made US assistance to Britain conditional on opening up the Imperial Preference system. At the Atlantic Conference Sumner Welles indicated that closed systems had been disastrous in the past. Churchill identified a duplicity, that Washington expected others to open their systems when the United States maintained adverse trade barriers.[36] The

Cold War reduced US influence on colonial matters as it increasingly integrated the West and the Soviet model provided alternatives.

Historical ironies: decolonisation in the Cold War

With the death of Roosevelt and the accession of Harry Truman (1945–1953), the Cold War emerged gradually through Soviet domination of Eastern Europe, US integration of Western Europe, mutual misunderstanding which divided first the continent of Europe and then conceptually the world. Within the bipolar vision decolonisation suffered. Third World states did not share Washington's view of itself as a champion of decolonisation, democracy or self-determination. In the increasingly universalistic framework of US policy, decolonisation became an awkward phenomenon that could at once bolster the political traditions of US diplomacy and undermine the security and cohesion of the West. And similarly, with the increasing integration of the global economy, decolonisation could work both ways. Independent nations could remain tied to the West by choice or through colonial economic connections that endured or they could withdraw from the western economy through the pursuit of autarky.

It was ironic that Washington portrayed Soviet domination of Eastern Europe as colonial, just as the European colonies became crucial to the western economy. It was ironic too that, just as US ideology was finally backed by power, it increasingly lost credibility in the Third World.[37] Pragmatism tempered US policy. Washington may have had some leverage over the European metropolitan centres, but they too had leverage over Washington, which the 'Soviet threat' provided. Compromise was the obvious outcome. But neither the colonial powers nor the independence movements trusted Washington. US traditions suggested that to maintain stability in the Third World, to win allies there it had to support decolonisation; and yet potentially such independence could provoke instability in an increasingly hostile environment. Moreover, if independence movements leaned towards Moscow then Washington considered that decolonisation and self-determination were incompatible.[38] Their political systems would be compromised by Soviet power, which within years were credited with all the characteristics that the United States had resisted in its diplomatic history. Fundamentally they were communist. Soon the pernicious attributes of Nazi Germany were grafted onto their identity through increasing reference to 'Red Fascism'. And finally their action in Eastern Europe and Africa constituted a form of colonialism.[39] The conflation of these noxious identities facilitated the conflation of the more benevolent identities associated with the West, around US characteristics, that eclipsed the West European past. The reductionism enhanced the Manichaean quality of US foreign policy.

The conflation of such identities both simplified and complicated the US stance on decolonisation in the Cold War. George Kennan objected to the use of universalistic language because it created expectations of and within the United States. In his Policy Planning Studies he argued that this 'universalistic approach has a strong appeal to U.S. public opinion; for it appears to obviate the necessity of dealing with the national peculiarities and diverging political philosophies of foreign peoples; which many of our people find confusing and irritating. In this sense, it contains a strong vein of escapism.' Kennan was arguing against the US inclinations to force other nations onto the Procrustean bed; the attitude 'assumes . . . all countries could be induced to subscribe to certain standard rules of behavior . . . [and] instead of being compelled to make the sordid and involved political choices inherent in traditional diplomacy, we could make decisions on the lofty but simple plane of moral principle'.[40] Such an outlook simplified the construction and domestic acceptance of US diplomacy, but the constructs eventually led to complications when such attitudes, outlooks and resulting policies were applied to a complex and heterogeneous world. It was not just that Washington misunderstood the situation; it was unprepared for the nationalist revolt in Asia that followed the Japanese collapse.[41] The binary formula could only be sustained in an atmosphere of fear and insecurity. The tendency to universalise made it more difficult to deal with Indochina when its self-determination combined political independence derived from the US Declaration of 1776 with models of social organisation derived from Ho's communist beliefs, which it considered more appropriate for its autonomous development. Washington found accommodation with this formula in Yugoslavia where Josip Broz Tito had broken with Stalin but maintained communist rule. But as Gardner writes, 'while one Tito demonstrated that even Communists could not tolerate Stalin's heavy-fisted rule, two Titos would suggest that the idea of a world Communist conspiracy needed serious re-examination'.[42]

Washington did not seriously try to understand the relatively new phenomenon of Asian nationalism. When the Pentagon tried to decide whether Ho Chi Minh was more of a communist or a nationalist, they were ultimately persuaded by the logic advanced by Secretary of State Acheson, that 'all Stalinists in colonial areas are nationalists'.[43] Moreover, Vietnam, unlike Yugoslavia, was a vital link in the increasingly integrated western economy. The French depended on Vietnam for reasons of economy and prestige; they insisted on maintaining their colonial connections, but now they could put forward their case for continued occupation within the new Cold War context. As early as 1945, and not for the last time, General de Gaulle tried to blackmail the United States into support in Indochina. He told the US Ambassador in Paris, Caffery, 'If the public here comes to realize that you are against us in Indochina there will be terrific disappointment and nobody knows to what that will lead. We do not want to become Communist; we do not want to fall into the Russian orbit, but I hope that you do not push us into it.'[44] Washington could deal with dissident communist regimes that undermined the unity of the Eastern Bloc. But if it had the power, it would not deal with regimes, communist or not, that undermined the unity of the western economy. By the mid-1950s it was increasingly evident that regimes were increasingly defined as communist if their autarkic tendencies did not 'complement the industrial economies of the West'.[45]

Washington was caught in a terrible irony compounded by Cold War myopia. On the one hand there was the ideological tradition of anti-colonialism that had informed US attitudes from Jefferson through Monroe, Wilson and Roosevelt. From this perspective it is no wonder that nationalists felt betrayed when Washington stood with the colonial powers and supported the reinstatement of French rule in Indochina. The ideological traditions of anti-colonialism, especially the US Declaration of Independence, resulted from an attempt to break out of the engulfing world system. Political independence and self-determination afforded greater consent on the form of government, its policies, commerce and destiny. Within decades of independence the United States had itself become an imperial power, colonising the west and integrating increasing territory first; in the twentieth century, as the centre of the world system shifted, economies increasingly revolved around its growing hegemonic power.

India's experience suggests an ironic course. Though Washington provided belated support for India's Swaraj, relations remained tense throughout the post-independence period. Both the United States and India had emerged from the interdependent British world system, though by the twentieth century their experiences were extremely divergent. The United States had become the hegemonic world power, whereas, in an attempt to reject the binary division, India remained in what soon became known as the Third World. And here nationalism limited the aspirations of the hegemonic power. Merrill explains:

> As the Cold War replaced World War II as the defining crusade in US foreign policy, Washington's antipathy toward Third World nationalism deepened, and Indo-American relations suffered. Indeed, the troubled history of America's relations with independent India suggests that the ironies of world history, enduring cultural barriers, and the vagaries of power politics continued to keep the two nations apart.[46]

The ideological constructs and constraints of the Cold War period 'hopelessly distorted' US perceptions of the situation in South and South East

Asia. Viewed in the wider historical perspective, the inability of the Truman administration to deal with the challenge of nationalism in Asia was short sighted in its attitude towards decolonisation, which must be regarded as 'the most profound and far-reaching developments in modern world history'.[47]

If, on the other hand, one considers the US colonial history, the irony is not so acute. US foreign policy is characterised by an almost continuous attempt to integrate various areas or systems. It pushed west to colonise and integrate vast areas of the North American continent. It presided at the centre of an informal empire in Central America and the Caribbean,[48] and a formal system in the Philippines. It exercised a 'preponderance of power' over Western Europe in the post-Second World War period, integrating the economies and binding the states through security alliances. There was an enduring tradition of economic integration, political and ideological hegemony. Herein lies a fundamental contradiction: for the United States to maintain its political, economic and ideological system, its way of life, it was necessary to impose certain constraints on various other forms of governance and nationalities that sought self-determination. US positive liberties often encroached on the negative liberties and human rights of others. Human rights and both positive and negative liberties were denied to 'others' when Jefferson and Jackson promoted western colonisation, McKinley and Roosevelt imposed Progressive ideas on Cuba, Central America or the Philippines, and so on to the point when the United States shied away from assisting anti-colonial nationalist movements.

What began as thirteen independent states on the Atlantic seaboard, through Madison's injunction to extend the sphere ultimately led to the expansion of the United States across the entire mid-section of the North American continent, laying the basis for its extraordinary productive power during the twentieth century, the 'American Century'. A more comprehensive understanding of the century requires a view beyond bipolarity in space and time. The continentalism of US history in the nineteenth century is crucial to understanding its power in the twentieth. To acknowledge the success of US federalism and the failure of secession is fundamental. The economies of north and south were integrated and industrialised, and resources were plentiful.[49] 'Freedom' implied a form of imposition, a denial of self-determination, an acceptance of the 'American way'. Lincoln, sensitive to what was going on, hoodwinked the people with the rhetoric on the new nation. The plurality of states in the Union became singular; the United States 'are' became 'is', the Union became the nation.[50] In Cold War rhetoric the plurality of the states increasingly acquired the singular collective noun: the West. Its identity rested on the grand narrative of liberty and democracy, it 'gave the NATO West a prehistory of Magic Moments starting with the Greeks and ending with the final Magic Moment of the Atlantic Charter'.[51]

Integrating the 'West'

Unity of purpose was not confined to political relations or security concerns. Unifying and integrating the western economy was essential, but this meant not only those countries around the Atlantic Ocean, but also 'their' colonies or 'dependencies'. The autarkic structures of the 1930s and economic nationalism would undermine US power and hegemony. US visions contained not only Soviet ideology and power but also rival forms of state capitalism. Crucially, the US attempted to secure the US 'way of life', necessitating the maintenance of 'a position of disparity' in world income.[52] The Truman Doctrine made it difficult to support colonialism, but the 'western' economy with its tentacles and trade routes spreading across the periphery was vital for western prosperity and the attainment of the West's objectives. Kennan thought an integrated Europe needed Britain, which in turn needed either North America or Africa, or a 'second possible solution would lie in arrangements whereby a union of Western European nations would undertake jointly the economic development and exploitation of the colonial and dependent areas of the African Continent'.[53]

Colonial areas were vital as Europe's suppliers of raw materials from which the essential US dollar could be earned. These triangular links between the United States, Europe and the Third World pushed the Cold War to these areas. Robert Wood suggests: 'The European Recovery Program was not simply about either Europe or recovery; it was much more ambitious than that.' The Marshall Plan addressed the economic problems of the 1930s with a vision of a global integrated economy. With Eastern Europe cut off and Latin America loosely closed, Africa and Asia were crucial to the health of the western economy.[54] Washington had to collaborate with European colonialism, ideals notwithstanding, to foreclose Soviet opportunities and to assure the survival of 'liberal democratic' capitalism. Rapid decolonisation might both undermine the European economies, and cause instability in the Third World, which could only benefit 'the communists'.[55] While Europe came first, the two spheres could not be separated, Leffler explains: 'The periphery had to be held or the Eurasian industrial core would be weakened. To simplify, Japan needed Southeast Asia; Western Europe needed the Middle East; and the American rearmament effort required raw materials from throughout the Third World.'[56]

The shackles of such systems were presented in terms of progress and freedom, especially in the Cold War. Free trade went with political liberty and democracy, which were conceptually the antithesis of what the Soviet system stood for. But even as Washington insisted on opening economies, it failed to lead through example. The language of 'free trade' was tempered with the practice of a mixed system: freedom of access combined with a managed protectionism. The narratives of liberalisation often clouded the situation. The International Bank for Reconstruction and Development (World Bank) and the International Monetary Fund (IMF), largely brought into being through agreement between Britain and the United States, soon found that even their operations were curtailed. US hegemony was characterised by an 'anti-free-trade' application of power. 'The free trade ideologized and practised by the US government throughout the period of its hegemonic ascendancy has been, rather, a strategy of bilateral and multilateral intergovernmental negotiation of trade liberalisation, aimed primarily at opening up other states to US commodities and enterprise.' Roosevelt's New Deal for the United States was transformed into a 'new deal' for the world. Despite the enormous power of the United States and its virtual control on global liquidity, the attempt to extend the American economic image could only become operational in a smaller sphere, the western sphere, after the pronunciation of the Truman Doctrine in 1947.[57] Trade liberalisation was brought about by the state, not by allowing market forces free play. The 'invisible hand' was always restrained, at times liberated by the state's boxing glove.

The process was evolutionary. The idea of free trade was based largely on a series of myths and self-deceptions or self-serving constructs. Rosenberg traces the stages of governmental involvement with the business world from the 'promotional state' to the 'cooperative state' and on to the 'regulatory state'. Liberal principles were selectively applied by post-war institutions 'upholding those that would favor American expansion and modifying or ignoring those that might not'. Yet these 'liberal principles' were central to the 'development strategies' for the newly decolonised nations. But US development had not emerged along such lines; the state was never far removed. Tariff barriers were erected, when these were lowered import quotas were imposed, and export subsidies became available to US businesses.[58] But rhetorical identification of such regulation would compromise the American dream and the fidelity to the belief that free trade enhanced prosperity, peace and democracy. The unequal terms of trade meant that US independence was enhanced while that of others was compromised.

Washington used its economic muscle to its advantage. Colonialism was eroded through the articles in the Lend-Lease agreement and the Atlantic Charter. Further, the British loan of December 1945 gave the United States an open door to Britain, the colonies and the Commonwealth. Similarly, US aid was a political weapon against the Soviets. When autarky persisted into 1946, Washington sharply restricted loans to the emerging Soviet bloc. Whether or not it made good business sense, politics came first. Stalin believed opening up to the West would compromise their system and the Eastern Bloc remained somewhat closed for the subsequent decades. Washington and London also had severe disagreements on both economic matters and on colonialism, but self-interest, not the 'clichés of "free trade" or "independence", helps to explain the course of events after 1945', according to Louis.[59]

The West was in conceptual chaos. It had grown to form alliances with the empires of old. The US nationalism centred on universal ideologies vied with its nationalism of state security. The Cold War 'national security state' was maintained at the political level, yet nationalism or autarky was considered anathema in the economic sphere. The traditions of the Westphalia model of sovereign, equal and strong states was enhanced by the Soviet challenge, providing the executive branch and the institutions of national security greater sway in the United States. As decolonisation and the US-centred economy spread across the globe, European powers too 'rescued the nation-state' through further combination. The inter-war economic nationalism gave way to a post-war political nationalism.[60] In the Third World decolonisation spread the creation of nation-states across the globe. The triumphs of particular nationalism were at once anti-western, anti-imperial, anti-European, but the process, a derivative of Westphalia, was entirely western. Moreover, in the apotheosis of nationalism, Wilson's self-determination was one of the most influential forces. After the Second World War Washington often had to paddle the tricky waters between 'western' solidarity and ideologies on self-determination and anti-colonialism; but the contradiction can never be resolved, because it would be difficult to describe the United States as anti-western. One quotation will illustrate the conundrum. On the eve of Africa's decolonisation, the National Security Council considered the dilemma. The resulting policy document stated:

Premature independence would be as harmful to our interests in Africa as would be a continuation of nineteenth century colonialism, and we must tailor our policies to the capabilities and needs of each particular area as well as to our over-all relations with the metropolitan power concerned. It should be noted that all the metropolitan powers are associated with us in the NATO alliance or in military base agreements.

Under policy guidance the document suggested that Washington support the principle of self-determination, stressing, however, that such a reality incurred associated responsibilities. Moreover, care should be taken to 'avoid U.S. identification with those policies of the metropolitan powers, which are stagnant or repressive, and, to the extent practicable, seek effective means of influencing the metropolitan powers to abandon or modify such policies'. And for good measure, 'emphasize through all appropriate media the colonial policies of the Soviet Union and particularly the fact that the Soviet colonial empire has continued to expand throughout the period when Western colonialism has been contracting'.[61]

Extending 'the West': the irony of self-determination

The revolt against the West was very western. Decolonisation is often situated in the post-war period between the late 1940s and 1980s. But earlier waves of decolonisation had occurred in Europe and in the Western Hemisphere between the 1780s and the 1820s. The rivalry between European nations was such that when they began to be driven out of the Western Hemisphere, they went in search of colonies elsewhere. The British, for example, having 'lost' the thirteen colonies in America, set sail for Australia. Denis Judd writes, 'without the loss of the American colonies there would have been no First Fleet sailing into Botany Bay in 1788'.[62] Their ideas and institutions followed their commercial interests. By the early twentieth century European rivalry and the 'age of empire' came to an end in the First World War.

As far as this essay is concerned, one of the effects of that war was to integrate parts of the various European empires further. Asia, Africa and the Middle East adopted western ideas on nationalism. From the Japanese victory over Russia in 1905 they learned that European powers were not invincible (reinforced during the Second World War). From the Russian revolt of 1905 the idea of social revolution and national liberation spread throughout Asia. From Woodrow Wilson's pronouncements the idea of self-determination was firmly placed on the agenda for the twentieth century. Finally, from Lenin's denunciations of imperialism to his dismembering of the tsarist regime, the revolt against the West and independence was only a matter of time.[63] The two new powers, the US and the USSR, espousing ideologies that derived from the Enlightenment, both opposed the colonial form of imperialism.

The irony of the 'revolt against the west' was that its method, in adopting the form of the nation-state, 'ensured the universalisation of Western political practice'.[64] The further irony may be that, just as these states were achieving the formal recognition they had sought, the Open Door was simultaneously eroding their nascent power. As Arrighi summarises:

> By the end of the Second World War, the main contours of the new world order had already emerged: at Bretton Woods the foundations of a new world monetary system had been established; at Hiroshima and Nagasaki new means of violence had demonstrated what the military underpinnings of the new world order would be; and at San Francisco new norms and rules for the legitimation of state-making and war-making had been laid out in the UN Charter.[65]

The division of the states in Africa was entirely western, following patterns agreed at the Berlin Conference of 1884. The tribal, ethnic, or linguistic divisions of the continent were largely irrelevant to the process, as far as Europeans were concerned. As far as Africans were concerned, the state was an external, authoritarian, dominating entity. Prior to colonialism, Hawthorn contends, 'there is almost nowhere an established habit, pre-dating the colonisation from Europe, of exercising central authority or of submitting to it. Over the *longue durée* . . . "Africa's most distinctive contribution to the history of humanity has been the art of living in a reasonably peaceful way without the state".' Even today the states remain alien forms in many ways.[66] Of course other forms of democratic governance were eroded or destroyed during the western ascent in World History. By the time the Europeans had left Africa from the late 1950s to the mid-1980s, they had no further interest in the political administration of these areas. The borders drawn despite their irrelevance to the peoples of Africa made absolute sense to the national élites, many schooled in Europe, who now guarded and policed their territories with determination.[67]

The nationalism that emerged in the anti-colonial movements and then in the Third World was almost entirely based on western ideology, which could be reflected in the domestic political arenas of the metropolitan powers. Traditional forms of governance were not widely mobilised in the search for self-determination. Prior to the 1970s no major movement appealed to any non-western ideology to legitimate its quest for independence or social revolution.[68]

Western models dominated. Until 1917 the only model to develop a state upon was that of western capitalist and bourgeois society. But the Russian Revolution introduced an alternative form of anti-imperialism to Wilsonian self-determination. The anti-imperial movements, national liberation movements, grew ever more conscious that their ideological inclination was towards the left. This is where the logic of the western alliance had taken them, this is where 'socialism' had a strong appeal, and this is where they would find their allies in the colonial countries. The left was reunited with nationalism, according to Hobsbawm, in part because of the resistance to Hitler and in part because of the decolonisation process after 1945.[69]

In the new states of the Third World, without ethnic or linguistic homogeneity nationalist sentiments often took expression against the state, not necessarily against the former colonial power. It was also directed against 'western-derived ideologies' associated with modernisation and the élite, who were seen as serving these foreign interests.[70] National problems were linked to the global economy. Neo-colonialism, economic domination, became a catch phrase for the nationalist opposition in Africa by the mid- to late 1960s. Earlier nationalists from José Matrí to Ho Chi Minh had experienced similar disillusion. The reconfiguration of nationalism with the left led to continual problems for US foreign policy, not least of which were the Vietnam wars. The recasting of the Soviet Union as non-western at the onset of the Cold War (the barbarians to the western civilisation) further meshed the ideas of nationalism and communism, a point on which US diplomacy was continually confused. The hostility that Washington showed nationalist movements (despite being derivatives of Wilsonianism) was in part because of their anti-western rhetoric and policies. In part it was because national self-determination meant not playing the Open Door game, either through autarkic practices, import substitution, or erecting tariff barriers, and in part because the Soviet Union opportunistically provided the necessary aid to these nations isolated from the western system. Washington was recast as Rome not Athens.

Liberation was confined to the nation-state. The extension of the Westphalia system was adequate proof of progress in World History, rather than any form of economic progress for the inhabitants of these new and sometimes repressive states. The United Nations guarded the sanctity of the national borders though not the sanctity of the life within them. Just as in the Good Neighbor policies of the 1930s, it was the stability and order of the Latin American nations that impressed Roosevelt and prompted him to renounce intervention, not the democratic aspirations of the inhabitants who lived under Washington's strong men.

Thus the era represented the extension of Wilsonianism, the Westphalia system, with a twist. The disintegration of empires and the formation of all the new nation-states since 1945 initiated a period of political fragmentation coupled with economic integration where possible.

6

CONTAINING THE EAST;
INTEGRATING THE WEST

Duality, orientalism, bipolarity operated as powerful and pervasive constructs throughout the Cold War. Certainly, US policy makers went to some lengths to try to create a culture of the Cold War in which the conflicts were seen as universal, all-encompassing and zero-sum. This served many purposes. Public pronouncements were alarming: they asserted the existence of a permanent 'clear and present danger'; they made society more cohesive; they gave it a new mission; they created a new myth to activate or motivate its people; they infused the 'West' with meaning and characterised the 'other' as barbarian. The internal characteristics of the various 'communist' regimes notwithstanding, what needs to be kept clear here is that the 'other', despite rhetoric to the contrary, was not monolithic or homogeneous. The Cold War was a unique period of history for several reasons, but the duality, though it climaxed during the period, derived from the earlier traditions of US diplomacy. All the major concerns of the period 1945 to 1989 (roughly) cannot be reduced to Cold War considerations. To be sure, the Soviets presented a challenge on certain issues, but the concerns with integrating economies and resisting Third World revolution were largely separate phenomena, though they unfolded within the Cold War context. Still, the pervasive ideological constructs created by the Cold War planners, unwittingly in many cases, cannot be ignored even if one is looking at a situation that may be little related to the central antagonism of these past decades.

The Manichaean outlook (the tendency to regard the world in a dualistic framework) derived in part from the traditions of the Monroe Doctrine. During the Cold War the spheres of influence were extended and hardened. The outcomes of the Second World War divided Europe into two spheres and the struggle to consolidate these spheres exacerbated the tensions. The Soviet challenge further entrenched the divisions through the fusion of ideology with the geopolitical contest. The Open Door traditions and the fear of depression spurred the strategies of economic integration. And finally, the combination of the above with the traditional antipathy towards revolution and disorder, from the French Revolution to the Mexican, made Washington hostile to the emerging phenomenon of Third World revolution. This chapter explores the divisions and hostilities centred on the early Cold War period, while the following chapter examines revolution and development within the contexts of the Cold War and the longer traditions.

Spheres of thought: the clash of ideologies

During the twentieth century the distribution of power was rapidly transformed, moving outward from the European empires to the United States and the Soviet Union. The Second World War brought these powers together, not only in a strange alliance to defeat Nazi Germany but also in a very physical sense at the centre of Europe. US and British tacticians had opted for invasion of North Africa in 1942 and the move through Italy, rather than opening a second front in Northern Europe, much to Stalin's chagrin. In many ways the situation played into Stalin's hands in the post-war period. Wary of his allies, he retained a strong Soviet presence in what came to be known as Eastern Europe. The Cold War divisions, whether reflected in the Churchill–Stalin secret agreement, the Iron Curtain speech, the Truman Doctrine or the Berlin Wall, the division in Europe was a result of the conclusion of the Second World War. Power was not asserted immediately, but interrelated events hardened perspectives and consolidated blocs emerged. The Soviets sought to rebuild their economy and military power, and to safeguard against potential German aggression through the creation of a buffer zone in Eastern Europe. They had lost the sense of security that the former divisions in the West had afforded them. Such objectives clashed with those of Washington, to secure their western allies and protect their 'way of life' which necessitated an open door in Europe and the wider world.[1]

Moreover, apart from the direct contact they had through the geographical division of Germany and later Europe, the powers also represented two universalistic ideologies. Both US-style liberal democratic capitalism and Soviet-style communism were descendants of the Enlightenment. Both powers sought to impose a total vision on the world. Pluralism and the recognition of nations' and peoples' positive liberties suffered as a result of the globalised clash of ideological and geo-political opponents. Ideological differences had existed since the Wilsonian period, but now these powers were the two most influential in the world, the resolution of the Second World War brought them together, and their differences became much more apparent. The cultural and academic disagreements over the meaning of the Cold War are still acrimonious because they relate so closely to the identity of the United States and less to that of the former Soviet Union.

For the purposes of this study it is sufficient to look at the formal US ideologies in the Cold War and some of the informal assumptions and the symbolic politics that attended policy making during the period. The formal ideologies included matters such as extending democracy, protecting liberty, now represented by the members of the 'Free World', and securing self-determination where possible from the 'Soviet colonial' impulse. The informal Cold War assumptions created a host of ideas that remain strong in US foreign policy. Concepts of 'national security' were infused with meaning beyond the immediate sense of protecting US territory. They became bound up with concerns for the protection of the US economy, the credibility of the Americans as self-appointed leaders of the western world, and their ability to propagate the formal ideologies associated with the nation. Containment and 'rollback' became important, not just as policy options but also as near-ideological imperatives for the survival of US credibility and consensus. And perhaps most importantly, the timing of this clash with the Soviet Union at the highest level infused Washington with universalistic aspirations that ultimately posited that the Cold War was a zero-sum game and that there could be little deviance from the mentalities and structures of this conflict. The Cold War pulled society together with a war like mentality. National crusades were pervasive with the subsequent War on Poverty, the War on Drugs and so forth.[2] When society did not pull itself together, the likes of Senator McCarthy did some of the tugging, as an extreme example of a pervasive phenomenon. Discourses on national security sometimes suggested Civil Rights protests were anti-American, though Jefferson's rhetoric was a clear reference point for these protesters. National security suggested that the anti-war demonstrators were somehow un-American because they opposed a very American crusade in South East Asia. Doctrines of national security reduced the ideological latitude within the Union and simplified perspectives on a complex world. Orientalism thrived when so much was apparently at stake. National identities were affirmed through interpretations of foreign crises that fed the meta-narratives and mental constructs with which US society evolved. Such 'cognitive' miserliness[3] informed major policy documents and created simple blueprints for action in a complex and heterogeneous world. This type of approach resulted in often misguided policies, of which the most costly was Vietnam.

Fusing ideology and economy

The extension of the ideological construct of 'the West' masked other tensions within which US policy developed. Monroe's opponents, the European colonial powers, were integrated in the enlarging concept; the Third World was lured with 'words softly spoken' or bludgeoned with a 'big stick'; US culture was infused with a new mission; but *the* conflict was reduced to a dualistic framework. The Soviets loomed large in ideological constructs, but they were not the only 'challenge'.[4]

Several considerations had to be borne in mind. First, Western Europe could not be pushed too hard on issues relating to decolonisation. Washington needed those countries to join the struggle against Moscow and the struggle against 1930s-style economic fragmentation. Western Europe provided the link to global economic integration and the most lucrative potential market necessary to ensure the 'American way of life'. In some ways Washington wanted Western Europe to look like the United States. Not quite a United States of Europe, if the political divisions were still too deep, but economic integration advanced the process. Integration secured viable markets for US exports, generated income, and secured access to colonial areas rich in resources necessary for the rearmament efforts. As Truman put it, 'without foreign trade . . . it would be difficult, if not impossible, for us to develop atomic energy'.[5] Ultimately, Washington boosted the European economies through Marshall aid, which affected the future shape of Europe.

Second, Marshall aid reached deep into the politics of Europe. It limited socialist activities and affected the various European colonial areas. These 'peripheral' areas remained the focus of Great Power competition. As Washington sought to open the economies of Europe they attempted to keep the Western Hemisphere within the US orbit. The Rio Pact of 1947 and then the Organisation of American States (OAS) Charter of 1948 (created under the exclusive auspices of Article 51 of the UN Charter) provided Washington with a preponderance of exclusive power. Political and military leverage could be deployed to inhibit 'the growth of ideologies favouring state ownership and control of industry', as identified as an obstacle to US investment by Truman's Treasury Secretary; it was another attempt to contain Latin America. Washington sought 'a closed hemisphere in an Open World'. Elsewhere in the Third World, the process of decolonisation closely paralleled the rise of US power in the twentieth century. The 'rise of the masses' may have taken support from US rhetoric on decolonisation and self-determination and 'millions stood poised to end the age of imperialism, violently if necessary'.[6] These so-called liberated peoples soon made competing demands on the raw materials and resources that lay within their nations. Frustrated by the lack of progress, recourse to revolution was a frequent phenomenon.

Third, ideological parameters were constrained through the ludicrous extremes of Senator McCarthy's accusations. More generally, the culture of the Cold War narrowed the parameters of debate. The culture moved towards greater homogeneity in national outlook, rival ideologies were not generally encouraged or tolerated. Politically viable policy options were limited as a result.

The Cold War conflated the differences with Europe, the Third World and within the United States with the global struggle. Ideological imperatives helped to reduce a rapidly changing and complex world to finite terms of reference.[7] The simplified public presentation of the Cold War began to take place in late 1945. Public pronouncements were cast in terms of a morality play of good and evil. The simplicity generated urgency and bound the society together around a new crusade.[8]

The premises of the Open Door economy, free trade and prosperity were blended with notions of democratic freedoms with which, in abstract philosophical terms, they had little connection, or which worked against each other. William Appleman Williams argued that 'the various themes which went into America's conception of freedom and the necessity of open-door expansion . . . had been synthesised into an ideology'. The potent cultural import of the ideology allowed Americans to 'consider themselves democratic because they were prosperous and prosperous because they were democratic'. Not only had there been a synthesis of 'free trade' with democracy, but there was also a synthesis of communism with fascism, or as J. Edgar Hoover called it: 'Red Fascism'.[9] Both constructs polarised the Cold War and the cultural conceptions of it.

The process of synthesis and ideological reduction began to find greater private and public expression during 1946 when a series of documents and speeches made as part of a programme of public diplomacy began to close the door on potential accommodation. There was an extraordinary turnaround in US opinion on Stalin and the Soviet Union after the war. During the war 'Uncle Joe' was relatively popular in the United States, but within a matter of months Stalin became a national focus of evil. The propaganda was powerful.[10] If an enemy did not exist it was necessary to create one.

In these public narratives the Cold War was a defence of the assumed traditions of US diplomacy, the protection of liberty, democracy and self-determination. The Soviet 'threat' had to be contained to preserve US liberal internationalism. In practice, the 'free world' was preoccupied with anti-communism rather than the more positive promotion of the assumed traditions. The Cold War consensus began to emerge which dominated US policy for almost a quarter century. Generally, the consensus included beliefs that the United States must reject its isolationist past, become an international power creating a stable order and promoting an open economic system. Policy makers believed that US security interests were global and that the Soviet Union posed the greatest threat to these and therefore must be contained.[11] Soviet control of territory, resources and influence around the world must be limited. George Kennan initially believed US interests could be limited to Europe, Japan and the Western Hemisphere,[12] the vital strategic points, but soon such strategies were eclipsed by a more universal global containment.

The initial policy statement was put forward in the now famous Long Telegram. Its effect was to harden US attitudes, formulate an intellectual rationale for US foreign policy during the period, and contribute to the misperception of the emerging bipolar world. It responded to Stalin's speech to the Supreme Soviet, which outlined a series of five-year plans, suggesting the need to revert to economic autarky. Stalin's speech was received in Washington as the announcement of the Third World War, because it argued that there could be no peace as long as capitalism existed, though there was little in the speech which threatened to initiate conflict with the West.[13]

George Kennan, assistant to Ambassador Averell Harriman, wrote a long telegram known, not surprisingly, as the Long Telegram, putting forward the basic arguments for the US containment of the Soviet Union. He argued there could be no long-term prospects of co-operation with Moscow, whose worldview was neurotic, and that the suspiciousness and the aggressiveness of the Soviet leadership derived from 'basic inner Russian necessities' not from any 'objective analysis of the situation beyond Russia's borders'. Soviet leaders were bent on the total destruction of the US so compromise or concession would not improve the relationship. 'We have here a political force committed fanatically to the belief that with the US there can be no *modus vivendi*, that it is desirable and necessary that the internal harmony of our society be disrupted, our traditional way of life destroyed, the international authority of our state be broken if Soviet power is to be secure.' The telegram did not call for military containment. What Kennan envisioned, and spelled out in public with his Mr X article in the summer 1947 issue of *Foreign Affairs*, 'The Sources of Soviet Conduct', was the use of political and economic leverage to contain the Soviet Union. Though Kennan's writings became very influential in official Washington, it was an irony that Kennan did not believe that the Soviet Union wanted to initiate a world revolution, the Marxist–Leninist ideology was more a justification for domestic oppression, and a Soviet invasion of Western Europe was 'highly unlikely'.[14] Kennan was brought back from Moscow later to serve as the first Director of the State Department's Policy Planning Staff.

Though this telegram was widely accepted and read, and formed the intellectual basis for the strategy of containment, Kennan grew increasingly disenchanted with the manner in which interpretation of it was altered and implemented. After much critical comment on his own writing and role in the formation of containment Kennan reviewed the situation in the *New Yorker* in 1985:

> To explain this I sit down to draft a preposterously long telegram – some 8000 words – going right back to the beginning and describing, as though in a primer for school children, the nature, the

ambitions, the calculations of these men. It is a grim and un-compromising picture. . . . I seem to be on the same wavelength as official Washington. But more important and more significant than that, I seem to have aroused a strain of *emotional and self-righteous anti-Sovietism, which in later years I will wish I had not aroused.*[15]

Ultimately, with the increasing militarisation of US policy, Kennan resigned from the Policy Planning Staff in 1949.

Within ten days of the Long Telegram the logic of bipolarity, Soviet 'indefinite expansion', the division of Europe, and the need for western democracies to stand together were enunciated in Churchill's Iron Curtain speech at Fulton, Missouri. No longer the British Prime Minister, his words formulated some emerging assumptions, and with Truman's presence they appeared to echo official thought. In turn, the concept of the Iron Curtain lay at the heart of Truman's doctrine a year later. Stalin characterised the speech as an effort to 'sow discord' and as 'a call to war with the Soviet Union'.[16]

The Long Telegram was one of the most 'influential explanations of post-war Soviet behaviour' because it provided an intellectual basis with which to 'fuse concerns about totalitarianism and communism in dealing with the Soviet Union'.[17] This fusion was born out of the need to over-come the isolationist sentiments lingering within Congress, and from the lessons learned from appeasement of the ghosts of Munich.[18]

The very employment of the word 'containment' carries ideological connotations suggesting a continued Soviet impulse to expand. Such ideo-logical reductionism was reflected in the language of the internal docu-mentation, which is 'usually reserved for crusades'. But Kennan's conceptualisation provided intellectual credibility to the anti-communism that was 'gripping Washington'. In this environment containment was conflated with the traditional narratives on the defence of freedom.[19]

But the Cold War also resulted from the much longer trend of continued US expansionism. Economic autarky threatened to limit the US sphere, inhibit its freedom and undermine its cultural values. Economic expansion, deemed vital for US well-being, concurrently inhibited the liberty and self-determination of other societies and nations. As Williams put it, 'the tragedy of American diplomacy is not that it is evil, but that it denies and subverts American ideas and ideals'. The pursuit of positive liberty was also responsible for the onset of the Cold War; the Open Door ideologies rejected a 'sphere of influence' deal.[20] Secretary of State James Byrnes (1945–1947) clearly recognised foreign and domestic policies were insepar-able. Peace, he argued, could not be built on the basis of exclusive eco-nomic blocs. The lessons or ghosts of the 1930s were evident. The United States had to confront ideologies that resisted US imperatives.[21] It was essential for corporate America to pursue opportunities and markets wherever possible.

Noam Chomsky points out that 'the Iron Curtain deprived the capitalist industrial powers of a region that was expected to provide raw materials, investment opportunities, markets and cheap labour'. The anti-communism of the period was an ideological necessity to justify or explain the logic of US intervention, should a region or a nation close itself off to the international trading system. Moreover, it was necessary always to couch the policy of intervention as a form of self-defence, to convince a reluctant populace that there existed an implacable threat that must be resisted. Hence, the 'Cold War is in effect a system of joint global management, a system with a certain functional utility for the superpowers. To mobilize the population and recalcitrant allies in support of costly domestic programs and foreign adventures, it is necessary to appeal to the fear of some Great Satan.' The primary aim of the United States was therefore not the defence of democracy or its territorial integrity, but the need to maintain open societies, open, that is, to US economic penetration. Understanding ideology helps to overcome the disparity between the rhetoric on democracy and self-determination and the reality of US foreign policy. Part of the Soviet aggression against the West was not a physical one but one of interfering with its designs on Eastern Europe or the quest for 'open societies'.[22]

The conflict over Eastern Europe is central to understanding the Cold War. Russia was not intrinsically important to the United States. (Even if the possibility had existed integrating Russia might have been counter-productive given the associated costs of the Marshall Plan.) The Soviets viewed Eastern Europe as essential to their security. They remained there in pursuit of reparations and for security while the United States had a nuclear monopoly. But Eastern Europe was also important to a western integrated economy. US economic vitality depended on West European recovery and this in turn, traditionally, depended on Eastern Europe for food supplies, raw materials and markets. Soviet control of these areas broke a link in the traditional world system. Moreover, the psychological effects of Stalin's five-year plans were not lost on the West either. With the huge aggregate growth of the Soviet economy in the 1930s, and with the assumed lessons of western depression, US hegemony was challenged with a seemingly viable alternative economic model.[23]

Assistant Secretary of State, Dean Acheson, realised US domestic prosperity required a 'constantly expanding trade with other nations' and the key powers of the world remained central to US plans. Acheson regarded neutralism as suicide, therefore 'neither an integrated Europe nor a united Germany nor an independent Japan must be permitted to emerge as a third force or a neutral bloc'. These key economies had to be integrated into the western system. In turn these economies relied on their peripheries or colonial areas, again 'the periphery had to be held or the Eurasian industrial core would be weakened'.[24]

The immediate 'Soviet threat' was negligible. Soviet policy was confused and often contradictory, its contacts with foreign 'communists' relatively limited. Moreover, Washington did not consider the Soviet Union an imminent military threat. It did not have that capacity. The Soviet Union could only compete with the United States if it could make use of the western industrial infrastructure, its skilled labour and its resources. Washington feared that West European communist parties would serve Moscow's interests even if they were not directly under its control. This assumption, coupled with Soviet control of Eastern Europe, constituted the long-term threat. Concepts of 'national security' had expanded to incorporate the defence of US values, ideological preferences and the US political and economic way of life. The perception 'that a whole political economy of freedom was at stake shaped the U.S. diplomatic offensive in 1947'.[25]

A defining choice in World History?

In 1946 attitudes hardened and thus intellectual debate was limited. Kennan's telegram forged a consensus on US foreign policy, which eschewed compromise. In July 1946 Truman commissioned the first inter-departmental assessment of Soviet intentions. Its authors Clark Clifford and George Elsey concluded that the Soviets intended to project their military power into areas which would threaten the United States. Self-determination was being violated in Eastern Europe, reparations were being demanded of Germany, and Soviet policy in Iran threatened US access to Middle Eastern oil. In short, they aimed at world domination. It was an uncompromising picture that further galvanised the US consensus.[26] Championing democracy and self-determination were fused with anti-communism.

The construct had yet to be sold to the wider culture. In the months pre-ceding the congressional elections, and at a time when the administration needed to present a single clear, almost palliative message, the Secretary of Commerce, from the liberal wing of the Democratic Party, challenged policy. Henry Wallace delivered a speech on 12 September 1946 that pro-vided a provocative test case for Truman's commitment to the general policy of 'getting tough' with the Soviet Union. Truman had hastily cleared the speech, but Wallace committed an electoral error by mention-ing a 'sphere of influence' approach and berating British imperialism, which complicated the Manichaean constructs. Such complexity was unhelpful. Truman fired Wallace.[27]

The narrowing debate reinforced the bipolar consensus and the grim caricature of reality. Such reductionism had tremendous impact throughout the twentieth century, but in terms of implementing a policy ostensibly in defence of democracy the consequences have been profound. The executive branch was strengthened,

> Congress has been overshadowed, the public left in the dark, and a cult of national security has flourished. These trends have undermined constitutional checks and balances, restricted the flow of information, impeded intelligent debate, and diminished the electoral accountability of policymakers – all serious blows to the workings of a democratic political system.

The impact of meaningful congressional debate was reduced from this time by the unquestioning bipartisan and public acquiescence in the rhetoric on the 'clear and present danger'.[28]

Even though the Cold War in Europe emerged from a series of disputes on Poland, Germany and Eastern Europe generally, the situation in Greece was emblematic of the expansion of US power, the formation of an enduring doctrine, and an example of intervention that did not directly involve the Soviet Union. Nevertheless, significant US Cold War policies and attitudes were formed as a result of the British withdrawal from Greece. The Truman Doctrine was presented as a response to the threat from insurgents to the Greek government during their civil war. Potentially Moscow could not only extend its sphere beyond the Iron Curtain, or on the wrong side of the 1944 Percentages Agreement between Churchill and Stalin, but it also applied pressure on Turkey for control over the Dardanelles.[29] Under this scenario Soviet power had to be limited in the eastern Mediterranean.

The Soviet Union did not supply the Greek insurgents. They had limited ties to Moscow. The Greek National Liberation Front (EAM) had a wide and growing membership, resulting from the harsh government repression and the jailing of up to 50,000 supporters in 1945. As the repression intensified, EAM, with supporters of the People's Liberation Army (ELAS), moved to the mountains 'to escape terrorism exercised by the extreme Right'. The left and the nationalists were a heterogeneous group without a coherent position. The irony of the situation was that Stalin had kept his 1944 agreement with Churchill and stayed out. Yugoslavian communist leader, Josep Broz Tito, provided the aid. In the bipolar vision there was little difference in the official Washington mind between an independent nationalist movement led by communists and monolithic communism. 'Truman believed that all Communists took their orders from Moscow.'[30]

On 21 February 1947 the British informed Washington they could no longer maintain their commitments to the Greek government. In the State Department the announcement signalled the end of Pax Britannica. After two world wars and over 150 years of varied hegemony Britain was exhausted. It not only withdrew from India and Burma, but also relinquished Greece and Turkey.[31] Secretary of State George Marshall (1947–1949) saw obvious opportunities. Dean Acheson argued that, should Greece fall, the situation in Turkey would soon deteriorate. With Soviet control of the Dardanelles, the effects on morale and credibility in the Middle Eastern and European countries would be damaging. The precursor to the domino theory suggested the 'rot' would spread through the apples in the western basket. Truman gathered congressional leaders to explain the situation. Most importantly he sought an alliance with Senator Vandenberg, chairman of the Senate Foreign Relations Committee, who persuaded the Republican-controlled Congress to support the request for $250 million for Greece and $150 million for Turkey.[32]

But since the war the US had undergone a rapid demobilisation, reducing its military budget and personnel dramatically. Congress was looking inward, but Vandenberg agreed to support the request if the president made a personal appeal to Congress presenting Acheson's scenario, intimating that Russian control over vast portions of the earth would jeopardise US security. Truman's presentation could not be designed to address the particular situation in Greece, to protect a monarchy – this would be to repudiate the Monroe Doctrine – but had to be couched in universal terms: a fight by democracy against communism. The deception of the domestic populace was largely successful. It would be unseemly for the United States, ostensibly the supporter of self-determination, to act against a relatively indigenous movement fighting the repression of its failing government. The problem had to be presented in global terms even though empirically this case did not fit the ideological necessities.[33]

Probably Truman's request would not have been approved had he argued that the US intended to ensure regional stability by propping up a brutal Greek monarchy. Vandenberg had told Truman's speechwriters to frame the request along the same lines as Acheson's comments to the congressional committees some weeks earlier. The bottom line, as Vandenberg told Truman officials, was that if they wanted the money they would have to 'scare hell' out of the American people.[34] The speech Truman ultimately delivered to Congress on 12 March 1947, known as the Truman Doctrine, steered clear of particularities or actualities and enhanced the consensus for US foreign policy based around a world-wide defence of 'freedom' and anti-communism. Truman drew a conceptual line, much like the Monroe Doctrine, that divided the world geographically and ideologically:

> At the present moment in world history nearly every nation must choose between alternative ways of life. The choice is often not a free one. One way of life is based upon the will of the majority, and is distinguished by free institutions, representative government, free elections, guaranties of individual liberty, freedom of

speech and religion, and freedom from political oppression. The second way of life is based upon the will of a minority forcibly imposed upon the majority. It relies upon terror and oppression, a controlled press and radio, fixed elections, and the suppression of personal freedoms.

The construct had little relation to the existing situation. But with this language necessary to gain congressional support, US foreign policy had been redefined in crusading terms for the next decades.[35]

In terms of the local Greek situation the speech smacked of hypocrisy. From March 1947 the prison population doubled, thousands were 'exiled to detention camps without trial', strikes were outlawed (violators faced the death penalty), and later the regime admitted to the extra-judicial execution of 3,100 people. Secretary of State George Marshall warned that such practices had succeeded in 'stigmatizing Grk [sic] government'. A US congressional committee found there had been a 'sweeping abrogation of civil liberties' and those communists represented only a tenth of the guerrilla units. Still, conceptually the Truman Doctrine divided the world and even the South African government found itself on the western side of the divide because of its uranium deposits. Given the lack of civil rights within the United States, it is little wonder that liberty and democracy in South Africa were ignored. The Cold War brought a new reductionism to the thinking in US foreign policy. While Washington sought to fashion the 'free world' along US institutional and ideological lines, essentialising the western world and obscuring realities, there was a negative side to the construct:

> Call it missionary zeal, a sense of manifest destiny, conceit, arrogance, or chauvinism, Americans had it: a self-satisfaction that they were an exceptional people. This self-image ... obscured blatant violations of American ideals, evident, for example, in racial segregation at home. In fact, the notion of American exceptionalism was laced with racism – with assumptions about a 'hierarchy of race' that placed white Americans of Anglo-Saxon stock at the top.[36]

Washington knew it would have to assume the British role. It knew the Greek insurgents were not receiving aid from the Soviet Union, that the Greek government was repressive and inept, but it was not concerned merely with the position in Greece but with the Middle East in general. The Truman Doctrine signalled the US intention to replace the British in the region. Its strategic importance and oil reserves were essential in war; they could not fall into 'unfriendly hands'.[37] But Stalin was not encouraging leftist movements in Greece; in fact he frowned on such autonomous developments and urged the principal suppliers of the Greek resistance, Yugoslavia, Albania and Bulgaria, to curtail their support. In the Middle East Arab nationalism was a threat that was positively encouraged against Soviet influence, but discouraged and subsumed to Cold War concerns when it affected US policy. The day the Truman Doctrine was declared, US oil companies signed agreements granting them increased access to the riches of Saudi Arabia.[38] It was this threat of indigenous forces aspiring to control their own resources which contributed to US and Soviet fears.

Middle Eastern oil was vital for post-war European reconstruction. The British had invited Washington to assume the role of hegemonic power on the edge of the Middle East so that access to oil supplies purchased with sterling, not vital dollars, could be maintained. Oil was particularly important for the dollar gap because the United States was becoming a net importer, so it would be cheaper and easier for Europe to get oil from outside the Western Hemisphere.[39] Thus oil and access were essential parts of the strategy, not only the fear that Greece would 'drop out of the United States' orbit and try an independent nationalistic policy'. Had the Greek left won, their example for various forms of Arab nationalism or socialism might have been considerable. There was a second form of the Rotten Apple theory: 'the rot that concerns planners is the threat of successful social and economic development outside the framework of U.S. control, development of a sort that may be meaningful to poor and oppressed people elsewhere'. The possible demonstration effects or what is known as the 'threat of a good example' had to be mitigated.[40]

The tone and the content of the Truman Doctrine amounted to a globalisation of the Monroe Doctrine. The US sphere of influence was no longer limited to the Western Hemisphere, but now would encompass at least the western world. The situation in Greece and Turkey was described as 'twin tempests in a teapot' because Soviet action in the region before the Truman speech was 'subdued and cautious'. Even after the speech Stalin still sought co-operation and peaceful coexistence.[41] The Greek insurgence was expendable in the emerging bipolar tensions. Stalin had withheld aid, recognised the British sphere of influence, and wanted to destroy Tito's example of an independent communist power outside Moscow's control. Washington also feared the potential of independent development. The Greek left 'was now crushed between the Tito–Stalin conflict on the one hand and the combined hostility and power of the Anglo-American and Athens governments on the other'.[42]

The Truman speech immediately created numerous doctrinal problems. The policy was enunciated in response to a local situation but took on the language of a universal crusade. In Washington's political context the limits of the policy and the objectives could not be identified; the mobilisation of domestic opinion depended on reference to the spectre of communism. According to Theodore Draper, the 'mixture of an universal doctrine with limited means of action created a dangerous mixture of illusion and reality which we have yet to rid ourselves of'. With the universalisation of the policy the implications required a conceptual universalisation of the Soviet threat.[43] The illusion continued through various administrations until the end of the Johnson era with tragic consequences for millions.

By the summer of 1947 the containment policy was made public in Kennan's (Mr X) article, 'The Sources of Soviet Conduct'. The inexorable Soviet attempts at expansion would have to be met by the United States with the policy of 'firm containment, designed to confront the Russians with unalterable counter-force at every point where they show signs of encroaching upon the interests of a peaceful and stable world'. The US would have to enter a period of 'long term, patient but firm and vigilant containment of Russian expansive tendencies'. He had not intended a military response with western forces, but with economic and political 'counter-force'. He had not made it clear that he was talking about an ideological threat from the Soviet Union, not a military threat. By the time X was published, Kennan had begun to move away from the idea of a universal response. Instead he began to advocate the defence of the vital 'strongpoint' areas such as Europe and Japan. Within the year Kennan and his policy planning staff criticised the universal response and suggested that the Truman Doctrine should not establish precedent, as unlimited resources were not available to the US. Containment entered US culture through widespread publicity.[44]

Walter Lippmann immediately criticised Kennan for failing to distinguish between vital and peripheral interests, which would drain US resources. The universal policy of reacting with counter-force to Kremlin initiatives at the periphery is to place too much importance on 'dubious and unnatural allies'. Moreover, it placed Washington in a reactive mode, waiting for the Soviet Union to 'mellow' or 'break up'. It was, therefore, a 'misuse of American power'. Lippmann also criticised containment for neglecting the option of negotiations. He wrote: 'for a diplomat to think that rival and unfriendly powers cannot be brought to a settlement is to forget what diplomacy is about'. The doctrine imposed an 'ideological straitjacket' which trapped US leaders in the confines of their rhetoric, and ultimately made it difficult for them to respond to Moscow's conciliatory gestures after Stalin's death, which 'contributed to the perpetuation of the Cold War'. In 1995, when Kennan was asked if the West had prolonged the Cold War, he replied that the US 'did not exhaust our possibilities for arriving at solutions that would have been better than the continuation of the Cold War'.[45]

The Marshall Plan: extending hegemony

The Marshall Plan was a stroke of genius. Washington wanted to avoid
the economic, political and military consequences of the closed world of
the 1930s. The Second World War ended with the creation of a system
based on the Open Door. The Bretton Woods system created in 1944 provided a vision to which the Soviets gave tacit ascent even though they were
minimally involved in its creation. Revolutionary agendas and the Open
Door are uneasy bedfellows but Moscow's primary objective was to
rebuild its power. When Washington cancelled Lend-Lease in late 1945,
Moscow turned to Germany and Eastern Europe for reparations to begin
reconstruction.[46] Gardner suggests the division of Europe was probably
necessary from Washington's perspective:

> It is difficult to imagine how the United States could have man-
> aged economic recovery without the Soviet sphere of influence in
> Eastern Europe. What incentive would Congress have had to sup-
> port Truman's major initiatives without the cold war? After both
> the German and Russian armies had trampled over Eastern
> Europe and stripped it bare, not simply of material resources but
> of experienced managerial capacity, would not the economic
> "drain" in that region have overwhelmed the Marshall Plan?
> Without an "enemy" to focus on, how could the bedevilling
> European rivalries of the interwar years have been overcome?[47]

The US invitation to Moscow to join in the plan was at best symbolic.
There was no intention that it should participate.

Though the Marshall Plan resulted in a strategy designed by and for
Western Europe, it was an essential element of containment. The plan was
implicitly linked to the Truman Doctrine and therefore always conceived
in terms of ideology, economic imperatives and geo-strategy. On his return
from the foreign ministers' conference, Secretary of State Marshall,
decided to proceed with the economic programme for Europe with, without, or against Russia. Towards this end he announced his programme at
Harvard on 5 June 1947:

> It is logical that the United States should do whatever it is able to
> do to assist in the return of normal economic health in the world,
> without which there can be no political stability and no assured
> peace. Our policy is directed not against any country or doctrine
> but against hunger, poverty, desperation, and chaos. Its purpose
> should be the revival of a working economy in the world so as to
> permit the emergence of political and social conditions in which
> free institutions can exist.

Washington did not want to appear responsible for the division of Europe hence Marshall's rhetoric was inclusive. If division was to take place, 'the responsibility had better rest with Moscow than with Washington'.[48]

The economic situation in Britain, France, Italy and Germany was desperate. Though productivity had reached pre-war levels, there was a shortage of dollars to purchase US goods (as Marshall recognised in his speech), inflation was high, distribution was poor and potential political unrest loomed large in Washington's mind. Washington was made aware of the humanitarian concerns, but its response was driven by 'self-interest, by fear of chaos and subversion'. In such circumstances the political left fared well. Because communism was perceived to thrive on poverty, desperation and chaos, the plan was partly conceived in an attempt to keep Europe out of the Soviet sphere, for both political and economic reasons, but also 'because it was the repository of the shared values of Western civilisation'.[49] Anyone could participate so long as their economies were integrated, the PPS gathered that 'Russian satellite countries would either exclude themselves by unwillingness to accept the proposed conditions or agree to abandon the exclusive orientation of their economies'.[50]

Washington insisted the plan was multilateral. Individual plans were unacceptable because the subtext was both to exclude the Soviet Union and to accelerate West European and US economic integration. Britain and France, in line with Washington's injunction, stressed that the outcome had to be an integrated plan for European recovery. Soviet Foreign Minister, Vyacheslav Molotov, left Paris warning that national sovereignty would be undermined, Germany would be revived, the United States would control Europe and that the continent 'would be divided into two groups of states . . . creating new difficulties in the relations between them'. Moreover, the plan reoriented German economic policy towards Western Europe and the world economy away from its links with the East. Germany was central to Washington's conception of a revived Europe, which had to be arranged with security guarantees to placate fears of German unilateral revival.[51]

With the arrival of Marshall aid Europeans had the necessary dollars to purchase US goods. With or without the 'Communist threat' US prosperity rested on a 'vigorous export market'.[52] European economic stability required a reduced presence of the left in national politics, and conservative and subservient governments.[53]

US hegemony prevailed even if it had to address particular concerns. Washington had to accommodate the British on currency convertibility, which would drive down sterling reserves and jeopardise the Labour government's welfare programmes. French fears of German remilitarisation were assuaged as Germany was integrated into the US-centred economy. Charles Maier refers to the relationship as one of 'consensual hegemony'. Washington was bound to exercise hegemony given the basic inequalities in the international system after the Second World War. The European élite quickly came to realise that their national interests and their 'personal political fortunes' were served by forming an alliance with Washington; 'such a transnational élite forms the backbone of any imperial system'.[54]

The Bretton Woods system of currency convertibility ended in the economic crisis of 1947 and prompted the Marshall Plan, which was essentially a response to the European payments problem or the dollar gap. Without the German supply of capital goods and the decreased output from other parts of the world West Europeans did not have enough dollars to pay for US imports. The goal of the European Recovery Program (ERP) was to reduce the dollar gap to move the system back towards the Bretton Woods model of currency convertibility. It was the success of the short-run recovery of the European economies that exacerbated the problem. The US aim was to sweep away the nation-state and to integrate Europe in a single economy and ultimately into political union. But Alan Milward argues that the European intentions were very different from those of the United States and that the various European states pursued different national aims; *integration* was the rescue of the European nation-state. 'Marshall Aid was not in fact important enough to give the United States sufficient leverage to reconstruct western Europe according to its own wishes. The main economic importance of Marshall Aid over the whole duration of the programme was the imports, particularly capital goods imports, which it permitted.' Ultimately the Europeans frustrated the United States and designed their own schemes for integration.[55]

The plan succeeded in terms of controlling inflation, reviving production and boosting trade. The substantial economic growth during the period 1948 to 1952 provided the various European coalitions with a range of options that precluded the extremes of political response from both the left and the right. The post-war US strategy was essentially aimed at boosting production in an attempt to eliminate 'ideology' from politics, which should be more concerned with economic growth. US ideological constructs were not seen as such, but assumed to be the 'natural order'; the 'American way of life' and its democracy were seen as essentially anti-ideological, that is, it pursued the politics of production between the extremes of communism and fascism. Hogan suggests that

> Economic growth, modest social programs, and a more equitable distribution of production would immunize participating countries against Communist subversion while generating the resources and mobilizing the public support necessary to sustain a major rearmament program. In addition, economic integration, supra-national coordinating mechanisms, and transnational patterns of

corporative collaboration would create an interdependent unit large enough to reconcile Germany's recovery with France's economic and military security.[56]

Washington envisaged a larger Europe within the process of global integration. That the ultimate market was more regulated than it would have preferred does not deny the US influence. 'Europe was only half Americanized' though plans were more ambitious.[57]

The Marshall Plan facilitated the extension of US hegemony. The hegemonic power usually tried to overcome economic nationalism and protectionist practices, and to 'accept a world of free trade, free capital flows, and free currency convertibility'. Its power was used to promote the ideologies associated with the Open Door, free trade, comparative advantage and a division of labour around the world. It forcefully resisted alterations to the system.[58]

The Marshall Plan was an attempt to save the capitalist system. When the system moved from the 'spheres of influence' deal envisaged at Yalta to the suggestion of a more open system, the Soviet Union decided not to participate; and in the summer of 1947 the Soviets walked out of the Paris Conference. Thus to some extent the Cold War was brought about by the Soviet refusal to accept US hegemony and its vision of the future world order. The differences between the United States and the European economies prevented the latter from bridging the 'dollar gap'. Europe had held a trade deficit with the United States since the First World War, and in the immediate post-war period was paying for US imports with the resources of the various colonies or the 'peripheries' of the system. The dollar gap grew in the years 1946 to 1947 from $8 billion to $12 billion. Had the trend continued, perhaps autarkic policies would have been revived. Worse still, if the Europeans were either co-opted or threatened by the Soviet Union, a key industrial core would be lost to the capitalist world system. As Kennan noted, 'the greatest danger that could confront the US security would be a combination and working together for purposes hostile to us of the central European and Russian military-industrial potentials'. The Marshall Plan consequently provided Europe with sufficient dollars to bridge the gap and continue its westward orientation.[59]

Washington was as much aware of its capitalist economy and domestic economic health, as it was about the prospects of the Soviet Union luring either a part of the periphery, or Germany or Japan into its orbit, thus eroding West European power and concomitantly that of the United States. US policy makers did not envisage a direct military threat from the Soviet Union, but thought rather that the challenge would remain at the political level. Europe had to be kept in the western economic system, which would provide a 'magnet' for the Soviet satellites in Eastern Europe. Washington had identified the nationalist feelings in the region and had also realised Moscow's control lacked any consent on the part of East Europeans. However, the plan required the revival of Germany's industrial potential, which generated reaction from other European powers. Ultimately Washington accepted British Foreign Minister Ernest Bevin's Western Union and associated the United States with a system of Atlantic security. Thus, the containment of a possible revival of Germany by securing the West European countries and integrating the German economy made Soviet retaliatory moves inevitable, which General Omar Bradley recognised as a cause of the 1948 Berlin crisis. US actions, in the knowledge of a limited Soviet response, were provocative. Leffler argues:

> the very actions they had to take to rebuild Western Europe, defeat local communists, co-opt Germany, and reassure allies constituted potential threats [to the Soviet Union], whether intended or not. 'The present tension in Berlin,' Marshall told the cabinet, 'is brought about by loss of Russian face in Italy, France, Finland. . . . It is caused by Russian desperation in face of success of the ERP.'[60]

If the motivations and the impetus to the Marshall Plan contributed to the strategy of dual containment, they also contributed to the security dilemma, setting up a process of action and reaction which ultimately solidified the various Cold War institutions, perceptions and assumptions. The process can be seen two ways. The declarations of Cold War came from the West first, whether it was the Iron Curtain speech or the Truman Doctrine. The Marshall Plan preceded the Molotov response, the Federal Republic of Germany preceded the German Democratic Republic, and NATO preceded the Warsaw Pact. The Soviets, on the other hand, had occupied large parts of the East against western designs.[61]

The division of Europe in 1947 exacerbated the economic problems of Western Europe. These countries had already been cut off from traditional economic links to Eastern and Central Europe, which made it more difficult to bridge the dollar gap. Markets in the Third World replaced economic activity normally conducted with Eastern Europe. With integration Washington not only provided dollars and security safeguards but also stimulated the extraction of cheap raw materials and food supplies from the periphery to assist European economies and therefore that of the US.[62]

Though Washington may have had indirect concerns for their security, it had calculated the Soviet Union would not go to war at that point. Instead, the security dilemma produced a system which exacerbated tensions in Cold War Europe, and various bloody and hot wars on the periphery or in the Third World. For the United States there seemed to be little threat to its physical existence. 'The peculiarity of the Cold War was that', Eric Hobsbawm writes, 'no imminent danger of world war existed'.[63]

The US way of life, its economic system, its ideologies, however, had to be maintained, and to muster the necessary domestic support the creation of an external threat was vital.

The Manichaean world of NSC 68

Any hegemonic system needs to act according to the realities of its power and its national interests. But to inspire and to mobilise society it needs the myths of the 'other' and the ideals, the constructs, of its traditional identity. Despite such 'realist' ambitions the nation was loath to talk about its politics and foreign policy in these terms. The narratives suggesting a higher purpose usually prevailed. The 1950 National Security Council Document 68 used a series of linguistic devices that enhanced the sense that the nation faced an imminent threat; it grafted its agenda onto the 'fundamental purpose of the United States', and it enhanced the binary opposites of 'us' versus 'them' that were a part of US tradition. Such constructions deny nuance and complexity in favour of consensus. 'NSC 68 . . . employs a familiar technique of militant nationalism: trying to forge a national consensus through the creation of a symbolic "other"' opposed to the cultural traditions of US diplomacy. Yet the document enhanced the power of the state and had far-reaching implications for US policy, defence and national budgets.[64]

Formal and informal ideologies legitimated the national interests, ensured domestic cohesion and consensus on the goals and identity of the nation. Through circular logic the success of US foreign policy reinforced the assumed ideologies; and in turn cohesion was enhanced by the traditional meta-narrative. Earlier, Kennan was aware of the effects that the supposed Soviet challenge would have on US society. He wrote in the X article that 'the United States need only measure up to its own best traditions and prove itself worthy of preservation as a great nation'. And:

> Surely, there was never a fairer test of national quality than this . . .
> the thoughtful observer of Russian–American relations will find
> no cause for complaint in the Kremlin's challenge to American
> society. He will rather experience a certain gratitude to a
> Providence which, by providing the American people with this
> implacable challenge, has made their entire security as a nation
> dependent on their pulling themselves together and accepting the
> responsibilities of moral and political leadership that history
> plainly intended them to bear.[65]

Kennan realised that the danger from the Soviet Union was political and not military. Later in 1947 he wrote a review of the world situation for Secretary of State Marshall indicating that 'the danger of war is vastly exaggerated in many quarters. The Soviet Government neither wants nor expects war with us in the foreseeable future.' Though the Soviets had attempted to dominate the Eurasian landmass, that process had largely been brought to a halt through several US initiatives including the psychological relief provided by Marshall's speech at Harvard in June 1947.[66]

Further realism was injected by the Policy Planning Staff in their review of 'trends' in US foreign relations early in 1948. West European economic and therefore political security would be enhanced through a European union, including Britain, though excluding the East, which would benefit through greater trading relationships with either Africa or the Western Hemisphere. West European nations would possibly 'undertake jointly the economic development and exploitation of the colonial and dependent areas of the African Continent'. The Middle East was treated as a security issue in terms of its strategic position and its resources. Russia would be prepared to do business with the United States over Germany after the European Recovery Program had become effective. Kennan thought Moscow would seek a 'sphere of influence' deal that the United States would have to reject. But beyond the areas of seemingly immediate interest Kennan was more suspicious of US influence. On the Far East he argued that Washington was deceiving itself if it thought it could provide answers to Asian problems though the region was vital to the integrated world economy, especially French and therefore European recovery. Kennan advised:

> we have about 50% of the world's wealth but only 6.3% of its population. This disparity is particularly great as between ourselves and the peoples of Asia. In this situation, we cannot fail to be the object of envy and resentment. Our real task in the coming period is to devise a pattern of relationships which will permit us to maintain this position of disparity without positive detriment to our national security. To do so, we will have to dispense with all sentimentality and day-dreaming; and our attention will have to be concentrated everywhere on our immediate national objectives. We need not deceive ourselves that we can afford today the luxury of altruism and world-benefaction.

Washington was too preoccupied with the desire to '"be liked" or to be regarded as the repository of a high-minded international altruism'. Kennan thought 'we should stop putting ourselves in the position of being our brothers' keeper and refrain from offering moral and ideological advice. We should cease to talk about vague and – for the Far East – unreal objectives such as human rights, the raising of living standards, and democratisation. The day is not far off when we are going to have to deal in straight power concepts. The less we are then hampered by idealistic slogans, the better.' Concluding the entire review, Kennan returned to this theme. The rhetoric and ideological propagation of US values had created straitjackets for Washington; it would be measured up to the standards it professed and would be found wanting. He concluded, 'In all areas of the world, we still find ourselves the victims of many of the romantic and uni-versalistic concepts with which we emerged from the recent war.'[67] Kennan saw the myths as constraints on a more realistic US programme. The world of NSC 68 regarded such myths as potent forces for the mobilisation of society, partly as an instrument to gain legislative consent for the significant militarisation of US policy and through this the introduction of military Keynesianism.

Truman attached an order to review US foreign policy to his instruction to proceed with the development of the hydrogen bomb in order to 'reassess US Defense policy . . . in the light of loss of China and Soviet mastery of the Atomic bomb'. Increasingly marginalised, Kennan had resigned from the Policy Planning Staff in 1949. Early in 1950 Paul Nitze was mainly responsible for the content of the extensive study of US strategy. The document, ready by 12 April 1950, set out in simple and ahistorical terms both the fundamental purposes of the United States and that of the Kremlin. The document reinforced the Manichaean view of the world as a bipolar struggle between the two powers. The fundamental US purpose was 'to assure the integrity and vitality of our free society, which is founded upon the dignity and worth of the individual', with obviously no mention of African or Native Americans or others. The fundamental purpose of the Soviet Union was to solidify its control in areas under its domination, and subvert and destroy the 'integrity and vitality' of the United States. A failure to resist Soviet expansion would result in a 'serious decline in the strength of the free world relative to the Soviet Union'. The co-ordinated western response must therefore, 'by means of a rapid and sustained build-up of the political, economic, and military strength of the free world . . . confront it with convincing evidence of the determination and ability of the free world to frustrate the Kremlin design of a world dominated by its will'.[68]

The document can also be situated within the context of a continual US expansionism stemming from the early days of the republic. Nitze's pro-gramme resulted in a trebling of the US defence expenditure. It advocated 'efforts to re-establish an international economy based on multilateral trade, declining trade barriers, and convertible currencies'. Commerce was subsumed within the security analysis. Gardner suggests that while the West was never on the defensive militarily, it was philosophically. The Soviet 'design' was apparently the threat it posed to US political and economic systems. The collapse of the international capitalist system in the 1930s, the rise of Hitler and the devastation of the war 'contributed to a malaise of doubt and uncertainty about the future of capitalist democracy'.

The Soviet ability to weather these storms, albeit at tremendous costs, primarily in terms of the millions of lives lost, gave rise to the perception of a 'plausible alternative to capitalism and political democracy'.[69] Any attempts to alter the US process of international economic integration, withdraw from the system, or provide alternative examples, was seen as an extension of the Soviet 'design'.

The domestic economy was just as important. The authors of the document were well aware of the economic lessons of the Second World War. Just as Roosevelt had justified rearmament in terms of its contribution to economic growth, the application of Keynesian economic theories to expansion of the military suggested that defence stimulated growth. In most cases the bargain would, according to Michael Sherry, remain tacit, but he cites the *U.S. News and World Report*, 'that "government planners figure that they have found the magic formula for almost endless good times . . . [the] Cold War is an automatic pump primer"'.[70]

It became a fairly standard refrain in many subsequent histories to suggest that NSC 68 was not such a sharp departure from the earlier assumptions of the Truman administration. In 1994 Nitze continued to insist it was a misconception to regard the document as a sharp departure: 'to the contrary, the report concluded by calling for the reaffirmation of policy already approved in NSC-20/4' written by Kennan in 1948.[71] Similarities undoubtedly have to be acknowledged, but there were differences. Kennan resisted writing a systematic exposition of his ideas on containment because this would limit the US ability to choose its method and moment of response. Kennan resisted the universalisation of the Soviet threat, which is exactly what NSC 68 presented. Kennan argued for a selective US response. He thought that 'unfriendly regimes . . . posed little threat to global stability so long as they lacked the means of manifesting their hostility'. But NSC 68 viewed the Cold War as a zero-sum game: any gain for the Soviet Union was a defeat for free institutions everywhere. In effect, the earlier distinctions between peripheral and vital interests had been lost in the new document. While traditionally budgetary considerations may have imposed a need to distinguish between vital and peripheral interests, military Keynesianism changed that logic. The economic lessons of the Second World War suggested that the economy operating 'at a level approaching full efficiency, can provide enormous resources for purposes other than civilian consumption' and simultaneously provide for an increased standard of living. While Kennan did not believe that the Soviets were likely to attack Western Europe or pose an insurmountable threat to the United States, NSC 68 lost that nuance of selective response. Gaddis writes, 'at the heart of the differences between Kennan and the authors of NSC-68 was a simple inversion of intellectual procedure: where Kennan tended to look at the Soviet threat in terms of an independently established concept of irreducible interests, NSC-68 derived its view of American interests primarily from its perception of the Soviet threat'. Hence, apart from 'real' US interests, attention also had to be paid to 'image, prestige, and credibility'. The interests and therefore threats thus vastly increased.[72]

The Soviet threat was exaggerated. The authors of the document probably concentrated on this because the more immediate fear of West European neutralism was too vague to form an official consensus around, and Truman stated earlier that only a national emergency could justify a major increase in government spending. As Acheson pointed out later, NSC 68 'was supposed to bludgeon the mass mind of "top government"'. The shift away from Kennan's economic containment to NSC 68's military containment, and the lack of room for neutrality or alternatives, infused US diplomacy with an offensive spirit.[73]

NSC 68 was closely associated with the outbreak of the Korean War. The war radically altered US perception of the Soviet threat. An aide to Acheson also indicated the government was 'sweating' over how to 'sell' the implications of NSC 68 to the public, when 'thank God Korea came along'. Acheson 'remarked that in the Korean hostilities "an excellent opportunity is here offered to disrupt the Soviet peace offensive, which . . . is assuming serious proportions and having a certain effect on public opinion"'.[74]

Such a world of compromise and pluralism, however, might undermine the importance of US security measures in Europe. Europeans might feel less obliged to the United States, and pursue more centrifugal economic policies. The world had to be made safe for capitalism. The process of integration from continental to hemispheric to western proportions had to be secured; even if a global economy would have to wait. The United States was in a unique position, as Acheson put it, to 'grab hold of history and make it conform'.[75]

7

REVOLUTION AND DEVELOPMENT
IN THE COLD WAR

The constructs explored in the previous chapter had a pervasive influence on US policy in the Third World throughout the height of the Cold War. The Manichaean outlook, driven by a set of security concerns and policies associated with containment and rollback of the 'Soviet expansive tendencies', was coupled with attempts to integrate the economies of the decolonised states with an integrated Western Europe and then the United States. For many Third World states such US global strategies undermined their national self-determination and often the negative liberties associated with individual human rights. Attempts by Third World states to pursue various forms of nationalism, where they thought the Cold War inhibited their self-determination, or attempts by radical or revolutionary movements were predominantly viewed through the Cold War constructs, and were subjected to various US reactions. Throughout the period from the 1940s onward, US policy reacted negatively to Third World nationalism that was driven by revolutionary groups or by economic models that detracted from the preferred US agenda for increasing liberalisation of trade and economic openness. This was not exactly new to US policy, but now it was conditioned by the Cold War constructs that lent it increasing intensity. Therefore independent or leftist nationalism was frequently undermined and was justified through ideologies derived from the new Cold War constructs. On the other hand the self-determination of US-backed regimes was enhanced through the provision of economic and military aid. The most extreme of these 'national security states', however, conducted gross violations of human rights against the so-called socialists or communists within the states. Throughout the period these conflicts were also informed by the struggle over the most appropriate form of economic development. US antipathy towards radical nationalism, revolution and alternative forms of economic development undermined political and economic self-determination, and frequently within various nation-states it undermined the democratic process.

An analysis of US ideologies explains the various constructs that conflated ideas on nationalism, revolution and economic development with the Cold War, but the propensity towards increased economic integration and US hegemony continued the materialist narrative that also informed US policy. The consequences of conflating these ideas and interests had serious negative consequences for pluralism in a constructed bipolar world. The intolerance shown to independent development undermined democracy, liberty and self-determination in many cases. The universalisation of the Cold War constructs and models of progress inhibited freedom and democracy. Isaiah Berlin argued 'that subjection to a single ideology, no matter how reasonable and imaginative, robs men of freedom and vitality', and that 'the richest development of human potentialities can occur only in societies in which there is a wide spectrum of opinions – the freedom for what J. S. Mill called "experiments in living" – in which there is liberty of thought and of expression, views and opinions clash with each other, societies in which friction and even conflict are permitted'.[1]

History, progress and revolution

Viewed from afar, the Cold War was a struggle over History and for the mantle of Progressivism. In the pursuit of building their state and economic might both superpowers undermined the formal ideologies of which they were supposedly representatives. Each imposed a political framework on their economic activities. The systems of state planning and economic liberalism vied with each other for the awareness of peoples and allegiance of the emerging Third World nation-states. These systems were not faithful to their intellectual origins, but the states that pursued them required social legitimacy.[2] Societal compliance required the states to be successful, progressive, and in the cases of both the United States and the Soviet Union politically messianic. It is not the intention here to enter into a discussion of the Soviet version of progress, especially not the Stalinist depredations, which were still derivatives of Lenin, communism, and ultimately the Enlightenment.[3] For its part the US system proved enormously more successful. It had harnessed the engines of modernisation much more coherently and the cultural constructs were attuned to the ideologies that served its global agenda.

The main engines of modernisation, the nation-state, industrialisation and capitalism,[4] were all closely associated with the purpose of US foreign policy throughout the twentieth century and before; it was assumed that 'progress' informed their direction. Cultural assumptions on a continued Manifest Destiny, reinforced by the US preponderance of power, took the nation through economic and political success in a world that had vastly increased its wealth. Now only the Soviets, revolutionaries and nationalists stood in the way of these ideas and material pursuits. But US-style progress was buttressed by the ideas on democracy, liberty, self-determination and the Open Door economy that galvanised and motivated the society.

Success in war and economy further enhanced the strength of the ideologies. Development through modernisation theories provided a conceptual framework, which reinforced acceptance of US economic penetration of the post-colonial economies. If the decolonised states aspired to similar lifestyles, the effective message from Washington suggested, economic 'modernisation' was best suited to that end. However, the applicability of the model was not universal. Furthermore, US motives were viewed with some suspicion given their close association with colonial powers. Many Third World nations looked to the Soviet model as an appealing alternative; its economic success during the 1930s stood in stark contrast to western depression. Moreover, for half a century Central American or Caribbean states had been tutored in US-style progress without much evidence of the fruits of modernisation.

Progress was a contested issue,[5] not just between superpower conceptions but also between the presence of these dominant powers and the states and peoples who aspired to greater independence within these spheres. Washington pursued economic integration, while revolutionary movements and some states wanted to limit their involvement in the global economy; notions of state and individual self-determination collided with each other. Washington alleged that revolutionary movements undermined the sovereignty of their nations through the extension of the 'Soviet design', while obviously the localised revolutionaries argued that they in fact enhanced their national self-determination, in part by resisting the effects of the global economy. Vietnam initially tried to integrate US conceptions on national self-determination with socialist ideas. Ho Chi Minh's 1945 Vietnamese Declaration of Independence took the model of the US declaration listing colonial grievances against France. US inspiration ended there; socialist ideas were used to inspire the nation's internal organisation. The two traditions are not without precedent. US self-determination required breaking ties with the metropolitan centre in London and asserting the rights of man in the 1770s and the 1790s. Decades later (1848) Karl Marx and Friedrich Engels asserted the rights of men against the effects of industrialisation.[6] Both traditions spoke of different conceptions of liberty, which remained at the heart of the struggle between Washington and the revolutionaries during the Cold War.

The Enlightenment narrative still informed the struggle in the 1950s and 1960s. Third World nations sought development and progress in one of the two forms. Even if development was bound within the nation-state, it still adhered to models and programmes derived from the West. It was not until the 1970s that there was a substantial revolt against progress and the western idea. Decolonisation distributed the western nation-state throughout the world. But because Third World nationalism was also asserted against the western economy it was seen as a perversion of the idea of nationalism, borrowed and reproduced in an inferior form. Such sentiments created recurrent problems for Washington throughout the post-war period. 'The history of all cultures is the history of cultural borrowings.' So, the radical departure of Indian independence was that it incorporated an opposition to modern civilisation within the concept of the nation-state. Through colonialism and integration the West had undermined so many of its ideas on self-determination and individual rights. Western civilisation, Gandhi quipped, would be a good idea. Prime Minister Jawaharlal Nehru took the nation, 'liberated from modernity by Gandhi', and deposited it within the state.[7] By the mid-1950s India's development agenda was back within the modernist project at the Bandung Conference. Notwithstanding this example, the process of revolutionary change examined here was by and large conducted within the narrative of progress. Not until the Ayatollah Khomeini's revolution of 1979 in Iran was another justification successfully advanced.

The main contention between revolutionary movements and the metropolitan centres in Washington and New York was related to the fruit of progress. The roots of revolution were found in the internal socio-economic conditions of Third World states that were products of a transnational economic system. Revolutionaries sought greater control over national resources to enhance self-determination, in some cases democratic rights, and in all cases to remove the neo-colonial ties with foreign powers and the local élites who served them. Improved living standards and self-determination were at the heart of the agenda whatever form the revolution took. Economic inequality and the quest for material progress motivated very real individual needs, which were expressed through nationalist sentiment and socialist programmes because they countered western hegemony.

However, given the consensus in Washington on the nature and purpose of the 'Soviet design', it is hardly surprising that the understanding of revolutions was filtered through a Cold War prism. Political change, reform or revolution was filtered through US geo-strategic and ideological aspirations. In the bipolar world of the 1950s and 1960s there was little space to countenance alternatives. The Cold War consensus and the logic of NSC 68 had posited an irreducible conflict in World History. US aspirations to maintain its standard of living, 'to maintain the position of disparity', and to enhance economic integration set up a contradiction between the aspirations of Third World states and those of the United States. Nationalism and the failure of the promise of material fulfilment fuelled revolution; but poverty alone did not a revolution make.

Third World revolution and the Cold War

Several trends merged in the post-Second World War period which dramatically exposed the material differences amongst the world's population.

First, decolonisation increased the number of nation-states rapidly. Independent states in Asia increased fivefold, in the Caribbean twelve were added, in Africa there were about fifty when the process of decolonisation ended. Political representation at the United Nations and assertions of their positive liberties were often caught up in the politics of identity. Second, a population explosion, unprecedented in World History, ensured that there was acute pressure on resources that moved to the northern industrial centres; yet the migration of labour, essential to Adam Smith's ideas, was limited by state borders and immigration laws. Third, the post-war period saw unprecedented economic growth in both the advanced industrial countries and many Third World states, but this growth has to be tempered by the demographic explosion in the latter. As Hobsbawm relates, it is one thing to distribute an expanding gross domestic product in a state with a stable population, quite another to distribute resources amongst a population that has grown much faster. Relativity is essential to understanding wealth. The obvious consequence of these trends was vastly to increase the gap between the rich and the poor, not only between First and Third World nations but also within them. Often a small élite in Third World nations maintained power and wealth at the expense of the vast majority of people.[8]

The conflation of the liberal ideas on wealth creation and open economies leading to pacific relations were enhanced by the phenomenal postwar economic growth and increased western multilateralism. The welfare state modified the raw edges of the capitalist states in the First World: 'post-war prosperity had induced the Western working classes to settle for good enough rather than Utopia; the horrors of communism had put up the price of Utopia, and the welfare state had lowered the costs of capitalism'.[9] But the unprecedented period of economic growth went hand in hand with the relative impoverishment of the bulk of the world's population. Third World states, a creation of the colonial legacy, adopted political systems which rarely enjoyed societal legitimacy. Repression was widespread. Where instability was a frequent occurrence, the military was often the guardian of stability and order. Cold War paradigms were imposed on national unrest, facilitating Praetorian opportunities for the frequent abuse of power and human rights in both the client states of the Soviet and western 'democracies'. Elections were held when possible, often to provide a facade of legitimacy either for internal stability or because US appropriation procedures mandated support for 'democracy'. One thinks of Ngo Diem's astounding electoral victory in 1955 securing 98.2 per cent of the vote or elections such as those held in El Salvador during the 1980s, for instance.[10] In Latin America states dominated by the military acquired the identity of 'national security states'. While the nominal number of 'democratic' states increased in the Third World, the internal characteristics of the Soviet-style 'people's democracies' or western 'national security

144

states' conditioned the actual prospects for democracy. Democracy was a luxury not a right in much of the Third World. As Hobsbawm writes: 'military politics, like military intelligence, tended to fill the void left by the absence of ordinary politics or intelligence'.[11] The superpower struggle, mostly enacted in the Third World, purporting to extend various notions of democracy to these countries, was ultimately a cruel joke for most of the inhabitants of the Third World. Democracy, in any meaningful sense, remained elusive for much of the world, despite its titular or adjectival presence.

The Third World emerged simultaneously with the Cold War. The credibility of the preferred US economic system required its adoption by the Third World and enhancement in Europe and East Asia. US prosperity necessitated integration of the European and the Japanese economies, which in turn led to demands for the resources of the Third World. Europe needed most of Eurasia, not to mention resources from Africa. The Japanese economy required the integration of most of South East Asia. The United States needed a vital Europe and Japan plus stability and order in its 'backyard'. As the US enhanced economic integration amongst the industrialised West (Japan included) through the Marshall and Dodge Plans, the process of political fragmentation was simultaneously under way through the formation of nation-states. As Clark explains:

> cumulative pressures were to draw the United States into military commitments in the Third World as the only way of protecting the political framework, and hence the economic space, of multilateralism. Although unintended in the late 1940s, the 1950s had found active military engagement necessary to support the US-preferred economic order. In part, this became necessary as a consequence of the rapid atrophy of European colonial power.[12]

In many ways the modern Third World revolution resulted in reaction to these global processes.

The Cold War context was crucial to understanding the US reaction to revolution, but not to understanding the origins or direction revolutions took. It would be necessary to suspend belief in the will to survive, to endorse the suggestion that countless people in the Third World went in search of abstract ideological monsters to destroy.

Revolution occurred for a variety of reasons and it is always necessary to examine the particular context of each situation. Nevertheless, some general observations can be made for the purposes of this analysis. Two things are important. First, there is the body of knowledge that has made the literature on comparative revolutions both voluminous and contested, but suggests why revolutions are closely linked to particularities in time and space. Second, these studies on the causes of revolution must be linked with studies on US paradigms, informal ideologies and constructs to understand the reaction. US perception was often only loosely related to reality.

The motivation for revolution is primarily an indigenous affair, though the opportunity can often be affected by politics beyond state borders. Several considerations are pertinent. First, revolutionary ideology was important. An intellectual and political purpose inspired groups, often disproportionately from the middle classes, to act. Though they acted as a catalyst, such groups rarely succeeded alone. Second, conditions had to be ripe for revolution. Sufficient grievance, in terms of political or economic exclusion, usually existed in the state. But economic conditions alone are insufficient to explain the particularity of Third World revolution. Third, revolution occurred when the domestic regime was weakened by international or structural opportunities in space and time. And finally, nationalism was a key ingredient. Singular explanations never sufficed, though such constructs were powerful tools in public discourse and US policy making.

Revolutions and US reaction need to be situated in the long-term process of economic integration. As far as the Western Hemisphere was concerned the process accelerated in the first few decades of the twentieth century. Presidents Roosevelt, Taft and Wilson crafted a response deemed most suitable to contemporary opportunities. After 1950 the Third World was increasingly integrated into the western economic system. The reactions that became most symbolic occurred where revolutionary movements impinged on western economic imperatives. The 1950s Iranian Revolution was caught up in the region's strategic significance and the politics of oil production, vital for European recovery. Guatemala (1945–1954) and Cuba (1959–) threatened specific interests, but more importantly favoured models of development, integration and US credibility. In Vietnam, the revolution was first conducted as an anti-imperialist venture against French control and then against US and Japanese interests. In all cases the revolutionary states were integral parts of the world economic system.

US involvement in Guatemala, Cuba and Vietnam was in part a result of the Manichaean worldview, which was superimposed on the world system. The link between the wealth and poverty of the First and Third Worlds was crucial. Economic closure or autarky affected the liberties of both sets of states and undermined, in actuality or through example, the credibility of the free trade regime and western concepts of modernisation.[13] With liberal trade Third World nations may have gained in wealth in macro-economic terms, but because of the social structure and the economic distribution within the states people were impoverished. Relatively isolated dictators suppressed the poor, alienated and excluded the middle-class and élite groups and corrupted the military to ensure that it was not sufficiently organised to overthrow the regime maintaining political power. National security doctrines ensured stability and systemic endurance. It was imperative to assert the primacy of communism as the cause of instability to maintain order and legitimate or ignore the repression and absence of democratic rights. The Cold War construct proved essential.

There is a potent myth that Third World revolutions occurred when there was a congruence of destitution and a revolutionary movement.[14] Nationalism was also a key component. Revolutionary movements harnessed the idea that they, not the élite dictators closely associated with the colonial order or with the world system, represented the force of national self-determination. Authoritarian regimes were seen as quislings serving foreign interests or the global economy, not the national interest and the negative liberties of their citizens. They were the local agents of globalisation. The role of government they performed was limited and attuned to external interests, rather than the role promised by the revolutionary movement that was inward-looking. If the regime did not provide basic services and these were being offered by the revolutionaries, as was the case in Iran, Guatemala, Vietnam, Cuba and Nicaragua, then revolution was more likely.[15]

The accelerated economic integration in the post-war period provided additional cause for the revolutionary movements. The period from the late 1940s to the early 1950s was one of unprecedented economic growth and industrial output. Capital flowed more freely across borders than it had done before; the economies of the world became increasingly integrated. In part the Third World regimes against which revolutions were conducted failed to provide the services of government and were seen as serving external interests. Thus the regimes were identified as agents of foreign power or the world system. They kept the economies open and served the interests of foreign corporations or interests that the revolutionaries moved against. The world system and the ideologies that gave it credence obviously had an incentive to react to the challenges to the system.[16]

Material interests and nationalism still do not sufficiently explain Third World revolution. These conditions need to be accompanied by a structural weakness in the regime and the international order. Regimes were usually weakened because power was exclusive, not just of the poor but of other, middle-class groups, hence revolutions were usually conducted by broad cross-sections of society. The more exclusive the power structure the more likely it will be that a broad coalition will form in opposition. If the middle class, business and other élite are excluded, they are likely to join the revolutionary movements at a point when the authoritarian government is seen to be organisationally weak or 'suddenly weakened'. The history of failed revolutions is one of premature attempts to overthrow authoritarian regimes. Most successful revolutions are made up of a cross-section of society, unlike the traditional assumptions that peasant revolt or urban factions foment revolution. Hence, the non-materialist explanations for revolution need to be acknowledged. Economic conditions are necessary but not sufficient factors to explain Third World revolution. Skocpol argues,

> Not surprisingly, revolutionary coalitions tend to form around preexisting nationalist, populist, or religious discourses that legitimize resistance to tyranny and, just as important, are capable of aggregating a broad array of social classes and strata. Nationalism, in particular, has proven to be a more inclusive and powerful force for revolutionary mobilization than class struggle alone. Revolutionaries have fared best where they and not conservative or reformist leadership – have been able to harness nationalist sentiment.

Marxist groups have done better when they stress 'national liberation' over class struggle in these situations.[17] Ultimately, widespread support from below, peasant or wider, needed to be accompanied by 'administrative-military breakdown from above'.[18]

Washington perceived Third World nationalism as more of a threat than socialism, communism or leftist politics. There was a difference between revolutionary movements and revolutionary states which, after the accomplishment of their initial goals, set off to build the society that had originally motivated them towards action.[19]

The Cold War dominated US perception and presentation of revolution. Congressional acquiescence and appropriations were facilitated by such constructs. The costs of US policy, provision of aid programmes and defence of dictators were justified in these terms. It was necessary to reinforce the Cold War narrative. It was easier to believe that the fundamental purpose of the nation was to defend freedom, or to promote democracy and self-determination against the communists, than it was to mobilise policy around the politics of materialism, economic access and integration; the former were more universal, the latter quite particular. The study of the Soviet or communist influence, in Latin America in particular, disproves the thesis that in opposing revolution Washington was either protecting the 'free world' or promoting democratic opportunities.

Nationalism, which within the Third World context offered the best opportunities for the establishment of democratic opportunities and self-determination, was the main threat to the US vision and policy of global integration. Washington did not want to inhibit western growth by permitting the proliferation of autarkic economies and the politics of nationalism in the world system. (Incidentally, for nations and states outside the world system, that is, behind the Iron Curtain, or nations is the pre-global economic world, that is, the world of European empires, nationalism, the self-determination of Wilsonian politics was perfectly acceptable.) Within the global economy, nationalism was only acceptable in its symbolic political manifestations.

In the post-war period Washington preferred whenever possible largely to ignore the Western Hemisphere. European recovery and integration exercised its purse strings, as did the rearmament programme and the Cold War. East and South East Asia increasingly consumed US dollars as Washington first became involved in the Korean War and then those in Vietnam. Latin America was essentially designated an area for exports and the import of raw materials. Kennan outlined US aims as 'protecting our raw materials', the prevention of military exploitation by the enemy, and 'the prevention of psychological mobilisation of Latin America against us'. Secretary of State Marshall had told the hemisphere that US priorities lay elsewhere. Finances for local development had to be secured from private sources. The US Secretary merely encouraged the governments to exercise 'fair treatment of foreign capital'; a sort of Open Door in a relatively closed hemisphere. Latin Americans wanted a Marshall Plan and, when denied, threatened Washington with price fixing and economic blocs. Hence Washington persuaded the OAS to write a set of economic principles that conformed to its multilateral agenda. The State Department indicated that 'Foreign capital will not venture, and in fact cannot operate, in circumstances in which excessive nationalism persists'. Nationalism, even of a conservative variety, was seen as an incomparably greater threat than communism.[20] Self-determination and democracy were severely compromised.

The United States and Third World revolution

The US reaction to revolution needs to be understood within the contexts of the global economy, assertions of nationalism, and an understanding of ideologies and political processes in the State Department, CIA, or National Security Council. US perceptions are extremely important in understanding the reactions. The Cold War shaped the language and the response to revolution, but distinctions must be made between Cold War perceptions and the history of US intervention and pursuit of order. To some extent the Third World cannot be divorced from the Cold War because semantically and systemically it very much evolved from the collapsed European empires into overwhelming bipolarity. But US relations with the post-colonial South, that is, with Latin and Central America, under Roosevelt and Wilson illuminate ongoing US attitudes and interests. Attitudes to people in the Third World were similar to those that informed the early treatment of the Native American population, or the Filipinos at the turn of the century.[21] The broader context of this period indicates the significance of Cold War constructs. Ongoing interests and attitudes remain relevant. Yet Washington has downplayed the social and economic conditions behind instability and revolution.[22] Revolutions were caused or directed by 'outside' pressures according to the dualistic worldview. Such constructs facilitated the Cold War consensus and maintained the traditional narrative of US foreign policy.

Washington's reaction to revolution was also conditioned by the early Cold War in Asia. First, US omnipotence and the supposed appeal of its economic and cultural system were openly challenged by the success of the Chinese and Vietnamese communists. Second, a negative policy limited to containment was inadequate; more positive strategies centred on development programmes had to be devised to reduce the revolutionary appeal. Third, Washington was tarred with the same brush as the European colonial powers even though their self-perception suggested exceptionalism. Last, the success of the revolutionaries and the élite who led them openly rejected 'American guidance in no uncertain terms directly challenging the tutelary model of external patron–domestic client relations that Washington favored'.[23]

The Cold War created intellectual and institutional straitjackets that reduced most challenges to Cold War dimensions, whether communist or not. Within these mental and bureaucratic structures combined with residual McCarthyite tradition, policy makers' manoeuvrability was limited. In the early Cold War such conditions were compounded by a belligerent spirit. The Truman Doctrine conflated totalitarianism and all the assumptions that went with it with communism and the erroneous lessons of Munich ensured that appeasement and negotiation were out of the question. The cast of mind developed to deal with European problems was universalised and used to misunderstand the revolutions in Central America and the Caribbean. Anti-communism, of central importance to the domestic US political system,[24] formed another straitjacket within which US policy had to be conducted.

In some cases Washington was able to find accommodation with revolutionary regimes. This was largely related to financial resolution of US interests in the post-revolutionary period. Washington found accommodation with both the Mexican and Bolivian revolutions after the settlement of outstanding issues.[25] But no satisfactory resolution was found with either Guatemala or Cuba, which challenged US authority and credibility more directly.

The literature on Iran, Guatemala, Cuba and Vietnam is vast. The point here is not to relate the particular histories but to illustrate US attitudes and policies towards assertions of national independence against economic integration and US hegemony. Washington had divergent interests in these countries. Guatemala and Cuba were a part of the Western Hemisphere and were therefore likely to cause a reaction not only because of the ideologies and perceived threats associated with the Cold War but also the hubris that went with the Monroe Doctrine and its derivatives. Iran was a key strategic area in the post-war period. It had been an early site of contest over the Soviet withdrawal from Azerbaijan. It was the repository of oil supplies, and a US client, prior to the Mossaddeq government. And Vietnam, thousands of miles from the United States, was still a key part of the world system, first vital to post-war French reconstruction and then to the Japanese economy. Its assertion of self-determination, of communist independence, flew in the face of Washington's post-war aims. Ho Chi Minh had an unusual vision, fuelled by the nationalism of one who had experienced French and Japanese occupation and knew the history of Chinese rule too well. He used the US model of self-determination, heavily citing Jefferson in his own Declaration of Independence. But freedom, in Ho's mind, in the late colonial period, in the global economy, also necessitated a socialist solution.

As far as the traditional narrative on democracy and self-determination was concerned, Vietnam was best forgotten. It was the site of massive suffering. Millions of people were killed, of whom 58,000 were American. The enduring failure of US policy wounded the nation, questioned its credibility and its ideals, its power and its prestige. The sooner the war could be depoliticised and returned to the meta-narrative of US foreign policy the better. When the Vietnamese cause proved conclusively that Vietnam was not a place to exercise traditional containment or rollback, when its self-determination had to be 'destroyed in order to save it', it became a pressing need to contain the history of US involvement in the region. The struggles in the historiography and more pertinently the public representation of the US experience in Vietnam are arguments about the identity of the nation.[26] In the teleological gist of World History a linear narrative best served the idea of progress. Deviations proved discomfiting.

In all four cases one is struck by the constant return of nationalism as a defining feature of the revolution. National liberation was more important than more abstract metaphysical projects. It is not surprising that these most enduring examples (including Iran) were also places where the sense of nation extended further into the past than most newly created Third World states, which were derivatives of the colonial system.[27] Washington maintained that the Eastern Bloc had compromised its independence. Frequently, the Eastern Bloc was irrelevant except when it was drawn in through the regional isolation visited on Guatemala, Cuba and Vietnam.

In the post-war period nationalism was closely associated with the left, not only because the expression of nationalism grew out of the anti-fascist struggle, but also because it was associated with several anti-colonial movements. Furthermore, the Soviet Union, largely an Asian country, viewed the world in non-European terms, which later somewhat endeared it to liberation movements. Still, however socialist or internationalist these struggles were in theory, in practice their primary objective was gaining independence. The US national interest did not comport with the Third World nationalism. National security, the *Preponderance of [American] Power*, necessitated a constant vigilance against other assertions of nationalism to protect and preserve its way of life. Globalism vied with particularism. Bi-polarity suggested that opposition to the US and an unwillingness to complement the multilateral economy was a threat to US interests. The Wilson Foundation and the National Planning Association in 1955 viewed the threat of communism, Chomsky relates, as 'the economic transformation of the Communist powers "in ways which reduce their willingness and ability to complement the industrial economies of the West"'.[28] Hence, for example, Tito's Yugoslavia or Deng Xiaoping's China, though communist in political form, were acceptable because of their political utility. China's increasingly open economy facilitated an improvement in relations despite its political form and its response to demands for democracy in Tiananmen Square in 1989.

The internal US discussions about Iranian, Guatemalan, Cuban and Vietnamese nationalism largely took place in the 1950s. In Vietnam later, too much US prestige and personnel had been committed to the process of rollback, to destroying local efforts at self-determination. Well into the post-Cold War period there was some space for major figures to state the obvious. In 1995 Robert McNamara, former US Secretary of Defense, apologised to Americans for the government's miscalculations, including its underestimation of the power of Vietnamese nationalism, and the exaggeration of the threat to the United States.[29]

Mohammed Mossaddeq's greatest sin was to nationalise the Anglo-Iranian Oil Co. With his removal from office in 1953, the National Security Council document NSC 175 considered the potential impact of the 'loss of Iran'. Apart from the regional security issues and the potential Soviet control of vital resources, oil could be used as 'a weapon of economic warfare to disrupt the free world pattern of petroleum production and marketing'. And the loss could 'have serious psychological impact elsewhere in the free world'. Washington wanted 'An independent Iran free from communist control' and (echoing Theodore Roosevelt) 'a strong, stable government in Iran, capable of maintaining internal security, using Iranian resources effectively, and actively co-operating with the anti-Communist nations of the free world'.[30] The problem was that, while Iran remained outside the Soviet orbit and muted its nationalism, the Shah's regime remained closely associated with the United States as a not altogether loyal client state, but more or less dependent on US largesse and security assistance. That identity came back to haunt the regime in the late 1970s, culminating in its removal in 1979.

Guatemala's experience is illustrative of US ideological and economic inclinations. After ten years of reform, and four years of the elected Arbenz government, the regime was overthrown. Washington's rhetoric was alarmist. Secretary of State Dulles indicated that a 'Communist type of terrorism' existed in Guatemala, that the leaders of communism had exposed 'the evil purpose of the Kremlin to destroy the inter-American system' and US Ambassador John Peurifoy talked of a Soviet Republic being established between Texas and the Panama Canal.[31] Cold War constructs facilitated Washington's use of covert means to subvert the democratic process, and various economic, diplomatic and military means to support the subsequent brutal 'anti-communist' regime. The original principles of the Monroe Doctrine were flouted. National independence and self-government had been undermined through means not dissimilar to those employed by the European autocrats that Monroe wanted to distance the United States from.[32]

For Arévalo, Arbenz's predecessor, democracy related to economic and social conditions not just electoral politics. His outlook included a balance between individualism and community. He was motivated by the idea of *vitalismo* (the vital minimum) 'or providing everyone with minimum standards for housing, nutrition, education, health, work, justice, and rest'. In many ways his reforms were less radical than Franklin Roosevelt's New Deal.[33] But within the inter-American system and as an example to the emerging Third World such options were intolerable. The State Department understood the motivations of the revolution and knew Soviet connections were minimal. The 1953 National Security Council's top secret document NSC 144/1 recognised that there was

a trend in Latin America toward nationalist regimes maintained in large part by appeals to the masses of the population. Concurrently, there is an increasing popular demand for immediate improvement in the low living standards of the masses, with the result that most Latin American governments are under intense domestic political pressures to increase production and to diversify their economies. . . . A realistic and constructive approach to this need which recognizes the importance of bettering conditions for the general population, is essential to arrest the drift in the area toward radical and nationalistic regimes. The growth of nationalism is facilitated by historic anti-U.S. prejudices and exploited by Communists.

Specifically, Louis Halle of the Policy Planning Staff argued the revolution in Guatemala was an 'expression of the impulse to achieve equality of status' for both individuals and groups within society and for 'the nation-state within the international community'. And that Guatemala's historic

153

conditions provided 'fuel to fire the revolution'.[34] Such thoughts, however, could not be expressed in public. Anti-communism was the defining principle to maintain cohesion within the United States and in the western world. A new US Ambassador, John Peurifoy, with experience in local crises that were inflamed to global proportions (he was in Greece in 1947), indicated that 'if [Arbenz] . . . is not a Communist he will certainly do until one comes along'.[35]

Before the government was overthrown, the Guatemalan Foreign Minister, Guillermo Toriello Garido, rose to speak after Dulles at the March 1954 Inter-American meeting in Caracas. Widely applauded, he delivered a stinging rebuke to the United States. Gleijeses writes:

> Never before had a banana republic dared to challenge the United States in an international forum. Dulles had spoken of the menace of communism – but Toriello spoke of the menace of the United States. Dulles had sought to enrobe his country in the Pan-American mantle, but Toriello assailed the arrogant meddling of the United States in the internal affairs of the Latin American republics. Dulles's resolution, he argued, was not aimed at a threat from across the seas: it was aimed at Guatemala. It sought to legitimize aggression. Guatemala's only sin, Toriello concluded, was its attempt to assert its sovereignty.

The US reaction had little to do with security concerns relating to the Cold War but is better understood in the long inter-American tensions and the processes old and new of continued economic integration.[36]

Cuba presented a whole host of other problems, not least because it was in the Western Hemisphere and had once been considered as a potential state of the Union. Fidel Castro's stance was not clear in the early days; he moved from humanism to socialism to communism in his public pronouncements. He moved towards the Soviet sphere after Nixon rebuffed him in 1959. First trade agreements and then weapons followed. The CIA's badly planned operation at the Bay of Pigs in 1961 deepened Havana's relationship with Moscow. But it is an irony of history that even after the CIA orchestrated the Bay of Pigs invasion the Policy Planning Staff were still not quite sure about Castro or Cuba's inclinations. The director of the staff, Walt Rostow, wrote a strategy paper on 24 April 1961 on US–Cuba policy. Five potential threats were identified. Cuba might join the USSR and set up an offensive missile base; it might conduct a conventional military build-up leading to a regional arms race; Latin American nations might be threatened by the development of a 'covert subversive network'; then Rostow argued that 'its ideological contours are [a] moral and political offence to us; and we are committed, by one means or another, to remove that offence', because the ideological contours might 'inflame' others in Latin America, 'accentuating existing economic, social, and political tensions which we, in any case, confront'. Later in the document Rostow explained these ideological contours:

> The roots of Castroism lie in Latin American poverty, social inequality, and that form of xenophobic nationalism which goes with a prior history of inferiority on the world scene. The vulnerability of the Latin American populations to this form of appeal will depend on the pace of economic growth; the pace at which social inequality is reduced; and the pace at which the other Latin American nations move towards what they regard as dignified partnership with the US. What is required here is a radical acceleration and raising of sights in the programs being launched within the Alliance for Progress. . . . We do not know what Castro's policy towards the US will be; nor do we know what Soviet policy towards Cuba will be.[37]

Development and development theory became hotly contested areas of concern, which will be discussed below. Castro had enjoyed the sincere admiration of the Cuban people, his revolutionary aims were described as lofty, but the State Department viewed the situation differently:

> Dr. Castro has chosen to follow another path. He has rejected the tenets of representative democracy to embrace the Marxian concepts of class struggle and dictatorship of the proletariat. He has forsaken the democratically inspired American family of nations to identify Cuba with the totalitarian system of the Sino-Soviet bloc. In the process he has placed the Cuban people under bondage. He has at the same time created a serious threat to the peace and security of the hemisphere by sowing distrust and discord and by serving as a bridgehead of Sino-Soviet imperialism within its inner defenses. This stark fact confronts the American Republics with the crucial test of their ability, through the inter-American machinery established for this purpose, to act to protect their individual and collective security.[38]

Washington tolerated nationalism if it was confined to political self-determination. The Westphalia system was useful against political empires; both the European and the Soviet empires could be put under pressure through references to self-determination and the mobilisation of nationalism. But nationalist opposition to US power and hegemony was rarely tolerated. Autarky diminished the sphere of the global economy, questioned the certainty of the preferred model of development, and questioned the credibility and prestige of the US civilisation.

Progress and development

The issues of self-determination and democracy lay at the heart of another problem for the United States. Apart from the political struggles against communism in the Cold War, Washington needed an economic formulation to win the allegiance of Third World peoples. Development in the Third World became an adjunct to the policy of containment. In the theoretical debates and practical implementation development was a hotly contested issue. At the political level Washington surmised that poverty and disorder were breeding grounds for discontent and communism. The same logic that applied to the Marshall Plan was used in Truman's 1949 Point Four Program.[39] Much of the aid was used to support or conserve authoritarian rule. The guardians of national security could better protect the self-determination against 'outside pressures' at the cost of domestic repression and sacrifice of democratic potential. Order and stability were deemed essential for the continued operation of the global economy, the protection of free trade when advantageous, currency convertibility and the free flow of finances. Modernisation theory provided the intellectual justification for such conditions. However, many saw in these economic formulae the continued source of poverty and the erosion of Third World self-determination by the power of international institutions such as the IMF or the World Bank, and the suppression of democratic opportunities. Washington preferred it that way. To paraphrase Kennan, it was better to have an authoritarian government that maintained order than to have a liberal government that was riddled with communists. Economic democracy opposed US interests. It placed the interests and human rights of the people over those of the state, which in the Manichaean worldview was interpreted as being either excessively nationalist or pro-communist. Authoritarian regimes were pressured into holding elections to justify receipt of US aid and to provide the legitimating veneer of democratic acceptability. But many in the Third World saw their opportunity in the search for the foundations of real power and personal security in material satisfaction. Economic security underpins democratic rights. But as peoples in the Third World organised to secure greater control over their resources, this diminished the ability, as Kennan put it, to maintain that position of disparity, and thus weakened US power. The Open Door and promotion of self-determination traditionally regarded as goals of US policy underwent dramatic change. 'Once the fusion of geopolitical, economic, ideological, and strategic considerations occurred, traditional foreign policy goals were transformed into national security imperatives.'[40]

Modernisation theory, just like discourses on 'civilisation' earlier, facilitated the link between Open Door concerns and US national security. The rise of US power in the post-Second World War period and the proliferation of nation-states within a bipolar context necessitated a formula that could ensure the preservation of the Open Door, the promise of modernity and material progress, and national security. Liberal development models proliferated as the solution to the dilemmas. Modernisation theory stemmed from two strands of nineteenth-century thought, one positing a dualistic opposition between the modern and the traditional, the other Auguste Comte's theory on evolution. Together these ideas posited that economies would evolve from a traditional base to modern societies. The universal model of linear development maintained that nations would pass through various stages of growth through the application of technology, industrialisation, capital accumulation and investment, which would eventually inculcate values similar to those held in the West. Rostow's *The Stages of Economic Growth: A Non-Communist Manifesto* was perhaps the most influential tract in this vein. He later served as Kennedy's head of the Policy Planning Staff. It was initially assumed that modernisation would bring with it democratic and liberal values; 'Westernisation, industrialisation, and economic growth would generate the preconditions for the evolution of greater social equality and hence, it was assumed, the rise of stable, democratic institutions. Progress, as defined by the West, would transform the underdeveloped world and propel it headlong into the twentieth century and modernity.' But this was largely optimism bred out of a fidelity to certain ideological assumptions.[41] Such concepts of modernisation were closely associated with political authoritarianism.

In the short term such regimes better served US interests. The authoritarian rulers could maintain order and secure the nation's participation in the global economy. In the longer term, Washington's continued association with authoritarianism undermined its identity and exceptionalism, unless the imperatives of national security could be credibly invoked. With the rise of nationalism, the problems became more acute. Eisenhower's National Security Council realised that 'if aspirations for economic development are frustrated, the likelihood will be increased that extremist elements will come to power'. Yet these extremist elements could be suppressed by military regimes, or regimes that maintained a facade of democracy and civilian rule, still keeping real power in the hands of the military. By 1959 the NSC documents related that 'Military regimes do not necessarily threaten U.S. interests in the underdeveloped world if they can be influenced to deal effectively with the developmental problem'. They noted that there would be a long-term problem with US identification with unpopular authoritarian regimes, 'but point to the fact that authoritarianism is the norm throughout the region and that this is not without certain short-run advantages'. And further, 'a military takeover can advantage the U.S. by imposing stability and decisiveness'. The National Security Council was fully cognisant of the implications. 'Political authoritarianism unquestionably weakens the tenuous fibres of democratic beliefs and values', which tend towards forms of communist economic control. Such changes damaged US interests because it made it more difficult to exert influence. 'Hence, the correlation between political authoritarianism and economic authoritarianism, and its dangers, must be impressed on the minds of military leaders and must remain one of our principal policy guidelines in exploring and developing techniques whereby Western values can be grafted on indigenous varieties of non-Marxist socialism.' The Council document concluded:

> In sum, if the U.S. quietly proceeds to make its own democracy work, stands unequivocally for the independence and development of emergent nations, and assists the regime in power to confront its problems of security and development – each in balance – we shall have made the best of the necessity of working with and through military authoritarianism in this stage of Asian development.[42]

The polarisation of the global conflict and the attitudes that went with it ensured that every corner of the globe was considered vital to the struggle against the Soviet Union. As Washington preserved self-determination through policies of national security, the democratic rights and opportunities of inhabitants within a state were often destroyed. The dichotomy in the political world order fuelled the integration of the western economic order.[43]

Dependency theorists did not accept the modernisation premise that all boats would rise on a rising tide. The post-war origins of the theory, largely formulated by ECLA (the United Nations Economic Commission for Latin America), began to externalise the sources of Latin American underdevelopment. Frequent US intervention and international free trade were seen as major contributors to the underdevelopment of the region. Constitutionally sovereign, the states of the region remained economically dependent on world capitalism. The global economy linked the two worlds of developed and underdeveloped nations. Simply stated, wealth creation in the North resulted in poverty in the South. Dependency theory was refined over time but it had considerable influence on the left and Third World nationalists. Andre Gunder Frank wrote about the development of underdevelopment. Latin American underdevelopment was caused by its economic penetration, not by its traditional culture or 'backward' structures. His writing was closely linked with the political thoughts of Régis Debray, who advocated revolutionary solutions. Such ideas, coupled with the success of Castro and the adventures of Ernesto Guevara, alarmed Washington, given their suggestions and impact. In addition, import substitution industrialisation (ISI) proposed to reverse the negative effects of operating in the international economy. It provided an alternative to Washington's vision of a multilateral economy. Doors could remain open, but as in the successful US model, doormen would attend to exclude unwanted commodities. Domestic industries would be protected by tariffs just as they had been in the United States during its period of development. Government subsidies and exchange controls would be implemented to stabilise and promote national models of development.[44] The ideas were anathema to Washington. They were opposed whether their practitioners were leftist or not. Inward-looking nationalism troubled Washington more than Cold War ideologies practised within particular states.

Kennedy's response to the revolutionary spirit and import substitution came in the form of the Alliance for Progress. Announced shortly before the Bay of Pigs, the plan envisaged an injection of US finance into Latin America to 'jump-start' the economies and use western liberal economic techniques to improve and reform the conditions within Latin America. Latin Americans, in the end, received half of the proposed twenty billion dollars, and paid 87 per cent of the Alliance costs. The development model Washington had in mind was based on western assumptions and did not go down well with the indigenous reforms. The Kennedy administration, like Wilson's earlier, intended to act against both the 'extreme' left to stave off revolution and the 'extreme' right to stave off reaction, but in practice it failed to move against the undemocratic right because it was assumed that this would assist the communists. The Alliance failed to provide the reform necessary to stabilise the hemisphere. Its main beneficiaries were the élite, the military and US companies. The injection of finance did little to introduce reform. Income distribution became more skewed towards the rich, a significant proportion of the disbursements went to military regimes: by 1965 half the population was under military rule, with the concomitant denial of individual liberties and democracy. The militaries were redirected to combat 'internal subversion' rather than external security, and with the overall growth in the economies, there was a corresponding rise of 'misery and starvation for much of the population'. Chomsky indicates that this 'development model has a necessary corollary: it requires an apparatus of repression to control the inevitable dissidence and resistance as the subject population endures its consequences. Death squads are not an accidental counterpart to the Alliance for Progress, but an essential component.'[45]

Washington's preference was the maintenance of order, even if these costs had to be accepted. The trend is a part of a long tradition in US foreign relations. The Monroe Doctrine was in part conceived to support new states in a volatile international period. The Roosevelt corollary was designed to stop outside powers taking advantage of the instability brought on by civil conflict; and the Alliance for Progress was serving the same ends for that brought on by economic upheaval and revolutionary potential. It was aimed at preventing another Cuban revolution.[46]

The Alliance formed part of the strategy of containing 'communism' in Latin America. Its purported goal was the defence of liberty against a foreign ideology. Modernisation and integration provided the economic part of the equation. Though restated in abstract form, Hunt argues, they repeated old recipes and 'ethnocentric platitudes about uplift and regeneration'.

> According to the gospel of development, peoples still laboring under a traditional way of life would acquire modern institutions and outlooks, the best guarantees of stable and free societies. Education would promote rationality in the place of superstition. A common sense of nationhood would emerge as a political system marked by a broad participation displaced one flawed by popular passivity or narrow family, tribal, or ethnic loyalties. Sophisticated science and technology would push aside primitive agricultural and handicraft techniques and create new wealth and prosperity. A closed, fragmented, stagnant economy would burgeon under the influence of outside capital and markets. In this process American institutions would provide the models, and American experience would serve as the inspiration. Thanks to American wisdom and generosity and to the marvels of social engineering, the peoples of these new nations would accomplish in years what had taken the advanced countries decades to achieve.[47]

But these thoughts, which accurately reflect the attitudes of the developmentalists and the politicians tasked with implementing the policies and strategies, suffered incredibly from the fallacy of presentism, the tendency to rewrite history according to assumptions commonly held in the contemporary culture. The narratives suggested that US economic success resulted from the pursuit of liberalism and democracy at home and open economies abroad. But this had not been part of the US experience. In its developmental stages protectionism was rife, and import substitution was a normal practice. The universal US ideology and its translation into policy not only created a new doctrine to enhance their legitimacy, but also denied other options. Modernisation imposed conceptions of development on sometimes unwilling recipients. Reluctance was often overcome by financial incentives. Participation in the Point Four Program or the Alliance for Progress, or the 'benefits' of IMF funds, came with certain expectations. Economic liberalism, open doors and private enterprise were catchwords, which were ideologically synonymous with democracy and liberty. Modernisation was the new rhetoric for a decolonised world of racial consciousness, political awareness of equality and freedom, but it echoed the rhetoric of 'civilisation', common at the turn of the century. Modernisation in many ways implied integration around the American economic model with the US at the core of the system. For hegemonic powers dissent was intolerable. Rosenberg writes, 'There could, American liberal-expansionists believed, be no truly enlightened dissent against the ultimate acceptance of American ways, and this faith bred an intolerance, a narrowness, that was the very opposite of liberality.'[48]

At the heart of US foreign policy, at the centre of its universal vision, the contradiction between freedom and the imposition of the US-centred system remains. Pluralism and decentred particularism are in constant tension with the centre and its universalism. The Cold War and the politics that went with it stifled freedom in the Third World. The universal ideologies of both superpowers, coupled with their geopolitical struggles, left little space for alternatives. At the end of the Cold War Ralf Dahrendorf caught the problem succinctly:

> The road to freedom is not a road from one system to another, but one that leads into the open spaces of infinite possible futures, some of which compete with each other. Their competition makes history. The battle of systems is an illiberal aberration. To drive the point home with utmost force: if capitalism is a system, then it needs to be fought as hard as communism had to be fought. All systems mean serfdom, including the "natural" system of the total "market order" in which no one tries to do anything other than guard certain rules of the game discovered by a mysterious sect of economic advisers.[49]

8

CONFRONTING 'EVIL' AND
IMAGINED EMPIRES

By early 1981 when Ronald Reagan entered the White House the world had undergone change. US hegemony was under pressure as the thaw in the Cold War created the political latitude to question the relevance of alliances and certain assumptions. Without the cement of an external 'threat', industrial centres moved in contradictory directions. Third World cartels had asserted their power in the 1970s against the West in the 'Decade of Development'. Vietnam had clearly exposed the divisions between Beijing and Moscow, and questioned the resolve and credibility of US foreign policy. The political, economic and mental structures that had seemed so certain in the past were unwinding in unpredictable directions. Political and economic multipolarity threatened hegemonic luxuries. Assumptions, attitudes and values were changing with the beginnings of what was eventually referred to as the 'postmodern condition'. Ronald Reagan was the perfect candidate to stop all the conceptual confusion. He presided over an intense but brief revival of the Cold War, which made the celebrations of 1989 all the more of a relief. But by 1991 the end of the Cold War, this time, witnessed the break-up of the Soviet empire, that supposed 'union' of Soviet Socialist Republics. The concepts of liberty and self-determination were celebrated throughout Europe and in the Atlantic alliance. Eastern Europe was free. But the decade was also a period in which Washington undermined democracy and self-determination in Nicaragua and propped up regimes that engaged in gross violations of human rights in Central America. Liberty, democracy and self-determination were once again evaluated in the context of the extent to which they served US interests or credibility; the extent to which they buttressed or detracted from the 'empire *for* liberty'.

World systems: political structures

The 1970s *détente* between the superpowers changed the character of the Cold War, though overall US objectives remained largely constant. The Nixon Doctrine (containment and order through proxy) and National

Security Advisor Henry Kissinger's system of 'linkage' continued containment but made it more politically acceptable because the costs of Vietnam were assumed by other regional powers. With *détente* the Soviets were induced to contain themselves, rewarded with economic carrots. US policy changed perceptibly. It did not harbour the visions of omnipotence that guided earlier policies. Its world 'leadership' was threatened; a period of retrenchment was necessary. As Kissinger indicated, it had to 'navigate between overextension and abdication'. President Richard Nixon (1969–1974) informed Congress on 18 February 1970 that 'the United States will participate in the defense and development of allies and friends, but that America cannot – and will not – conceive *all* the plans, design *all* the programs, execute *all* the decisions and undertake *all* the defense of the free nations of the world'. The limits of US policy were recognised. But the limits had to be situated within the traditions and ideals of the nation. Kissinger searched for 'a *sustainable* role for an idealistic America' – Wilsonianism and *realpolitik,* universalism, but most fundamentally national interest came first.[1]

Realism or *realpolitik* did not relate well to the ideals, values and the meta-narrative of US history. Though policy was often based on realism, the novelty of the Nixon/Kissinger period was in their willingness to frame policy publicly in these terms. The US was no longer willing 'to pay any price' or 'bear any burden' for the survival or success of liberty. Its illusion of omnipotence, or more specifically the failure to match interests with capabilities, had passed. The executive needed to find new strategies, not only because the external world was less malleable or compliant, but also because domestic consensus had fragmented. Washington had to learn to live with new limits. The Nixon Doctrine was basically an attempt to bolster regional 'strong' countries to maintain order in various limited spheres of influence. The search for order, the maintenance of stability and a balance of power were central considerations. The nation-state was considered the primary historical agent in an international environment characterised by anarchy amongst nations. The central objective was to increase the power of the state relative to that of its closest rivals. Interests were defined in terms of power; the balance of power was crucial, as was the primacy of the nation-state. With these considerations, the attempt to perfect a universal system was both myopic and dangerous. There was a distinct departure from the supposed ideals and universal approaches which had earlier driven the vision (or illusion) of US diplomacy, from Monroe through to Wilson, and on to Truman and Kennedy; overtly now, stability and order were central considerations. Freedom required order and liberty required authority. But given that Nixon also wanted to reconstruct domestic consensus, such realism had to be tempered with acceptable and inspiring rhetoric relating to the 'full generation of peace'. Kissinger's vision therefore combined Theodore Roosevelt's realism with

Wilson's messianic messages. Ultimately US ideals would spread their influence in the world through a realist engagement with older patterns of diplomacy.[2] Such realism, however, challenged US exceptionalism. Narratives of progress were rare, 'destinarian' language limited. Global politics took precedence over the pursuit of universal ideals. Kissinger wrote: 'no clear-cut terminal point beckoned'.[3] There was no End of History in this vision.

Détente facilitated increased multipolarity in the world order. US hegemony was eroded as Europe and Japan gained a greater proportion of global wealth and greater independence in the conduct of their foreign policies. The space created by the thaw in the Cold War allowed these new assertions of power to stake out independent destinies. Washington resented Europe and Japan's stance during the Oil Crisis (1973) and the Middle East wars, but Washington needed these allies (of a kind) to bear a greater burden of defence expenditure. *Détente* had taken the Europeans closer to the Soviet and Eastern economies. So finally, with the 1979 Soviet invasion of Afghanistan and Reagan's 1981 conceptual reaffirmation of bipolarity, both Europe and Japan felt squeezed; they had benefited from *détente* more.

The Cold War was indispensable for continued US hegemony. *Détente* threatened to undo the global structures. By 1971 Nixon told Congress that the world was 'at the end of an era. The postwar order of international relations, the configuration of power that emerged from the Second World War is gone. With it are gone the conditions which have determined the assumptions and practice of United States foreign policy since 1945.' The changes necessitated adjustment. Bi-polarity facilitated the cultural acceptance of narratives on modernisation, civilisation and barbarism. Such structures had proved useful to both superpowers within their 'alliances' and to inspire or control domestic aspirations.[4] Under such formulae Washington achieved a number of its post-war aims: the world economy was increasingly integrated, domestic prosperity had risen, the Soviets had been contained, and the colonial order had passed. But the world system had increasingly linked economies, access to which the US now depended on.[5]

But the dependence did not imply subservience. When the predominantly US-designed international economic order worked against Washington, it changed the rules of the game. Its mission in Vietnam, the 1960s military spending, its overseas investments and its trade deficit 'produced an unfavourable balance of payments' which pushed Europeans and the Japanese to cash their dollars in for gold and search for a new 'international monetary standard'. US leverage on its 'allies' diminished with the more competitive European Community and Japanese economies. Moreover, the 1970s recessions 'cumulatively constituted the greatest economic slow-down since the 1930s Great Depression'. Washington first attempted to force European and Japanese currency revaluation. Europe half-complied but the Japanese refused. The attempt to coerce the core economies of the western world necessitated a reconfiguration of the US strategy.

In Nixon's 1971 'New Economic Policy' the post-war economic system ended. Washington unilaterally wound up the Bretton Woods system and ended the convertibility of $35 dollars for an ounce of gold. The dollar was no longer as good as gold. Washington could have undergone a process of deflating its economy along lines associated with measures it commonly advocated for others: tax increases, wage cuts and redundancies. But such IMF-like packages were un-American, and certainly did not comport with attempts to secure better US standards of living. US needs provided a further stimulus to *détente*; the US searched for increasing access to the East European and the Chinese markets. By 1975 Kissinger described the new world political and economic order to the United Nations: 'the global order of colonial power that lasted through the centuries has now disappeared. . . . The Cold War division of the world into two rigid blocs has also broken down and major changes have taken place in the international economy. . . . Therefore it is time to go beyond the doctrines left over from a previous century that are made obsolete by modern reality. . . . The world is a single global system of trade and monetary relations.'[6]

Briefly, various agents and changes in the Third World destabilised the structures of the world system. Decolonisation rapidly increased the number of states in the international system. Nationalism was frequently asserted against the West; commodity cartels such as OPEC and CIPEC extracted higher prices. Talk of further solidarity and opportunity created aspirations for a New International Economic Order (NIEO), which demanded regulated prices for raw commodities, against major opposition from the core powers: the United States, Germany and Japan. Other Europeans were more conciliatory. Agreement on a new economic order passed as 'security concerns' pushed the West towards political reintegration. Third World nationalism represented in the politics of the NIEO had to be overcome. As Clark explains:

> For all the high hopes of the early 1970s, the sad irony was to be that further Third World integration into the world economic system was to be postponed until the 1980s and onwards, and was to be the direct consequence of Third World *weakness,* not of *strength.* Its integration was to occur, not on its own terms, but on those set by the West and its panoply of international financial institutions. Far from being an expression of the autonomy of the Third World, in which state control and national development were the top priorities, the terms of engagement denoted the final

capitulation of the Third World's struggle for separate national development in the face of a more competitive, and importunate, international economic system. Instead of the NIEO symbolizing the new political order, the old political order managed to thwart the NIEO.[7]

The West overcame its differences, at least on the surface, through the creation of the Trilateral Commission, which brought together the élite planners of the United States, Europe and Japan. Initial concerns were to gather 'significant groups of leaders' to work on 'matters of common concern' to lessen communication problems and develop a shared understanding of common problems. The commission's first report dealt with the *Crisis of Democracy*, both within the United States and in the international arena. Echoing Robert Lansing, it argued against the participation of 'ignorant and meddlesome outsiders'. Samuel Huntington looked back at the crisis of the 1970s and reflected on the past: 'Truman had been able to govern the country with the cooperation of a relatively small number of Wall Street lawyers and bankers' so that democracy functioned smoothly and without 'crisis'.[8]

With the apparent loosening of the global superstructure, the denial of economic aspiration, and material benefits, Third World revolution was more common in the late 1970s. Development and democratic opportunities had been frustrated.[9] *Détente* collapsed, and the world briefly returned to a bipolar construct. The centrifugal forces of the period were briefly held in check, until again towards the late 1980s when the Soviets withdrew from the system in stages, freeing the nation-states from the bipolar straitjackets.

The essential West: Reagan's crusade

Reagan's foreign policy essentially involved battering the Soviet Union with ideological rhetoric, rejecting the politics of *détente* and returning, at least in words, to dreams of US exceptionalism. But the fault lines of the modernist project were blurred. Reagan confronted revolution in the Third World and Soviet power at its centre, proposing to confine it to the ash heap of history, but continued relations with Communist China were unproblematic. Washington acted concertedly against a thoroughly western revolution in Nicaragua. Here the United States and the Sandinistas argued over the meaning of democracy, liberty and self-determination. In the world system, progress for Washington meant the eradication of a movement that had exercised independence, whereas progress for the Sandinistas meant the extension of democratic participation within their country, the improvement of social facilities and some control of the economy. But Reagan, bound by Cold War straitjackets and US absolutism, unlike the Carter administration, had to situate the Nicaraguan revolution in the ideological East to legitimate US aggression. In Afghanistan, Washington provided assistance to the Islamic Mujahedin against Soviet occupation. Yet in Iran the clash with Washington was presented by political leaders in both countries as a clash between Islam and the West. Despite all of these conceptual differences, so good for the politics of identity, legitimisation and mobilisation, the common strand that ran through all these conflicts was the assertion of nationalism.

Reagan possessed an uncanny ability to connect with the American psyche. The administration's rhetorical strengths allowed the president to recreate an image of a strong, determined, resolute nation. Reagan was elected more 'for an ability to soothe' rather than govern. The process of healing US 'wounds' after Vietnam and the crippling confusions of the Carter administration was enhanced through the effective use of symbols closely associated with the national narrative. These symbols were exploited to bolster the ideological basis of the nation, to secure and legitimate their identity in the face of particularly the Soviets and the Sandinistas. Reagan 'was able to talk so effectively with Americans . . . because he embodied so much of the American dream'. The power of his speech was virtually unchecked. Reagan used this platform to return Americans, almost dream-like, to the original morals the country is supposed to have stood for. He offered Americans a new (old) vision when 'they were still heartsick from defeat in Vietnam and the humiliation of the Iranian hostage crisis'. Hunt indicates that his foreign policy vision was largely shaped by the Munich analogy accompanied by a myth, referring back to the post-war period of seeming US omnipotence coupled with the moral crusade associated with the birth of the nation. Reagan's rhetoric largely looked back to the moral regeneration provided by either Thomas Paine or Woodrow Wilson, with promises to begin the world over again, though this president curiously lacked any detailed knowledge of foreign affairs. But for all the emphasis on the myths, the rhetoric and the lack of engagement, the simplicity had force.[10]

That Reagan's view of the world was simplistic was often obvious, though it is not clear that his strategies, if indeed they were preconceived, caused the Cold War to end. His worldview was predominantly Manichaean, everything was reduced to the bipolar conflict, despite evidence to the contrary. Excoriating the politics of *détente*, Reagan argued in the 1980 campaign that 'the Soviet Union underlies all the unrest that is going on. If they weren't engaged in this game of dominoes, there wouldn't be any hot spots in the world.' The Soviets were characterised as an 'evil empire'; Marxism–Leninism was to be confined to 'the ashheap of history'. Democracy, liberty and the American way were central to his rhetoric. Yet he was willing to align the United States with the most brutal dictatorships or militaristic regimes. For Reagan, exporting democracy was not 'cultural imperialism', he told the British Parliament in 1982, but 'providing the means for genuine self-determination and protection for diversity'. It is ironic that Francis Fukuyama's 1989 influential argument suggested that liberal democracy had indeed triumphed over rival ideologies and the world was becoming a more homogeneous place.[11] Reagan's coupling of rhetorical anti-Sovietism and a crusade for 'democracy' in the Third World was central to his vision. That one often had very little to do with the other was an inconvenience that would have to be finessed through 'public diplomacy'.

The administration was guided by general intentions that derived from constructs from the past. The Soviets were the principal threat, the barbarians at the gate. US militarisation would undermine them, forcing them to negotiate. To hit the Soviet periphery, as he regarded Third World revolutionary states, he needed to reconstruct a consensus on intervention after Vietnam. Proxy forces were used to achieve these ends without risking US morale or life, particularly in Nicaragua, Afghanistan, Angola and Cambodia. The Third World was integrated into the global economy more thoroughly and crucially through privatisation and neo-liberal policies. The United States would provide the 'model for other nations'; its mission was 'to reform a reprobate world'.[12]

Militarisation and the Cold War

The symbols of US power were self-evident during the 1980s. Militarisation generally characterised the endgame, with Soviet power at the centre and an insidious low-intensity conflict with 'hot spots' in the Third World. Tension was rife in the early 1980s, buttressed by Reagan's verbal attack on Moscow, and the public showdown he pursued with Nicaragua. Despite other divisions, there was a great deal of consensus in the administration on remilitarisation and its role in ending the period in World History dominated by the clash between the United States and the Soviet Union. Attributing this far-sightedness to Reagan is itself built on a partial myth. That he intended the collapse of Soviet power in actuality, beyond rhetorical inspiration, is contentious. The similarities between Carter's final year and Reagan's first term are more striking than their differences. It is one thing to look back with hindsight and identify the step-by-step retreat of Soviet power, from the Third World from 1987, from its empire in Eastern Europe in 1989, or the break-up of its own 'Union' two years later. It is another thing to suggest that this was the outcome intended in Washington. Reagan's efforts at bringing about 'peace through strength' are often credited with this result by administration memoirs and cultural assumptions. McMahon points out, however, that the argument closely resembles one of the oldest of logical fallacies: namely, that an event that follows another event occurs as a necessary *result* of the previous event. Because the Cold War ended and the Soviet Union collapsed *after* Reagan increased American defense spending, ratcheted up the vigor of his anti-Communist invectives, launched the Strategic Defense Initiative (SDI), and clung detrimentally to a set of unyielding arms control positions, his policies must have *caused* those developments.[13]

Still, a 'vindicationalist' school of thought has emerged among historians, largely reflected in the outlets of popular interpretation as well. The view suggests that the United States not only triumphed in their duel with the Soviet Union, but that its policies were justifiable and largely responsible for bringing about this victory.[14]

The defence budget grew rapidly in the 1980s. Reagan spent $1.6 trillion over five years. Expenditures expressed in constant 1990 dollars, according to John Kenneth Galbraith, jumped from $206 billion in 1980 to $314 billion in 1990. In 1985, the Pentagon was spending $28 million every hour of every day of every week of the year. The plans were ambitious. They were to build a 600-ship navy; to have the ability to fight three and a half wars around the globe simultaneously; to achieve the superiority to prevail in a nuclear conflict; to launch the SDI adventure; to enhance their counter-insurgency ability; to develop the MX missile, the Stealth Bomber, Trident II submarines and to procure $300 'manual excavation units', commonly known as spades. Reagan informed the Pentagon: 'Defense is not a budget item.' Without the necessary taxes to defray the costs, the national debts soared. But the United States was feeling good again. It was, as the refrain in 1984 went, 'morning in America'.[15]

There was some resistance. The initial military budgets were passed with little congressional rancour, but there were considerable doubts about the 1982–1986 defence programme totalling $1.5 trillion. The doubts centred on the policy's 'underlying strategic premises, economic sustainability and military necessity'.[16]

The policy was defined by 'spending, rather than the capabilities provided by that expenditure'. Spending was essential. Reagan argued that government was the problem in most issues of economic or social consideration. Yet, in terms of defence spending the intervention of the government was absolutely crucial; in a sense the government created a form of socialism for the rich, or for the 'culture of the contented'. Though in retrospect, Galbraith contends, the threat of a communist takeover within the United States was ridiculous, 'even mentally aberrant', in foreign policy that fear played an important role in the development and sustenance of military power at the heart of US culture. The Reagan arms build-up 'was a further enormous increase in military and defense spending as the constituency of contentment gained full power in the 1980s'; the result of this fear was a large military establishment 'standing above and apart from democratic control'. And even with these excessive increases justified by the dire threats Washington faced there was an anomaly in the excessive build-up and the unwillingness to use that power. The culture had become increasingly militaristic, but was unwilling to use its military power.[17]

The continued militarisation reflected a trend evident since the 1960s. The policy was aimed less at the outside world or the objective threats posed to the United States, and more at US needs. The huge dent in the treasury was not 'accompanied by . . . [a] coherent policy for using the increased power'. Militarisation had deep roots in a US culture which wanted the respect without paying the price; it wanted the glory of Kennedy's inauguration without Vietnam. Reagan satisfied the contra-dictory demands of a low-cost foreign policy (in terms of US lives) and the 'illusion of greatness' (in terms of arms procurement). The implications are disturbing. The militarisation and the narcissistic self-reflection that accompanied it would not end with the disappearance of the Soviet Union or the Cold War:

> the renewal of national security [was] lavish but short lived, ener-
> getic but empty. . . . A bit like Reagan himself, the Soviet threat
> appeared by the end of the 1980s to have been both formidable
> and insubstantial, impressive when viewed from afar but hollow
> when seen close up. Militarization did not halt, because it was a
> historical process never driven alone by the Soviet threat in either
> its real or imagined forms.[18]

With such cultural foundations of militarisation the new Cold War of the early 1980s was in part related to internal US pressures and conditions.

The US economy in the world system

The internal dimensions of the remilitarisation programme were linked not only to the psychological needs of society but also to that of its economy. Remilitarisation was intended to project US power in the world again and to manage the economic recession through 'supply side economics'. With the supply side injection of finance into the faltering economy the Reagan administration could reverse the downward trend of US economic strength relative to that of its main competitors Germany and Japan. Long-term problems relating to US competitiveness stemmed from spending up to 8 per cent of its GNP on 'defence', while the German and Japanese figures were much lower, 3.5 per cent and 1 per cent respectively, allowing them to invest more in the civilian sectors of their economies. Adam Smith's 'hidden hand' might direct the US civilian economy, but the military economy relied on generous government handouts.[19]

Though the economic kick-start produced impressive growth rates in the first term, the benefits were short. The trade deficit grew from $30 billion in 1981 to $130 billion in 1985, and the federal budget deficit expanded exponentially from $59.6 billion in 1980 to $202.8 billion in 1985. Much of this was related to the 'military Keynesianism' or deficit spending, borrowed from other sources. The solution to the situation was found in the Strategic Defense Initiative (SDI), more commonly known as Star Wars. SDI had an economic function. The huge government investment was intended to act as a major contribution to research and development to offset the advances made by Germany and Japan. The *New York Times* estimated that the spin-offs to the '*civilian* sector' could be considerable. Hence, SDI was tenaciously guarded at the 1986 Reykjavik summit, and spending on the discredited system continued into the Clinton years.[20]

Militarisation not only created problems for the Soviet Union and the long-term effects on the US economy, but also for Western Europe. McCormick writes:

> The term *Catch-22* might have been invented to describe the quandary of a hegemonic power in decline. If that nation sustains the high-level military spending necessary to carry out its global policing, it neglects civilian research and development, distorts the general economy, and reduces its ability to compete with others in world markets. On the other hand, if it cuts military spending to restore civilian productivity and trade competitiveness, it diminishes its role as global protector for a capitalist free world.

The disjunction between security and trade policy exacerbated tensions between Washington and Europe in the early 1980s. The tensions resulted from an 'asymmetry between Europeanism in the economic sphere and Atlanticism in the security field'. Since 1949 US and European security interests had been tied together through the structure of NATO and a shared view of the Cold War. But from 1958 the European Economic Community had grown increasingly independent and unreliable. Throughout the 1970s the disputes on various protectionist measures, especially associated with European agriculture, produced increasing friction between the 'allies'. Washington exercised considerable influence in NATO, but did not enjoy the same deference on economic issues, largely decided upon within the EC. And Washington was increasingly frustrated that it was bearing a disproportionate share of the defence budget, but when in 1983 to 1984 there was a revival of the West European Union (WEU), Washington then worried about a 'European caucus in NATO'.[21]

Continued conflicts of interest characterised the relationship between US hegemony and Europe's assertion of its own foreign policies. While Washington pursued heavy-handed superpower diplomacy, it seemed to disregard the fact that *détente* had continued between many West European governments and Moscow. In Poland, after the government cracked down on the Solidarity movement, Reagan imposed sanctions on the Polish government though the US had lifted them on Russia and continued to supply it with wheat exports at subsidised prices. Despite this, Reagan pressured six West European countries, but particularly Germany, to terminate a proposed deal with Russia to build a gas pipeline to supply western economies. When the Europeans refused to move, Washington prohibited the use of US technology in the venture.[22] Renewed cohesion on security matters was not shared in the post-hegemonic economic realm.

The Reagan Doctrine, Nicaragua and World History

This section concentrates on US–Nicaraguan hostility because, despite the very real causes for the other conflicts of the 1980s, the Sandinistas offered a symbolic alternative. In this conflict all the attendant ideologies and world systemic imperatives were present. The impact on Nicaraguan lives and the outcomes of the conflict speak to the US conceptions of democracy, liberty and self-determination. There was widespread violent conflict throughout the globe, some much more violent and larger than Reagan's war against the Sandinistas, but they captivated his attention and US media focus unlike any other. The Sandinista revolution vexed US assumptions on the Monroe Doctrine, or rather its twentieth-century derivatives. Theodore Roosevelt's corollary, with all its attendant ideas on proper conduct, efficiency, resources, barbarism and civilisation were present in Reagan's crusade. Ironically, Monroe's original injunction that prevented European intervention in the Western Hemisphere became operative again in attempts to limit EC and Scandinavian assistance to the Sandinista regime. The Truman Doctrine and the removal of the Arbenz government in Guatemala also informed Reagan's mindset and his vitriolic rhetoric. Communism, red tides in the Caribbean Sea and Sandinista helicopters leaping up the Central American isthmus characterised US public diplomacy. There was frequent mention of the Moscow, Havana and Managua axis, to much overseas derision. Issues of democracy, nationalism, self-determination and concepts of liberty were frequently at the centre of the diplomatic relations between Washington and Managua; development models and the world system were daily realities and concerns.

A brief contextualising of the Reagan doctrine will facilitate the discussion. The Reagan doctrine became operative shortly after he assumed office, though it was not publicly formulated, defended or identified specifically until the early days of his second term in January 1985. At face value the president declared the United States would defend 'freedom and democracy [on] every continent, from Afghanistan to Nicaragua'. Essentially the doctrine amounted to providing guerrilla groups with enough munitions and assistance to undermine leftist governments on four continents, principally: Angola, Cambodia and Nicaragua, and actual Soviet forces in Afghanistan. In Angola, Washington backed Jonas Savimbi, with the assistance of South Africa, against the MPLA and Cuban troops. In Cambodia, Washington moved against the Vietnamese-installed government of Heng Samrin, in the process siding with the Khmer Rouge, one of three main groups within a coalition of forces organised in 1982. By far the largest operation was conducted against the Soviet presence in Afghanistan. The administration backed the Mujahedin, who ultimately compelled a Soviet withdrawal in 1988–1989. Though the Afghan war was the largest in terms of US finance, Congress had little problem backing it, and in 1984 increased aid to the Mujahedin. With the direct Soviet presence there was little to argue about in Washington.[23] This was not the case in Nicaragua. US policy on Nicaragua specifically, and on Central America more generally, created acrimony.

Reagan's rhetoric against the Sandinistas, and for that matter most of the governments subject to his doctrine, focused exclusively on the East–West conflict. Without any sense of irony Reagan railed against Marxism and the Soviet–Cuban thrust into the Western Hemisphere: 'We must not break faith with those who are risking their lives on every continent from Afghanistan to Nicaragua to defy Soviet-supported aggression and secure rights which have been ours from birth. . . . Support for freedom fighters is self-defense.' There was constant reference to the growing Soviet presence in the region and a revival of the domino theory was used to graphically explain events. Career diplomats were removed from office because they favoured local particulars over the global view and militarist approach. They knew the area too well to be confined by Reagan's mental straitjackets. Early in the first term, Secretary of State Alexander Haig talked about 'drawing the line' in El Salvador against the Soviet advance, and 'going to the source' (meaning Cuba) to deal with the problem. But Washington had another problem. It somehow had to implement Truman's bipolar vision in the shadow of Vietnam. Its ambition was universal, but its means limited by concerns about sustained US troop engagement. Conceptually, solutions had to be found somewhere between the analogies of Cuba and Vietnam. That is, no more revolution, no more defeat. It is captured in one of Brands's inventive terms: 'The Reagan Doctrine might have been considered a corollary to the Nixon Doctrine, or perhaps an extension of the Truman Doctrine via the Doolittle lemma.'[24] US troops were often used as symbolic assertions of power. But if the dangers were real, as in Nicaragua, US troops were kept out or removed, as in Lebanon. Elsewhere, 'the guns fired along the periphery rather than at the core'. The victims or their governments were hardly client states of Moscow, but belonged, if the term can be used collectively, to various assertions of Third World nationalism, 'as if it were either easier or more necessary to do battle with non-Westerners. Against the only serious use of Soviet military force, in Afghanistan, American guns remained in their holsters. Nonetheless, alarm about Soviet power remained the touchstone of the leader's rhetoric and proclaimed policy.'[25]

The reluctance to fight limited the administration to a form of low-intensity conflict, which was still devastating to the lives, infrastructure and the economies of the region. The main components of the Reagan doctrine included low-intensity conflict, pro-insurgency, finessing potential revolutions, conducting 'anti-terrorism' operations, and asserting US power. The administration target was the Soviet Union, or at least at the edges of the Soviet empire. There was plenty of evidence suggesting that the Soviet presence was extremely limited but it was imperative to approach the situation through this prism to reduce conflict with Congress. In 1981 the administration began its propaganda campaign with a white paper that charged the Sandinistas with shipping arms to the Salvadorean Frente Farabundo Martí para la Liberación Nacional (FMLN). The charges were soon discredited in the media and later thoroughly refuted by various academic studies, but still the administration persisted. By September 1985 a State Department report, *Beyond Our Borders*, accused the Sandinistas of exporting their revolution. The title of the report was extracted from a statement made by the Sandinista Interior Minister Tomás Borge, who had actually argued that the Sandinista revolution was part of a revolutionary wave, which goes 'beyond our borders' but, he added, 'this does not mean that we export our revolution'.[26]

US security was never really threatened by the Sandinistas or any other revolutionary group during the 1980s. Christopher Hitchens most aptly described the Sandinista triumph of July 1979 as a 'revolution of revulsion'. The revulsion, however, was contained within the confines of the nation-state. It was a broad-based movement against a repressive regime backed by Washington from the mid-1930s to the Carter period. After July 1979 the Carter administration found a limited basis for co-operation with the Sandinistas, recognising that, in the words of its ambassador to Managua: 'it is very much a Nicaraguan phenomenon. There is no question about that. Sandinismo . . . is a Nicaraguan, home-grown movement. Sandino predates Castro. . . . There is no reason to believe they are going to go out and borrow from elsewhere when they really have something at home.' Carter indicated he was trying to maintain links with the revolution to prevent it from 'turning to Cuba and the Soviet Union'. Viron Vaky, Assistant Secretary of State, argued it was 'essential to supply aid to keep the monetary/economic system viable and enmeshed in the international economy'. To that end Carter appropriated $75 million for Nicaragua though the Congressional system tied it up with stringent conditions. If Carter tried to find a basis for a continued relationship, this was terminated shortly before he left office, and totally reversed when Reagan entered the White House.[27]

Security considerations were grossly exaggerated. The Sandinista revolution caught the Soviets by surprise, and was, as Carter's administration recognised, a 'homegrown' movement. The revolution had largely grown out of the socio-economic inequality within the country, exacerbated by declining wages throughout the 1970s, despite the impressive macro-economic growth rates of the country. The declining wages in real terms meant that 'employed, wage-earning Nicaraguans suffered a palpable drop in their ability to feed and shelter their families'. But Reagan's vision was one of global export of revolution. Thus, in turn, he charged the Sandinistas with exporting their revolution to neighbouring rebels in El Salvador, though no proof was unearthed to back up the claims. The International Court of Justice in 1986 determined that there had been an 'intermittent flow of arms' through Nicaragua in early 1981, but there was insufficient evidence to attribute responsibility to the Sandinista government. The activity soon dried up when the US ambassador explained Reagan's mindset to the Sandinistas. Still, the charges continued throughout the administration. Within weeks of Reagan's coming to office Washington started to back and organise groups of counter-revolutionaries (contras) operating out of Honduras on Nicaragua's northern border; a southern front was later initiated in Costa Rica. Though these groups were ostensibly set up to interdict weapons supposedly flowing north, they never captured any throughout Reagan's period in office, and this argument largely became a fig leaf for the attempt to remove the Sandinistas, though it was not until Reagan's second term that he could openly talk of such intentions.[28]

The Reagan administration redefined the traditional State Department approach to the sources of instability in Latin America. Originally they debated whether poverty or communism caused instability. Under Reagan the debate centred on how much communism existed? The administration focused on the presence of the Cubans and Soviet aid in Nicaragua and rarely questioned the purpose of the aid. Moscow assisted the Sandinistas from 1981, but sophisticated equipment did not arrive until late 1982, after the US covert war began. Reagan's ideas were based on the assumption that because the Sandinistas were leftist they were necessarily aligned to Moscow and must be internally repressive, externally aggressive and expansionist. But Moscow's support for the Sandinistas was cautious. It provided enough aid to sustain the defence against the contras but did not enter into any security guarantees. Ex-US marines pointed out that, given the nature and the vintage of the Soviet equipment, primarily the HIND helicopters and T-55 tanks, the Sandinistas did not have the capability of being externally aggressive. The Sandinistas had no plans for external adventures; they were aware that, should they go beyond their borders, they would invite immediate response. Even a 1984 State Department report indicated:

> The counterweights to Soviet influence are also more far-reaching and varied than sometimes appreciated. Extensive West European presence is often commented on, as is pervasive Church influence. Other actors have also moved in. UN agencies fund a large number of Nicaraguan development projects; Japan's trade with Nicaragua has risen in direct reverse proportion to Washington's economic disentanglement; Algeria picked up the sugar quota that America cancelled; the larger South American states have given Nicaragua significant support; even US and contra-aligned Honduras, El Salvador and Guatemala maintain trade with Managua.

In short, the contentious and graphic propaganda emanating from Washington misrepresented the nature of the Soviet presence.[29]

Security issues that concerned Washington were addressed in diplomatic fora, but Washington refused to talk seriously. Throughout the 1980s there were a number of diplomatic processes which dealt with the deteriorating situation. There were bilateral talks between Washington and Managua, regional talks organised by the Contadora group (Mexico, Colombia, Venezuela and Panama), predominantly active between 1983 and 1986, and ultimately joined by the Contadora Support Group including Argentina, Brazil, Uruguay and Peru. In these talks the main issues related to democratisation, self-determination, demilitarisation and non-intervention. The process continually faltered due to procedural matters or direct attempts by Washington to prevent a successful conclusion. In late 1984 a National Security Council memorandum indicated: 'we have effectively blocked Contadora group efforts to impose the second draft of the Revised Contadora Act. Following intensive U.S. consultations', the isthmian countries submitted a counter-draft consistent with US interests. From 1987 Costa Rican president Oscar Arias revived the peace process, taking the structure of the Contadora process largely designed by Mexico's Foreign Minister Bernardo Sepúlveda, but reduced the issues to democratisation and demobilisation. The Sandinistas adopted a strategy of concessions throughout the process to keep the US at the negotiating table. As Washington increased its demands to block settlement, the Sandinistas conceded on issues to perpetuate talks. Reagan was compelled to demonstrate that negotiations had been tried and failed to gain congressional funds.[30]

Mainly from 1981 to 1988, but more sporadically after that, the United States backed the contras in a devastating covert war against the

Sandinistas. The costs of the aggression were considerable. Over 40,000 Nicaraguans lost their lives during the 1980s. The contras concentrated on the social infrastructure that represented the advances of the revolution (widely commended by various development agencies), destroying health centres, schools, co-operatives, bridges, oil installations and so forth. In 1983 the CIA produced manuals to assist the contras, which, according to one contra leader, Edgar Chamorro, advocated 'explicit and implicit terror' against the civilian population, including assassination. 'Many civilians were killed in cold blood. Many others were tortured, mutilated, raped, robbed or otherwise abused.' Moreover, 'the atrocities reflected a consistent pattern of behaviour by our troops'. In early 1984 the CIA engaged in what Senator Barry Goldwater described as 'an act of war' by mining the harbours of Nicaragua. In 1986 the International Court of Justice found against the United States. It rejected the legal basis of self-defence, and found that in arming, training, equipping, financing and supplying the contras the United States was 'in breach of its obligation under customary international law not to intervene in the affairs of another country'. Washington, of course, did not participate in the process and simply ignored the decision and the request to pay Managua reparations.[31]

A key element of the Reagan doctrine was to support and promote democracy against Soviet influence around the world. Even though there was a growing transition towards a form of democracy during the 1980s, many of these changes occurred independently of US policy. Where Washington supported 'democracy', the content of the word could only be understood in the sense of an extremely exclusive system of electoral conduct, often coupled with support for a brutal regime. Throughout the 1980s Reagan insisted the Sandinistas introduce democracy to Nicaragua, while he championed the cause of other Central Americans. Apart from Costa Rica, the other isthmian countries, El Salvador, Honduras and Guatemala, could only be considered 'democratic' in that they were pro-US. Stephanson's distinction outlined in the introduction on the difference between the 'empire of liberty' and the 'empire for liberty' is acutely pertinent. The governments of both El Salvador and Guatemala backed death squads, presiding over a brutal period of history; by the end of the 1980s the UN Truth Commission on El Salvador estimated that, of the 75,000 people killed during the decade, the government was responsible for 85 per cent of them. The type of democracy Washington supported is best characterised as 'low-intensity democracy', designed to stave off either progressive reform or revolutionary change, to sideline popular aspirations while concentrating on the electoral process. In Nicaragua elections were held in both 1984 and 1990. Both elections were widely regarded as both 'free and fair' by a range of international observer groups. Simultaneously, elections in neighbouring countries were often faulted for many reasons.

Reagan's support for democracy within this region was a highly charged political construct.[32]

Perceptions of US credibility were important for understanding the extreme response. Reagan staked his reputation on prevailing in Nicaragua. In a limited sense it did not really matter what the Sandinistas did within their borders, whether they introduced reforms or democracy, whether they kept 60 per cent of the economy in the private sector, whether they remained in the world system, whether they improved on Nicaragua's human rights record, or introduced an IMF-style economic austerity plan backed by the US. The bottom line was that Reagan wanted them out of power. In 1985, safely re-elected, Reagan publicly indicated that he wanted the Sandinistas to 'say uncle'. Earlier, in 1983, he went before a joint session of Congress to persuade those gathered to side with him. In an alarmist speech, conjuring up the Soviet threat and the extension of its power into the Western Hemisphere, invoking the Truman Doctrine, as if the world were still bipolar, and totally ignoring the indigenous origins of the revolution, Reagan asked:

> If Central America were to fall, what would the consequences be for our position in Asia, Europe, and for alliances such as NATO? If the United States cannot respond to a threat near our own borders, why should Europeans or Asians believe that we are seriously concerned about threats to them? If the Soviets can assume that nothing short of an actual attack on the United States will provoke an American response, which ally, which friend, will trust us then?

But the Soviets had no intention of extending their sphere into the West. Still, they could only benefit from the situation. If Washington prevailed they could shout aggression, if Washington failed they could highlight its weakness, and if the conflict dragged on, their credibility would be bolstered in the Third World, and they could use the situation as a counterweight to Afghanistan. Another problem was that the European allies did not share Reagan's perspective. Many continued to trade with Nicaragua despite US pressure: France initially sold arms, Japan and other allies increased their trade with Managua. Nevertheless, by May 1985 Washington passed an Emergency Act, because Nicaragua constituted 'an unusual and extraordinary threat to the national security and foreign policy of the United States'. The threat related more to Reagan's credibility than to US foreign policy. The allies, the Congress, Latin American governments, largely did not share Reagan's concerns with the Soviet–Cuban–Nicaraguan axis. It was largely a fiction.[33]

There was another kind of threat though, the 'threat of a good example'. This is not to suggest the Sandinista revolution was faultless, or in any way perfect, but it does suggest that impressive gains were made by the Sandinista revolution in their initial years. Under Somoza, 1 in 8 babies died under a year old, 2 in 3 children were malnourished, 90 per cent of medical services were concentrated on 10 per cent of the population, 93 per cent of homes did not have safe drinking water, 6 out of 10 deaths were caused by preventable diseases, more than 50 per cent of the population was illiterate, 94 per cent of children did not finish primary education, export crops made up 90 per cent of agricultural produce. The Sandinistas began to change this situation. Illiteracy was reduced to 13 per cent, winning an UNESCO prize in 1980. There were 127 per cent more schools (before many were destroyed), there were 61 per cent more teachers, child-care was free and universal, medical care was universally available. There was a 90 per cent drop in deaths from preventable diseases. Advances were made in land reform, food production, and the move to eradicate death squads. Even the Inter-American Development Bank noted: 'Nicaragua has made noteworthy progress in the social sector, which is laying a solid foundation for long-term socio-economic development.' The costs of the contra war to all of these advances were horrendous. Apart from the direct infrastructure damage, the war forced Nicaragua to divert a large portion of its annual budget to defence. In 1982 the National Security Council acknowledged they had 'a vital interest in not allowing the proliferation of Cuba model states . . . the Sandinistas are under increased pressure as a result of our covert efforts and because of the poor state of their economy'.[34]

Nicaragua threatened the credibility of the US preferred world system and the 'development' models it advocated. The 'fears about the demonstration effect of Sandinista achievements are real, and it is understandable that they should be masked in hysterical rhetoric about Soviet missiles and military bases'. The bottom line was that the experiment could not be allowed to succeed. The US could not 'tolerate a government that diverts resources to the poor majority . . . and embarking on a course that may have dangerous demonstration effects if the experiment is permitted to succeed'. The US war had helped stagnate the economy by 1984, Washington embargoed it in 1985, and by 1988 it was thoroughly out of control. The revolution was not exported. Third World revolutions do not work like that; nationalism, as suggested in chapter 7, was a key factor. Eduardo Galeano has aptly put it thus: Washington's problem was not communism, but Nicaragua's solution to the dire state of its condition prior to 1979; it was

a dangerous and contagious example of a people that lost patience. To guard a criminal social order, the neighbour governments are forced into armed insomnia. With good reason they feel themselves threatened, but threatened by their own peoples, who may find out that they'd be better off making history from below and from inside than continuing to suffer history made by others from above and from outside.

The irony was that there was little attempt to export revolution or introduce economic autarky. Castro had warned them against it. But in the extreme bipolar vision of the Reagan doctrine, any assertion of independence, especially in the US 'backyard', was intolerable. Hegemony had to be maintained, at least in this region. Nicaragua threatened US hegemony, providing a role model that was inappropriate for the periphery, undermining neo-liberal modernisation and internationalism.[35]

The Reagan doctrine undermined western notions of democracy. Nicaraguan consent provided to the Sandinistas in the 1984 elections was undermined through externally driven counter-revolution and economic strangulation. National self-determination was similarly undermined through the application of US policy on a range of fronts. In Central America US support for the regional 'national security states' maintained regimes that constantly abused the most basic human rights. These features of the Reagan doctrine undermined the ostensible values that informed foreign US policy. But the American nationalism associated with its formal ideologies had long given way to its nationalism associated with perceptions of its state security, its hard-nosed realism.

US hegemony was contested. If the foundation of US hegemony in the Western Hemisphere can be traced back to the Monroe Doctrine (1823) and consolidated in the decades around the turn of the century, it was threatened increasingly after the 1960s. Castro's Cuba had invited Moscow into the Western Hemisphere; Venezuela in founding OPEC moved against Washington; Brazil moved away from Washington, in terms of arms purchases, during the Vietnam war; Peru purchased Soviet weapons; Argentina sold wheat to Moscow; Allende demonstrated that alternative ideologies could be constitutionally elected. *Détente*, with a world centred on five powers, actually provided Washington with the opportunity to consolidate the 'imperial net'. But the Vietnam syndrome, coupled with local conditions, pushed forward further revolutions or movements towards change, not in service of the Soviet Union but against the US 'hegemonic presumption'. In 1984 Henry Kissinger was briefly employed to write a report on the region. He concluded that the 'erosion of our power to influence events worldwide that would flow from the perception that we were unable to influence vital events close to home' would further exacerbate the US decline. In private, Kissinger indicated there was an anomaly in the Reagan strategy on Central America: that if the threat was as great as Reagan indicated, his expenditure really did not match his worry. Thus the direct US interventions against the Dominican Republic (1965), Grenada (1983) and Panama (1989) 'attested not to U.S. strength but to the loosening of the imperial net'. For all of Reagan's efforts to assert US power in the region, the resistance continued, the administration went to lengths that invited severe scepticism, the Iran–contra scandals further weakened his power, and created space for other extra-hemispherical actors to increase their roles in the Western Hemisphere. By the late 1980s the United Nations was considerably involved in mediating peace in Nicaragua, El Salvador and Guatemala, European powers had increased their influence, Latin American governments had designed their own solutions, and Washington was almost an outsider. In much of this manner US hegemony had been tested, and the Reagan administration had presided over the last years of the Monroe Doctrine.

The costs to US credibility would be considerable. Halliday posits:

> The most striking feature of the Reagan Doctrine was the way in which Washington itself came to be a promoter and organizer of terrorist actions. The *mujahidin* in Afghanistan, UNITA in Angola and the Nicaraguan *contras* were all responsible for abominable actions in their pursuit of 'freedom' – massacring civilians, torturing and raping captives, destroying schools, hospitals and economic installations, killing and mutilating prisoners. In his eight years in the White House Reagan was responsible for the deaths of tens of thousands of people through terrorism, many times more than the PLO or other favourite targets of his righteous wrath.[36]

As Washington celebrated the freedom and self-determination that resulted from 'people power' in Eastern Europe, it had presided over a severe limitation of them in the Western Hemisphere. Self-determination and democracy were thoroughly undermined through the Reagan doctrine. Nicaragua's reinsertion into the global economy was so thorough and so successful for US foreign relations. For Nicaraguans the changes were dramatic. Relative poverty under the Sandinistas became absolute in the 1990s, 'real wages dropped 50 percent in the first year, 69 percent of the population lived in poverty in 1992, and per capita food consumption fell by 31 percent between 1990 and 1992'.[37]

9

CONCLUDING THROUGH CONTEMPORARY DILEMMAS

The global political superstructure underwent tremendous change at the end of the 1980s and the beginning of the 1990s. The end of the Cold War meant many different things at different levels. Celebrations gripped Europe with the final collapse of the Berlin Wall. Elsewhere, no such dramatic symbols existed but there were clear signs of change. Two years earlier Moscow began to withdraw troops and finance from the Third World, most significantly in Afghanistan. Mikhail Gorbachev characterised the retraction as virtuous. Soviet ideology and its economy could not survive further imperial politics; he told the UN General Assembly in December 1988 that it was 'inadmissible and futile to encourage revolution from abroad'. And similarly he called for global tolerance, pluralism and restraint from settling conflict through force. He recognised that Soviet autarky had been compromised and that 'the world economy is becoming a single organism, and no state, whatever its social system or economic status, can normally develop outside it'. He argued that the very notions of progress were changing. International law, non-violence and human rights were supposed to be fundamental to his vision, though obviously not accorded to the Baltic republics trying to cede from the Soviet 'Union'. Perhaps because he could no longer defend the Soviet system he urged tolerance and pluralism, implicitly castigating the imperious US vision and economic system:

> More and more characteristic is the increasingly multi-optional nature of social development in different countries. . . . The diversity of the sociopolitical structures that have grown over the past decades out of national liberation movements also attest to this. This objective fact demands respect for the views and positions of others, tolerance, a willingness to perceive difference as not necessarily bad or hostile, and an ability to learn to coexist with others while retaining our differences and the ability to disagree with each other. As the world asserts its diversity, attempts to look down on others and to teach them one's own brand of

democracy become totally improper, to say nothing of the fact that democratic values intended for export often very quickly lose their worth.[1]

The Cold War was over. The inter-systemic conflict that existed since the 1940s and the ideological clash since the Bolshevik Revolution had ended. The celebrations disregarded the fact that over a billion people still lived under communism in China. China's economy had opened up sufficiently since Deng decided to pursue economic modernisation by the most effective means rather than through doctrinaire prescription, since he gave up caring whether a cat was black or white so long as it caught mice. China's half-open door made ideological discussions an irrelevance; concerns on negative liberties associated with human rights were muted. Conceptually, the 'evil empire' was Russia not China, and Washington presumably had faith that the market would eventually work to its assumed conclusions in China; US interests dictated such a course. The democratic agenda could wait, as the students in Tiananmen Square in 1989 bitterly learned.

Reagan had railed against the Soviet system. The simplicity of his vision, some historians suggest, helped break the logjam in superpower politics. But the collapse of the Soviet system did not necessarily vindicate the western system or ideology. One of the historiographical developments in US foreign policy since the end of the Cold War has been the rise of 'vindicationism'. In short, the victory was seen as a vindication of US policy:

> it is incontrovertible that the United States emerged the victor, but viewing victory as vindication claims more than mere triumph. . . . In the vindicationist interpretation the end of the Cold War demonstrates the superiority of the American political and economic system, not only because we won but because our former enemies now embrace our economic and political values. The world is better off because the United States met the challenge.[2]

No doubt the world is better off without the Soviet Union and especially without its most malign practices. But there is still a logical leap between this and the suggestion that US policies benefited the world beyond containment. That case needs to be made in a positive argument more conclusively, rather than in the negative yet triumphal arguments associated with the end of the Cold War.

It is not necessarily the case that the world system led to further democracy or the extension of liberty. There has been a strong ideological fusion of the ideas on democracy, liberty, Open Door capitalism and the idea of progress in history. In the twentieth century and especially during the Cold War these ideas have been caught up with the idea that the United States has been the major historical agent acting on their behalf. In turn, US nationalism has merged with these ideas. Prevailing over Soviet-style communism added further success to deepen such perspectives and the impact of such conceptual conflation.

Gaddis suggests that when Truman divided the world at the inception of the Cold War into a bipolar conflict, he probably believed what he was saying, even though the political aims are obvious and, moreover, 'most Americans and Europeans, at the time, probably agreed with him'. Ideology was important, the 'conflict was *primarily* about the difference between freedom and its absence'. Though there were many Faustian bargains and compromises along the way, the 'conflict came to an end only when it became clear that authoritarianism could no longer be imposed and freedom could no longer be denied'. To elaborate:

> Perhaps Harry Truman had it right after all: the struggle really was, ultimately, about two ways of life, one that abandoned freedom in its effort to rationalise politics, and another that was content to leave politics as the irrational process that it normally is, thereby preserving freedom. The idea of freedom proved more durable than the practice of authoritarianism, and as a consequence, the Cold War ended.

The US did create a sphere of influence in Europe, but US hegemony, when compared to the alternative, was the 'lesser of two evils'. US expansion was wedded to the liberal 'conviction that the prosperity capitalism generates prevents war and revolution'.[3] Hence, autarky and fragmentation were anathema to such ends.

Bush and Clinton: in search of monsters to destroy

The end of the Cold War deprived the United States of a mission; consolidation was never as attractive or inspirational as regeneration. The Soviet threat had imploded. The need for containment ended but the 'American way of life' demanded economic expansion that pre- and post-dated the Cold War. During the Cold War anti-communism was conflated with the pursuit of 'free trade'. The 'Free World' included various forms of government, repressive or not, that were anti-communist, ludicrously including apartheid South Africa. Members of the world system defined the free in terms of the economic realm. In either case social contracts that guaranteed human rights or state sovereignty against US intervention or economic penetrations were ignored. Freedom was closely associated with the Open Door. Free-trading authoritarian regimes were thus acceptable and worthy of US defence. Democratic regimes that sought to protect their national trade, often in order to protect the democratic rights of their citizens, were isolated and opposed. At the end of the Cold War goals could not be promoted exclusively in such commercial terms. US foreign policy works best in the domestic sphere when it occupies the moral high ground. Liberty and democracy were once more the clarion calls for both the Bush and Clinton administrations. The End of History thesis provided an intellectual framework at a time when the president lacked a 'vision thing' and the nation emerged into a bewildering future. A Popperian global 'open society' was a disorientating prospect. Spheres of conceptual conflict characterised US foreign policy from Madison and Monroe to Truman and beyond; various clashes of civilisations informed US diplomacy. There were several attempts to identify new enemies: Noriega, Hussein, Aideed, for example. A personalised conflict was much better for the politics of the collective ego. It was easier to articulate the US identity in negative terms. The commercial elements of its foreign policy agenda could never attract such reception, because the domestic benefits were never completely universal.

The post-Cold War doctrines for the United States borrowed from the past. Tony Smith points out that at the end of the three major conflicts of the twentieth century the United States had taken the lead in defining the contours of the new world order. In the First World War, Wilson set out his vision, articulated largely in the Fourteen Points of January 1918, of a world that universalised the Monroe Doctrine: a world that was safe for democracy and a world in which national self-determination was paramount, an open world of free non-discriminatory trade relationships protected by the League of Nations. In the Second World War Roosevelt, essentially a Wilsonian, adopted most of the earlier prescriptions, except in the UN Security Council, where power was clearly located with the five permanent members, and an informal 'spheres of influence' system was acceptable; Truman and Stalin took the spheres to extremes and solidified them. In 1989, without barbarians at the gate, it was difficult to formulate an attractive policy. George Bush essentially maintained the system at a high point in the trajectory of US power. Smith writes:

> to the extent the United States had an established doctrine in foreign policy, one that linked the definition of its national security to a particular structure of international relations, it was liberal democratic internationalism. . . .
>
> [Bush] had been vice president in an administration that had circled Jerico for eight full years trumpeting the virtues of democracy, and once the walls of the adversary had fallen, no other reliable formula seemingly existed for policymakers to help chart American policy in what was now a very different world.[4]

Bush lacked an enemy of equivalent stature to the Soviet Union. Encircling and trumpeting rock music over the walls of the Papal Nuncio's residence in Panama did not command the same enduring attention as earlier crusades, though US violation of Panama's sovereignty with thousands of troops did wonders for his presidential rating.

Freedom remained central to the constructions of foreign policy. In his inaugural address Bush updated Roosevelt's Four Freedoms: 'We know what works: freedom works. We know what's right: freedom is right. We know how to secure a more just and prosperous life for man on earth: through free markets, free speech, free elections, and the exercise of free will unhampered by the state.'[5] The theme was a centrepiece of US policy. Aid to the liberated countries of Eastern Europe was tied to various democratic criteria. The administration celebrated the democratic advance in Nicaragua when the Sandinistas were defeated in the 1990 elections, even though Washington had done so much to undermine democracy throughout the 1980s. Wilsonian self-determination was a part of the ostensible reasons for ejecting Iraq from Kuwait in the 1991 Gulf conflict. Yet there were numerous occasions when Washington opted for stability over democracy and freedom. Bush supported Gorbachev rather than the more democratically legitimate Boris Yeltsin. Frequently democracy and self-determination would have been better served had Washington stayed out of the internal affairs around the world. Yet for Smith,

> The virtue of selective liberal democratic internationalism is that policymakers hold it to be in the United States' security interest for democracy to expand abroad, yet are aware that this country's power is too limited for it to promote such reforms imprudently, meaning that important stakes must be involved or that the likelihood of success is high before the United States commits itself.[6]

Primarily, US support for democracy and self-determination was closely associated with the pursuit of national interests, which secured the two kinds of nationalism running through US history: that of state security and ideology. The selective response was not new in US history. The Good Neighbor policy facilitated the existence of dictators in Latin America, because the primacy of self-determination was placed above that of democratic opportunity, order above liberty. The universal discourses made selection on the primacy of national interests difficult. 'Since 1898', Brands writes, 'Americans had agreed that the national interest encompassed prosperity, democracy, and security'; but which came first and when depended on the contemporary opportunities.[7]

Credibility was at stake too. The universalism of the Truman Doctrine, NSC 68 and Kennedy's inaugural pledge to 'pay any price or bear any burden to ensure the survival and success of liberty' was myopic. The Vietminh and the Vietcong were determined to do their own nation building, and in the process US credibility suffered. As Steel points out, the US was not the 'first to define security by the length of [their] reach or the depth of [their] pockets'. The British had done so in the nineteenth century. Protecting interests at the 'periphery' drew the powers into areas hitherto unknown, imposing inappropriate agendas for development at particular stages of history. 'Powerful nations such as ours, particularly when they define themselves as "superpowers" are different. . . . They perceive all unwelcome changes as threats. Then they declare that their "interests" require them to counter such "threats." The result is to make interests universal. This was a hallmark of the American approach to the Cold War.'[8] Alternative developments were seen as threats to US credibility; a lack of response might undermine faith in their identity as guarantor of the system. The selective response might have been good for US national security, but its credibility was constantly undermined through such choices.

Bush's State of the Union speech in 1990 captured so well the tensions between freedom and order, and the universal and particular inclinations of US foreign policy. The pursuit of its national interest vied with the promotion of the national narrative:

> The anchor in our world today is freedom, holding us steady in times of change, a symbol of hope to all the world. And freedom is at the very heart of the idea that is America . . . America, not just the nation, but an idea, alive in the minds of people everywhere. As this new world takes shape, America stands at the corner of a widening circle of freedom – today, tomorrow, and into the next century. . . . This nation, this idea called America, was and always will be a new world – our new world.[9]

Clinton came to the Oval Office setting high expectations, echoing the sounds of the past, tapping into its traditions, sounding pluralistic, invoking more of the same. 'When our fathers boldly declared America's independence to the world and our purpose to the Almighty, they knew that America, to endure, would have to change; not change for change's sake, but change to preserve America's ideals – life, liberty, the pursuit of happiness. Though we march to the music of our time, our mission is timeless', he told his audience. Change was embedded in the theme of the speech, but change limited by the national traditions and opportunities. The United States had to meet the challenges in the world, 'a generation raised in the shadows of the Cold War assumes new responsibilities in a world warmed by the sunshine of freedom, but threatened still by ancient hatreds and new plagues'. But the United States would work to shape the changes and meet the international challenges:

> Today, as an older order passes, the new world is more free but less stable. Communism's collapse has called forth old animosities

and new dangers. Clearly America must continue to lead the world we did so much to make. . . . When our vital interests are challenged or the will and conscience of the international community is defied, we will act – with peaceful diplomacy whenever possible, with force when necessary.[10]

The United States had demonstrated resolve in the Gulf and Somalia, he argued, but soon found out that he could not match the resolve in Bosnia. In the shadow of Vietnam, US interests took precedence over the outrage to the 'conscience of the international community'. When Susan Sontag directed *Waiting for Godot* in Sarajevo, the refrain of the inactive hapless tramps suggested they were waiting for Clinton. But the United States continually postponed its arrival. Its leaders were strapped by tradition, a desire to be viewed as world leaders, as exceptional moral actors, but had to cut their response to suit the temperament of the post-Vietnam generation. In April 1993 the State Department released four criteria for US involvement in regional conflicts. A fifth was added a year later in PDD-25 (Presidential Decision Directive). As so often before, the United States would not become involved unless its vital interests were at stake or there was a threat to the international community (read a threat of instability). While Clinton had to respond in Haiti to reassure the world that the United States was not a paper tiger; in Somalia, in Rwanda and in Bosnia its response was initially more symbolic than effective. These were demonstrations of power rather than effective uses of it.[11] The bombing of Iraq in late 1998 continued the politics of symbolism.

Such demonstrations were necessary, even if ineffective in terms of stated objectives, because they were also demonstrations of US world leadership. Without consensus on a new vision, challenges to US leadership were all the more worrying. Without any significant 'other', US strategy had to be expressed in positive terms. But the constructs of confrontation were much more effective in uniting the people, in articulating a national purpose. The positive discourses on freedom might promote genuine democracy or self-determination, but the negative discourses contained the centrifugal forces within the West. While the administration crafted its positive agendas, it took action in the military sphere to shore up its credibility and assume global leadership. National Security Advisor, Anthony Lake, was conscious of the problem. US credibility was at stake in regional trouble spots. Just prior to the US invasion of Haiti in September 1994, he pointed out that Washington 'must make it clear that we mean what we say. . . . Our actions in Haiti will send a message far beyond our region, to all who seriously threaten our interests.'[12] There was a time lag between the construction of a new consensus and public expectations of one. Washington faced a myriad of problems but could not reduce its policy to the conceptually comfortable option pursued by Truman, Acheson and Nitze.

Ironically, Cold War cultures created dependencies; the world looked to the US for resolution. They waited for Washington, not for others. Tony Judt captured the sentiment well:

> That few in Europe any longer take President Clinton seriously may not matter much – he has long since been plausibly dismissed by policy makers and commentators alike as the most incompetent and ineffectual US president of the century. European politicians continue of course to look to the US to take the initiative in collective actions, as we have just seen; this is the natural product of habit and of the United States' overwhelming military power worldwide.[13]

The 1993 Pentagon study, *The Bottom Up Review*, was clear that with the demise of communism the threat had gone and that the most important challenges to the United States were economic. Despite this, little was cut from US defence budgets; peace dividends were postponed. By 1996 the US defence budget equalled that of all the other 'developed nations of the world *combined*'.[14] Militarism was the one area where the United States was exceptional at the end of the Cold War. Both Bush and Clinton had succumbed to its attractions. It was an area that easily commanded global attention. Sherry writes: 'The Cold War's end did not halt militarization, never caused in the first place by the Cold War alone, but it did destroy the most prominent rationale for militarization, and no sure replacement emerged.'[15]

The Cold War's end deprived America of a sense of victory akin to that at the end of the Second World War, for example. The Cold War was normal and overlapped with the height of US power in the 1940s and 1950s, a golden age in the collective memory of the nation. The duration of the 'Cold War had made obsolete that way of finding meaning in war's end'. Perhaps the overreaction in the 1991 Gulf War parade in New York was in part a celebration of a longer victory that could not be so jingo-istically expressed in 1989 or in 1990. These symbols powerfully counter-acted the post-Cold War malaise. The atmosphere was caught well by Sherry:

> This structure of memory, experience, and imagination accounted in part for the shifting, dyspeptic mood apparent in everything from cartoons to novels to learned commentaries on the public pulse. Comic-strip Congressman Bob Forehead gave his wife so much trouble that she took him to a "perestroichiatrist," who opined, "The fading of the Cold War has left a terrible void inside

him. He'll need a lot of care until he finds a new enemy," one the *New Yorker* saw many Americans finding in drugs. Novelist John Updike put his long time character Rabbit to rest in 1990, having him muse, "The cold war. It gave you a reason to get up in the morning," and lament, "Without the cold war, what's the point of being an American?" Updike explained that Rabbit's "sense of being useless" had "this political dimension. . . . Like me, he has lived his adult life in the context of the cold war," and Rabbit had a "concept of freedom, of America, that took sharpness from contrast with Communism."[16]

A sharp identity could not be constructed in the economic realm. The world system was more or less unified. Though the economy was considered a part of the national security structure, major competitors could not be publicly used to set off the US identity. They shared the ideas on freedom, democracy and the world system. Moreover, the state was supposed to leave the 'free hand' to guide market forces; theoretically states were supposed merely to ensure that the field remained relatively fair without favour. But this was not the case. The leaked 1992 Pentagon report *Defense Planning Guidance for Fiscal Years 1994–1999* warned: 'we must account sufficiently for the interests of the advanced industrial nations to discourage them from challenging our leadership or seeking to overturn the established political and economic order'. Further, the document noted that regional competitors must be deterred 'from even aspiring to a larger regional or global role'.[17] Europe and Japan had to be contained, albeit contained through hegemonic co-option. But why would these powers defer to US priorities unless they shared a joint political identity and purpose? There were two predominant options in 1993 and 1994: the thesis put forward by Samuel Huntington, the 'clash of civilizations', or that of the National Security Assistant, Anthony Lake, on 'backlash' or 'rogue' states. Either one, if it could gain acceptance and be grafted on to the positive statements of democratic engagement and enlargement, would promote US opportunities as World Leader.

The 'clash of civilizations'

Samuel Huntington's 1993 thesis on the 'clash of civilizations' attracted widespread comment. It captured the public imagination because it grafted the Gulf War, the most significant post-Cold War conflict, on to previous constructions. The Cold War institutionalised mental and cultural structures, attitudes and assumptions about US identity; there was considerable resistance to change in the 1990s. The reductionist thesis of a clash between Islam and the West facilitated some institutional continuity. With the apparent centrifugal tendencies of the European 'allies' and the predominance of Islam over the areas of vital oil reserves, the thesis worked quite well in US culture, especially as Saddam Hussein and the western media fed the hunger. Throughout the Cold War the Middle Eastern oil reserves had been regarded as a stupendous 'prize' in World History. George Kennan had talked about the US ability to exercise a 'veto power' over allies through control of their access to oil.[18] The region loomed large in US strategy and in the process of enhancing US identity, embarrassing though it was to Washington's regional allies.

Many differences with the West are not solely confined to religious ideologies. They relate to material exclusion from the world system (apart from the oil-rich élite), to the politics of dispossession, to the inability to assert self-determination, amply demonstrated in the post-Oil Crisis years, to the inability to implement non-western forms of economic development. At the broadest level there is in parts of society which command disproportionate western attention a fundamental rejection of western modernity, and the consumerism identified with it.

Huntington's central contention is 'that the fundamental source of conflict in this new world will not be primarily ideological or primarily economic. The great divisions among humankind and the dominating source of conflict will be cultural.' The past 500 years have represented a series of western civil wars. 'With the end of the Cold War', the world finally 'moves out of the Western phase' of history and the central concern for history will be 'the interaction of West and non-Western civilizations', and to a lesser extent 'among non-Western civilizations'. The thesis required the postponement of the peace dividend because there was no cause for western complacency. Washington would have to enhance co-operation within western civilisation, between the United States and Europe, to limit the possibilities of the other main challengers: the Islamic and Confucian worlds.[19] The vision recreated another bipolar world, essentially as a section of the article posited, the 'West versus the Rest'. And of course there was the ominous-sounding 'Confucian–Islamic Connection'.

'Civilization is the highest cultural grouping of people and the broadest level of cultural identity people have, short of that which distinguishes humans from other species.' The peoples of the other civilisations, Confucian, Japanese, Islamic, Hindu, Slavic-Orthodox, Latin American, and 'possibly' African, were simply different, they did not share the western values.[20] Their grievances against western domination and materialism would be enhanced as globalisation accelerated. Not only did globalisation marginalise the weaker states in the international system, but it also eroded others' identity through western cultural influences. The world system undermined autarky and compromised national differences. Cultural differences ensured that History could not end. Moreover, such an ending would remove the destiny and mission from US policy, it would undermine its purpose and its identity. That sense of struggle that animated the thought of Theodore Roosevelt would be lost, and with it the 'vigour' of US diplomacy would suffer.

The reductionist argument provided some coherence to the cultural interpretation of US foreign policy, though the Clinton administration openly rejected it. The thesis developed the same erroneous logic of the homogenisation of the 'other' that had occurred in the early Cold War, with tragic consequences in Vietnam for the millions of victims of the war. 'Islam' opposed the 'West', and supposedly rejected moderation, pluralism and liberal values. Said pointed out that the identification of the 'other' both posited a unified coherence to the 'other' and also a sense of superiority in the West. The thesis ignored many intra-Islamic conflicts, especially differences between Iran and Iraq. But perhaps more crucially it suggested a unified West, masking the very real economic tensions between the core powers of the world system.[21] Essentialising the difference also strengthened conceptual identities, with the West closely wedded to democracy and liberty. Yet during the Gulf conflict local democratic groups were marginalised because their prominence might have confused issues on regional order, predictability, and control of regional resources.[22]

Washington's alternative: the backlash states

Washington could not endorse the 'clash' thesis despite its cultural impact. Anthony Lake, Director of the National Security Council, articulated the argument that formed a centrepiece to the administration's identity. Washington's new task was to confront 'backlash states'. The end of the Cold War had enlarged the 'family of nations now committed to the pursuit of democratic institutions, [and] the expansion of free markets'. Washington's task was to promote these values and to confront those 'outlaws' who resisted these core values. As Lake put it:

> our policy must face the reality of recalcitrant and outlaw states that not only choose to remain outside the family but also assault its basic values. There are few "backlash" states: Cuba, North Korea, Iran, Iraq and Libya. For now they lack the resources of a superpower, which would enable them to seriously threaten the democratic order being created around them. Nevertheless, their behavior is often aggressive and defiant. The ties between them are growing as they seek to thwart or quarantine themselves from a global trend to which they seem incapable of adapting.[23]

Lake was eager to point out that the US strategy recognised that these countries were unique and that US policy had been specifically devised to deal with them individually. The associations with the domino theory and a homogeneous enemy would not trap Washington. Still, the regimes did share some characteristics. They were 'ruled by cliques that control power through coercion, they suppress basic human rights and promote radical ideologies. While their political systems vary, their leaders share a common antipathy toward popular participation that might undermine the existing regimes.' The thesis lacked coherence and consistency. There were several US allies that could fall into these categorisations, who consistently denied human rights. There were authoritarian governments that nevertheless kept their economies in the world system and were thus exempt from Washington's rhetorical wrath. Ironically, Cuba was searching for ways to lift the US embargo on its economy. Its isolation was not self-imposed. Washington had created a self-fulfilling prophecy.

The key to understanding the identification of these states was that they exercised a modicum of independence; their assertions of identity challenged the western narrative. Lake stated that 'their behavior is often aggressive and defiant'. It was not sufficiently supportive of the US-centred ideologies or not sufficiently compliant with Washington's preferred scenario of the 'family of nations'. Hitherto, the Soviet adversary helped US strategists define their purpose and provided the nation with a 'mental map' of how to understand the US purpose in history.[24] Writ large, Lake articulated that purpose again in 1994:

> In defeating fascism, and prevailing over communism, we were defending an idea that comes under many names – democracy, liberty, civility, pluralism – but has a constant face. It is the face of the tolerant society, in which leaders and governments exist not to use or abuse people, but to provide them with freedom and opportunity, to preserve individual human dignity. Societies in which the wonderful paradox of democracy is at work. The paradox is this: a society built around a central devotion to pluralism is a society best able to reconcile the divisions that would otherwise rip it apart. Today, those societies – from the fragile to the mature – remain under assault. Far from reaching the end of history, we are at the start of a new stage in this old struggle. This is not a clash of civilizations. Rather, it is a contest that pits nations and individuals guided by openness, responsive government and moderation against those animated by isolation, repression and extremism. The enemies of the tolerant society are not some nameless, faceless force. *They are extreme nationalists and tribalists, terrorists, organized criminals, coup plotters, rogue states and all those who would return newly freed societies to the intolerant ways of the past.*

For Lake and Washington the challenge lay in consolidating 'the victory of the idea of democracy and open markets', and whether the new structures 'can succeed in the face of the centrifugal forces at work within and among nations'.[25]

Globalisation and world leadership: engagement and enlargement

The centrifugal forces in the global environment were not just represented by the radical nationalists, tribalists and terrorists. Other states, well versed in the ways of international commerce and diplomacy, were emerging from the strictures of the Cold War to assume new roles and increased shares in the global economy. In the early post-Cold War period there was some rhetorical flak between Washington and Brussels about the barriers erected by the European Common Agricultural Policy, about iron curtains erected around the European Community and so forth. The United States was not bound to lead; its dominant position was increasingly questioned.

Clinton's vision was provided in the 1994 White House document: *A National Security Strategy of Engagement and Enlargement*. The goals pre-dated the Clinton administration, but the thrust injected into US foreign relations after the Gulf War was reinvigorated. The threat of communist expansion had gone, but the new threats were no less serious: rogue states, nuclear proliferation, environmental degradation, ethnic conflict and population growth. US goals in this period were essentially three: 'To credibly sustain our security with military forces that are ready to fight; To bolster America's economic revitalization; [and] To promote democracy abroad'. All of this was premised on an argument that was inherently circular and comfortable. The line between what was domestic and foreign had essentially disappeared, hence, 'we must revitalize our economy if we are to sustain our military forces, foreign initiatives and global influence, and that we must engage actively abroad if we are to open foreign markets and create jobs for our people'. The document indicated the importance of US leadership and the advance of the core values of US history. There was the simple acceptance of the formula that free trade enhanced democracy and vice versa. 'The more that democracy and political and economic liberalization take hold in the world, particularly in countries of geostrategic importance to us, the safer our nation is likely to be and the more our people are likely to prosper.' Hence Washington adopted the explicit task to 'work to open foreign markets and spur global economic growth'.[26]

Global economic growth did not necessarily comport with the ideals of promoting democracy. Individual rights were best protected through secure social contracts administered within nations in which the people were able to elect their representatives and give their consent to various initiatives. The issue of popular consent lies at the heart of any democratic system. Global economic growth often necessitated limiting, curtailing, or even eliminating the participation through which populations provide consent and therefore the political legitimacy a regime might enjoy. This was the case in Sandinista Nicaragua. And so often before it had been the case that expressions of democracy were sacrificed to the desire to maintain a set of economic relationships that favoured the Open Door and the tendencies towards globalisation. But the liberal assumption that democracy and free trade enhanced each other was an ideological imperative by the late twentieth century. That it was predicated on ideological views dating from the nineteenth-century is evident, and at that time may have made very limited ethnocentric sense. The nineteenth-century Manchester School of liberalism 'held that free trade would increase prosperity worldwide and thus contribute to peace by giving states a vested interest in cooperative political and economic regimes'. But by the late twentieth century, the US 'foreign policy community turns Manchesterism on its head by accepting the economic logic but not the political logic of free trade theory'. The foreign policy community looks to the government and US military might to guarantee an order in which 'free' trade is possible.[27]

Much of the world systems analysis suggests that Washington conducted many of its 'Cold War' interventions to ensure order and the maintenance of Open Door economies. Anti-communism was but one, albeit important, narrative. In the Third World its importance must be considered second to the struggle over development models and within 'national security' states. The Soviet Union may have been the focus of US security interests during the Cold War, but it was incidental to its capitalist interests. But capturing the paradox, 'the Soviet Union was indispensable to that policy's success'.[28] It is not that capitalism needs an enemy *per se*; but the state needs one to motivate and inspire society to pay taxes that pay for 'defence' budgets that largely benefit the élite, ensuring that 'free trade' occurs in relatively risk-free environments.

US world leadership was imperative for preventing other powers pursuing alternative orders. If the United States wanted a unified Europe with Germany at the centre after the Second World War, it had to guarantee European security and the systems that maintained Europe's prosperity. In practice this meant guaranteeing the stability of the periphery and access to the decolonised areas. Political independence was often not considered sufficient for self-determination. For those states that did successfully fragment from the global economic system, such as Vietnam, stability was no longer important to the West; instability, destruction or isolation of the state ensued. The 'backlash states' challenged Clinton's strategy of engagement and enlargement. Hence the paltry cuts in the post-Cold War defence budgets. The Soviet threat had disappeared, but the threat of a fragmenting international economy remained.

'The problem lay in the inherent contradiction between capitalism and international politics,' Schwarz writes. Successful capitalism has never been confined by the nation-state; and yet the political systems on which world organisation is based are predicated on the importance of the nation-state. There is a serious disjuncture in the two systems of power. Capitalism thrives on open economies. The closure and fragmentation of the 1930s brought misery to the western economies. The effects of open doors and globalisation are currently evidenced in widespread misery in the Third World.[29] In the current world system closure, autarky, or 'fair trade' proposals, may benefit democratic opportunities, human rights, negative and positive liberties. Economic nationalism in these circumstances may make rational sense for progress centred on human development as opposed to the 'wealth of nations'. Clinton's strategy of identifying rogue, backlash, or outlaw states that practise radical nationalism is nothing new; it merely had to be articulated in an environment without the preponderance of the 'Soviet menace'. Clinton, like his predecessors, had a 'remarkable opportunity . . . to "grab hold of history and make it conform"'.[30] US-style progress depended on it.

The End of History

If Reagan began the 1980s by reinvigorating the ideological crusade, promising to confine Marxism–Leninism to the ashheap of history, the decade ended with a metaphysical echo by Francis Fukuyama, the deputy director of President Bush's Policy Planning Staff. The widely discussed and very influential 1989 article and 1992 book posited that History had ended: 'The triumph of the West, of the Western *idea*, is evident first of all in the total exhaustion of viable systematic alternatives to Western liberalism.' History, as understood in a very specific sense, of the development of consciousness, could see no higher ground to pursue. This was the terminus on the road map, the final destiny; there were no more frontiers. Overall, the world was becoming increasingly homogeneous. Liberal democracy was spreading, economic liberalism marked the growing concern of most nations of the world: 'We might summarize the content of the universal homogeneous state as liberal democracy in the political sphere combined with easy access to VCRs and stereos in the economic.'[31] Such affluence, according to other interpretations, suggested that History's motor had been turned off, individual agency sidelined, 'by narcotizing its members – they were sexually gratified, well fed, well housed and fashionably clothed, and they were taught to think no thoughts that would derail the society in which they lived'. The costs of capitalism were reduced by the welfare state; people thus settled for lifestyles that were 'good enough'.[32]

Fukuyama's thesis is extremely important because it captures so much of the prevailing ideology and its recent variant on the neo-liberal global economic system. Halliday argues that his stress on the idea of progress in history is important because this kind of eighteenth-century assertion of universal criteria is welcomed against the particularities of nationalism and religious revivalism, and the idiocies of postmodernist confusion.[33] Yet Hegel, upon whose ideas Fukuyama builds his argument, found that the highest form of freedom and the application of the universal was to be found in the nation-state. This is a long way from the universalism of current ideologies. There is also another problem as far as this book is concerned. While state constitutions and institutions may theoretically guarantee freedoms within their spheres, there is no such social contract for the world system. Negative liberties are largely ignored or selectively applied. Self-determination may have been restored in the Gulf War of 1991, but numerous other examples persist from Tibet and East Timor to the West Bank. Human Rights as set out in the 1948 UN Declaration are constantly abused; the abuse of economic rights in that document may be a structural necessity of the world system.

Fukuyama brings liberal democracy to the fore in the historical narrative though, as Halliday points out, his idea of it is ahistorical, not only because most classical liberals did not believe in universal suffrage but also because there is an obvious selective process in Fukuyama's thesis in the world-wide liberal revolution. He charts the rise of liberal democracies world-wide. He argues that 'It is true that democracies have been relatively rare in human history, so rare that before 1776 there was not a single one in existence anywhere in the world. (The democracy of Periclean Athens does not qualify, because it did not systematically protect individual rights.)' And yet the table is content to mark the United States of 1790 as democratic though arguably it was not until the 1960s that it even sought systematically to protect individual rights.[34]

Such selectivity is essential to the endurance of ideologies and their acceptance as givens derived from history; in fact, as far as US foreign policy is concerned, historical reference provides cultural legitimacy. And so through an elaborate process all of these ideas are conflated and alternatives are lost through 'principled forgetting' or repressed. Various threads of US policy are sewn together though internal contradictions abound, for history is made by individuals in pursuit of their own objectives rather than through a fidelity to a set of ideas or the rationality of an economic system. This much the Founding Fathers of the United States recognised even if subsequent generations have chosen to ignore their knowledge that people are inherently selfish. Though the United States may not have needed external enemies, their presence assisted in the process of integrating these ideas. The society rallied round the symbols that represented certain concepts and national narratives; declarations, flags, social traditions further fuelled the sense of nationalism upon which the state fed. To question such ideas or symbolic representation was to question the basis of the society in many ways. In the process, the dominant narrative of 'freedom' obscured others. Global forces such as decolonisation, nationalism, revolution were understood within Cold War paradigms and superpower narratives.[35] The framework and the choices advanced in the Truman Doctrine forged unnecessary alliances, which inhibited the development of independent forces or historical agents. The bipolar vision dominated and suffocated other routes of historical agency towards liberty.

The final destination of History brought about increasing global homogenisation. Destinarian thinking throughout the history of US foreign policy promoted the desire to remake the world in the image of the US.[36] The messianic tendency that resulted in the End of History eventually produced the liberal democratic capitalist system. Capitalism does not need enemies. But as capitalism and the nation-state have been the driving forces behind globalisation,[37] one needs to distinguish between US state interests and those of the world system. The maintenance of US power at the core of the system has necessitated the acceptance, both domestically and within its alliance structures, of US hegemony. The catalyst for such cohesion has frequently been some 'imagined other' to maintain the 'imagined community'. Washington has often articulated its foreign policy through the rhetoric of opposition in order to galvanise support. A distinction needs to be made between the needs of capitalism and those of the United States. The two have often been wedded but are not the same.

Throughout the nation's existence US policy makers have tried to marry the discourses on civilisation, modernisation and the Open Door with those of democracy and liberty. Fukuyama likes to distance his argument from specific US policies. First, it was an empirical description of a universal, directional history, and second, a normative evaluation of liberal democracy. What he intended to deal with in the abstract became closely associated with events in the real world as the Berlin Wall came tumbling down. At the end of the Cold War, coincidentally, the world had arrived at the End of History:

> It is possible that if events continue to unfold as they have done over the past few decades, that the idea of a universal and directional history leading up to liberal democracy may become more plausible to people, and that the relativist impasse of modern thought will in a sense solve itself. That is, cultural relativism (a European invention) has seemed plausible to our century because for the first time Europe found itself forced to confront non-European cultures in a serious way through the experience of colonialism and decolonization. Many of the developments of the past century – the decline of moral self-confidence of European civilization, the rise of the Third World, and the emergence of new ideologies – tended to reinforce belief in relativism. But if, over time, more and more societies with diverse cultures and histories

exhibit similar long-term patterns of development; if there is a continuing convergence in the types of institutions governing most advanced societies; and if the homogenization of mankind continues as a result of economic development, then the idea of relativism may seem much stranger than it does now. For the apparent differences between peoples' "languages of good and evil" will appear to be an artifact of their particular stage of historical development.[38]

With the end of the Cold War and the ideological construct of the End of History, US foreign policy received an enormous boost. Not only had its repressive practices been forgotten in the dominant narrative, there was muted questioning of its curbs on domestic liberties and alternative ideologies. The national security state had become the norm (now including economic activity). Protecting the US 'way of life' through government action was seen as vital, even though this meant denying others the ability to practise their own ways of life. Homogenisation carried with it great costs. The universal vision displaced alternative forms of development and crushed the social and revolutionary experiments from Vietnam to Nicaragua, and from periods and places before and after these points. Liberty, democracy and self-determination were reduced to concepts compatible with the US model.

Conceptual reductionism through bipolarity limited plurality and political possibilities in the 'West'. In the process alternative systems and 'experiments of living' were opposed. Various expressions of nationalism, where this meant a real assertion of that power, were treated as forms of communism and subject to either covert or overt operations, political isolation and economic hostility. This occurred in Guatemala in the 1950s and Nicaragua in the 1980s when the governments sought to extend democratic participation *within* the country. A complex world was reduced through Manichaean visions; the evil other was usually present, whether the Soviet 'fascists', Theodore Roosevelt's 'barbaric' neighbours, or the 'Old World' of Monroe's formula. The barbarians were a kind of solution in that they permitted the society to accept expressions of an external threat and to cohere around various discourses on national security. With the end of the Cold War, such clarity and coherence disappeared; the consensus on the national purpose was contentious. An external threat was needed to ensure that society continued to make sacrifices to the state.[39]

The ends of US foreign policy

Progress that sought liberty through expansion lay at the heart of US strategies from the late eighteenth century. Negative liberties were advanced by the clash of interests within the Union. Those protected by the social contract largely benefited from a highly innovative and productive culture. Those outside the system were removed from their traditional living spaces, pacified or exterminated. US-style negative liberty was rarely applicable beyond the sphere. This was demonstrated through the erosion of self-determination in any real sense of the word. Notions of self-determination were limited to political structures that complemented the 'empire for liberty'. Human rights abuse was a widespread practice in the history of US foreign relations, whatever ideologies of race or 'national security' were attendant to explain or 'legitimate' them. And finally, democracy was considered a deterrent to the smooth functioning of economic systems within the expanding western sphere.

Progress in US foreign policy was closely related to the expansion and health primarily of its own economy. That US ideologies were grafted onto notions of progress in World History and deferred to widely is testimony to the force of the hegemonic power of the US and the appeal of its culture. It is a mistake to assume that the triumphs of capitalism necessarily enhance those of democratic rights and responsibilities. In the age of globalisation, of a tendency towards capitalist homogeneity, decisions that affect millions of lives are often taken beyond the confines of the nation-state. Yet democratic rights or responsibilities are confined to the nation-state. There is no global form of democratic governance, no institution through which people can participate in the decision-making process. The key feature of consent to democratic theory and notions of negative liberty is largely absent from the world system. Even nation-states, where there may be legitimacy in terms of liberty and justice, have their powers to protect democracy and liberty compromised by 'trends' in the global economy.

The Cold War may have helped reinvigorate the basis of the nation-state (the 'rescue of the nation-state') and the nation-state may even have enhanced globalisation. Yet during the Cold War the assertions of national sovereignty were welcomed in Europe, especially in the security field, but the assertions of national autonomy in the Third World were often opposed by the United States and other agents of globalisation. As Clark relates, the 1980s were seen as a period, finally, when 'the Third World was disciplined by the destruction of its vestigial "national development" and "revolutionary" projects and fully incorporated into the economic strategies set by the key capitalist institutions'. Moreover, the socialist road to development was destroyed in the process too.[40] The Cold War was a triumph for capitalism though not necessarily for democracy. Decision-makers' accountability is largely treated as irrelevant to the process of economic modernisation. Individual consent is an abstract formula in the type of democracy that Washington lauded in its triumphal tones at the conclusions of the NAFTA or GATT negotiations, or the initiation rites of the World Trade Organisation.

Size matters: the power of decision making was acutely affected by the power behind the decision-maker. Writing in 1995, Karl Magyar argues that the political equality accorded to states in the United Nations is a convenient and political fiction, which masks a much deeper economic inequality. The Third World, with the great bulk of humanity confined within its borders, has the least political influence in an age of 'Democracy'. There is a huge and widening gap between the wealth of the advanced industrial economies and the poorest states. 'The Third World contains just over 75% of the world's population but generates only about 15% of global wealth. By contrast, the members of the OECD (First World) comprise only 16% of the population but generate about 72% of global wealth.' Economic commodity transfers across borders much faster than any form of balancing agent. Immigration barriers contain population movement. After all, national security is about maintaining a standard of life, the disparity in the national wealth that George Kennan identified in 1948. Adam Smith has one hand tied firmly behind his back. Smith had envisioned the 'free circulation of labour . . . from place to place'.[41] 'Few doubt that this intense global economic interaction contributes greatly to gross world prosperity, but benefits are unequally distributed among states and within them. Those with established economic power are in a position to dictate the rules of such transactions and to influence the markets.' The disparity in the size and therefore the relative influence of nation-states and economies can be illustrated with a few examples. Consider this:

The GNP of South Africa, a country considered to be the power-house of Africa, is but one-fiftieth of the GNP of the USA – or equal to the gross product of the average US state: Missouri. Namibia, considered to be well off by African standards, has a GNP that is one-fiftieth of South Africa's, – which makes Namibia's entire GNP equal to that of a small US city. Black Africa's combined GDPs do not equal that of Belgium. Currently, the USA's single richest person has a personal net worth greater than the annual GNP of any black African country except Nigeria. . . . And a ranking of national GNPs and annual corporate sales places General Motors into the 20th position, considerably ahead of Finland, Saudi Arabia or Indonesia. . . . Exxon, as the second largest corporation, ranks ahead of South Africa. *These data should illustrate the realities of economic concentration, power and vulnerability in the international system. Countries may enjoy a fictitious sense of equality at the United Nations, but in terms of economic realities, this is a dangerous presumption* [emphasis added].[42]

Nevertheless, that presumption is necessary to legitimate the basis of a political system that is otherwise inherently unequal. The notion of consent, which lies at the heart of democratic theory, is almost absent from the decision-making processes that characterise our world system. Democracy may or may not be advancing within nation-states, but between and among nation-states the issue of democratic accountability is not yet on the political agenda. It is of course in the interests of the prosperous G7 + 1, EU, APEC, IMF and other such entities to keep it off the table. David Held writes:

> Territorial boundaries demarcate the basis on which individuals are included in and excluded from participation in decisions affecting their lives (however limited the participation might be), but the outcomes of these decisions must often 'stretch' beyond national frontiers. The implications of this are considerable, not only for the categories of consent and legitimacy, but for all the key ideas of democracy: the nature of a constituency, the meaning of representation, the proper form and scope of political participation, and the relevance of the democratic nation-state, faced with unsettling patterns of relations and constraints in the international order, as the guarantor to the rights, duties and welfare of subjects. Of course, these considerations would probably come as little surprise to those nations and countries whose independence and identity have been deeply affected by the hegemonic reach of empires, old and new, but they do come as a surprise to many in the west.[43]

It is commonly proposed that the process of economic integration enhanced the prospects for democratic participation. Both the Bush and Clinton administrations have repeated the message. Bush emphasised the liberal prescription; 'the power of commerce is a force for progress'. Open markets were supposed to enhance democracy. Or in Clinton's national security strategy, the point was articulated that 'All of America's strategic interests – from promoting prosperity at home to checking global threats abroad before they threaten our territory – are served by enlarging the community of democratic and free market nations. Thus, working with new democratic states to help preserve them as democracies committed to free markets and respect for human rights, is a key part of our national security strategy.'[44] Of course the rhetoric of solidarity and benevolence is there. The key words in the messages must be intoned with gravity without reference to the relationship between trade, growth, prosperity, democracy and human rights. That one may be inimical to the other is not considered. So the Clinton administration talked of Central America 'docking' up to NAFTA. Democracy went hand in hand with global economic integration;

as the Assistant Secretary for Inter-American Affairs put it, 'it is vital that the United States avail itself of this unique historic opportunity to enhance and deepen the commitment of all nations of the hemisphere to the core values of U.S. foreign policy'.[45]

Such notions can only be sustained with the most exclusive, non-participatory forms of democracy. The statistics of UNICEF, the World Development Report, UNDP are constant reminders of how meaningless democratic rights are without some form of economic security. In an attempt to engineer consent – and many have internalised a connection between democracy and capitalism – there is a constant tendency to universalise the identification between these two often-opposing forces. The instrumental function of such ideologies, enhanced by the success of the West, is that the conflation is pervasive and naturalised.

Animated by these beliefs, comfortable with their implications, the structures of the world system deepen. The attempt to create integrated markets based on unequal terms of trade required the exercise of hegemony, 'westernisation', and often force. The conjunction of the Westphalia system of nation-states with the world economic system has caused widespread instability, marginalisation and misery.[46] The modern world is characterised by immense wealth and dire and absolute poverty, of unbound liberty and of continued servitude. World History, written as a narrative on the progress of liberty and justice, will reflect the mixed results.

But singular narratives based on ideological conceptions ignore the pluralism in the world. To those who have consciously resisted integration, or sought better terms of trade, or the benefits of negative liberty provided by a social contract, the subjection to essentially western economic systems backed by western ideologies has caused deep offence. The concept of liberty embodied in US foreign policy is one of positive liberty enhancing the US national interests. It has been the 'empire for liberty' and not one 'of liberty'. Though self-determination and human rights have animated US ideology, in practice they have often been incompatible with the economic interests of the US. The messianic injunction to expand the sphere frequently trod on the negative liberties and self-determination of others. While Washington attempted to open doors within its spheres and then globally, it did not seek an international open society. Yet it promoted a myth, to use the words of Thomas Paine who railed against political and economic oppression, that 'the cause of America is in a great measure the cause of all mankind'. This sentiment was one thing in 1776, but in the crowded and reduced sphere of the twentieth century such visions of Utopia, to use Isaiah Berlin's reasoning, were unrealisable, 'conceptually incoherent' and often ended in tyranny.[47]

NOTES

INTRODUCTION

1 The Hegelian dialectic, which gives pre-eminence to the spirit and to the realm of ideas, is nevertheless still teleological and deterministic, and in the long run deprives the individual of liberty. David Ryan, Reviews, *Borderlines: Studies in American Culture* vol. 3, no. 1 (1996), p. 91.

2 Timothy Garton Ash, *We The People: The Revolution of 89* (Cambridge: Granta, 1990).

3 Francis Fukuyama, *The End of History and the Last Man* (Harmondsworth: Penguin, 1992).

4 Thomas McCormick, 'World Systems', in Michael J. Hogan and Thomas G. Paterson (eds), *Explaining the History of American Foreign Relations* (Cambridge: Cambridge University Press, 1991), pp. 89–94. For further material on both the world systems see McCormick, '"Every System Needs a Center Sometimes": An Essay on Hegemony and Modern American Foreign Policy', in Lloyd C. Gardner (ed.), *Redefining the Past: Essays in Diplomatic History in Honor of William Appleman Williams* (Corvallis: Oregon State University Press, 1986), pp. 195–220. See also Fernand Braudel, *Civilization and Capitalism: The Perspective of the World*, vol. III (London: Fontana, 1985); Immanuel Wallerstein, *Historical Capitalism with Capitalist Civilization* (London: Verso, 1996); Terence K. Hopkins and Immanuel Wallerstein, *The Age of Transition: Trajectory of the World System, 1945–2025* (London: Zed Books, 1996).

5 Filipe Fernandez-Armesto, *Millennium* (London: Bantam Press, 1995), p. 7.

6 Eric Hobsbawm, *The Age of Revolution: Europe 1789–1848* (London: Weidenfeld and Nicolson, 1995 [1975]).

7 See, for instance, Michael H. Hunt, *Ideology and US Foreign Policy* (New Haven: Yale University Press, 1987), *passim*; and idem., 'Conclusions: The Decolonization Puzzle in US Policy-Promise versus Performance', in David Ryan and Victor Pungong (eds), *The United States and Decolonization: Power and Freedom* (London: Macmillan, 2000), pp. 207–227.

8 See particularly Geir Lundestad, *The American Empire* (Oslo: Norwegian University Press, 1990); idem., '"Empire by Invitation" in the American Century', *Diplomatic History* vol. 23, no. 2 (Spring 1999), pp. 189–217; idem., *"Empire" by Integration: The United States and European Integration, 1945–1997* (Oxford: Oxford University Press, 1998).

9 See contributions by Tony Smith, H. W. Brands, Walter LaFeber, Joan Hoff and Bruce Cumings in 'The American Century: A Roundtable' in *Diplomatic History* vol. 23, no. 2 (Spring 1999), and my response in H-Diplo at http://

www.h-net.msu.edu / logs / showlogs.cgi?list = h-diplo&file = h-diplo.log9904d / 2&ent = 0, 22 April 1999.

10 Francis Fukuyama, *The End of History and the Last Man* (Harmondsworth: Penguin, 1992). See also Alan Ryan (ed.), *After the End of History* (London: Collins and Brown, 1992); Timothy Burns (ed.), *After History? Francis Fukuyama and His Critics* (London: Littlefield Adams, 1994); Arthur M. Melzer *et al.* (eds), *History and the Idea of Progress* (Ithaca: Cornell, 1995).

11 David Held (ed.), *Prospects for Democracy: North, South, East, West* (Cambridge: Polity Press, 1993), pp. 13–52, esp. p. 27.

12 Isaiah Berlin, *Four Essays on Liberty* (Oxford: Oxford University Press, 1969), pp. 122–134. For several alternative conceptions see David Miller (ed.), *Liberty* (Oxford: Oxford University Press, 1991).

13 Michael Foley, *American Political Ideas: Traditions and Usages* (Manchester: Manchester University Press, 1991), pp. 7–26, esp. 24, 13.

14 William H. McNeill, 'The Changing Shape of World History', *History and Theory*, Theme Issue 34 (1995), p. 11; Ashis Nandy, 'History's Forgotten Doubles', *History and Theory*, Theme Issue 34 (1995), p. 46.

15 Anders Stephanson, 'A Most Interesting Empire', paper delivered to the symposium, 'Reviewing the Cold War: Interpretation, Approaches, Theory', Norwegian Nobel Institute, 1998.

16 Berlin, *Four Essays on Liberty*, pp. 156–158. The literature on human rights and US foreign relations is considerable. See Noam Chomsky and Edward S. Herman, *The Political Economy of Human Rights* (Nottingham: Spokesman, 1979; and Montreal: Black Rose Press, 1979); David Louis Cingranelli, *Ethics, American Foreign Policy and the Third World* (New York: St. Martin's Press, 1993); David P. Forsyth, *Human Rights and U.S. Foreign Policy* (Gainsville: University Presses of Florida, 1988).

17 World Historians of the persuasion that economics is the driving force of history have tended to use the term 'world system', whereas those concerned principally with spirit, ideologies, faith and belief have often preferred the word 'ecumene'. See William H. McNeill, 'The Changing Shape of World History', *History and Theory*, Theme Issue 34 (1995), p. 14.

18 I try throughout to use US or United States to distinguish their identity from all the other Americans. At times, when discussing ideology, it is too awkward and 'American' is used.

19 Henry R. Luce, 'The American Century', *Life* (17 February 1941), p. 65.

20 Serge Ricard, 'The Exceptionalist Syndrome in U.S. Continental and Overseas Expansionism', in David K. Adams and Cornelis A. van Minnen (eds), *Reflections on American Exceptionalism* (Keele: Keele University Press, 1994), p. 73.

21 Filipe Fernandez-Armesto, *Millennium* (London: Bantam Press, 1995), p. 7.

22 McNeill, 'The Changing Shape of World History', *History and Theory*, p. 16.

23 Peter Novik, *That Noble Dream: The 'Objectivity Question' and the American Historical Profession* (Cambridge: Cambridge University Press, 1988), p. 4, discussing the ideas of Emile Durkheim, Georges Sorel and Claude Lévi-Strauss.

24 On the formation of collective memory see John Bodnar, *Remaking America: Public Memory, Commemoration, and Patriotism in the Twentieth Century* (Princeton: Princeton University Press, 1992); Paul Connerton, *How Societies Remember* (Cambridge: Cambridge University Press, 1989); Paula Hamilton, 'The Knife Edge: Debates about Memory and History', in Kate Daren Smith and Paula Hamilton (eds), *Memory and History in Twentieth Century Australia* (Melbourne: Oxford University Press, 1994); Patrick H. Hutton, *History as an Art of Memory* (Hanover: University of Vermont, 1993); Michael Kammen,

Mystic Chords of Memory: The Transformation of Tradition in American Culture (New York: Vintage, 1991); Jacques Le Goff, *History and Memory* (New York: Columbia University Press, 1992); David Thelen, 'Introduction', *The Journal of American History* 75, no. 4 (March 1989); Frances A. Yates, *The Art of Memory* (London: Pimlico, 1966).

25 Ashis Nandy, 'History's Forgotten Doubles', *History and Theory*, Theme Issue 34 (1995), p. 47.

26 Noam Chomsky, *Necessary Illusions: Thought Control in Democratic Societies* (Boston: South End Press, 1989), pp. 1–20. Chomsky relates that Walter Lippmann 'described a "revolution" in "the practice of democracy" as "the manufacture of consent" has become "a self-conscious art and a regular organ of popular government"'. And 'Reinhold Niebuhr argued that "rationality belongs to the cool observers," while "the proletarian" follows not reason but faith, based upon a crucial element of "necessary illusion"' (pp. 16–17). See also Jacques Ellul, *Propaganda: The Formation of Men's Attitudes* (New York: Vintage, 1973 [1965]); Herbert Marcuse, *One Dimensional Man: Studies in the Ideology of Advanced Industrial Society* (London: Routledge, 1994 [1964]).

27 Hobsbawm, *Nations and Nationalism*, p. 10; Joyce Appleby, Lynn Hunt and Margaret Jacob, *Telling the Truth about History* (New York: W. W. Norton, 1994), pp. 102–106; Said, *Culture and Imperialism*, p. xii.

28 Said, *Culture and Imperialism*, p. xiii.

29 Hunt, 'Ideology', in *Explaining*, pp. 193–194.

30 David Ryan, 'U.S. Ideology and Central American Revolutions in the Cold War', in Will Fowler (ed.), *Ideologues and Ideologies in Latin America* (Westport: Greenwood Press, 1997), pp. 105–124.

31 Edward W. Said, *Orientalism* (Harmondsworth: Penguin, 1995 edition), p. 333.

32 Richard H. Immerman, 'Psychology', in Hogan and Paterson (eds), *Explaining*, p. 160.

33 Said, *Culture and Imperialism*, p. xxviii.

34 The term is Benedict Anderson's.

35 Edward Said, *Culture and Imperialism* (London: Chatto and Windus, 1993), p. xiii; Joyce Appleby, Lynn Hunt and Margaret Jacob, *Telling the Truth About History* (New York: W. W. Norton, 1994), pp. 92–102; Garry Wills, *Lincoln at Gettysberg: The Words that Remade America* (New York: Touchstone, 1992), p. 38. This analysis is informed by Said's approach to identity. As he relates, via Vico, 'human history is made by human beings. Since the struggle for control over territory is part of that history, so too is the struggle over historical and social meaning.' It is necessary to make connections between the materialism of the first and the metaphysical qualities of the second. The development of culture for Said has necessitated the development 'of another different and competing *alter ego*. The construction of identity involves establishing opposites and "others" whose actuality is always subject to continuous interpretation and re-interpretation of their differences from "us"' (Edward W. Said, *Orientalism* (Harmondsworth: Penguin, 1995 (1978)), pp. 331–332).

36 Alex Callinicos, *Theories and Narratives: Reflections on the Philosophy of History* (Cambridge: Polity Press, 1995), p. 45; Alun Munslow, *Deconstructing History* (London: Routledge, 1997), pp. 9–11; Renan cited by Eric Hobsbawm, *Nations and Nationalism since 1780: Programme, Myth, Reality* (Cambridge: Canto, 1990), p. 12. See also Peter Novik, *That Noble Dream: The 'Objectivity Question' and the American Historical Profession* (Cambridge: Cambridge University Press, 1988).

37 Munslow, *Deconstructing History*, p. 13; Callinicos, *Theories and Narratives*, p. 51.
38 Edward Said, *Culture and Imperialism* (London: Chatto and Windus, 1993), p. xix.
39 Hunt, *Ideology*, p. 12.
40 Terry Eagleton, *Ideology: An Introduction* (London: Verso, 1991), pp. 18–19, 15.
41 Novik, *That Noble Dream*, pp. 61–62; Clifford Geertz, *The Interpretation of Cultures* (London: Fontana, 1993 [1973]), pp. 204–205.
42 Hunt, *Ideology*, p. 12.
43 Hunt, 'Ideology', p. 201.
44 Hunt, *Ideology*, pp. 125, 189; Louis Hartz, *The Liberal Tradition in America: An Interpretation of American Political Thought since the Revolution* (New York: Harcourt, Brace and Co., 1955), p. 289.
45 Serge Ricard, 'The Exceptionalist Syndrome in U.S. Continental and Overseas Expansionism', in David K. Adams and Cornelis A. van Minnen (eds), *Reflections on American Exceptionalism* (Keele: Keele University Press, 1994), p. 76.
46 Novik, *Noble Dream*, p. 552; Geertz, *Interpretation of Cultures*, p.5; Ricard, 'Exceptionalist Syndrome', p. 74; Hunt, *Ideology*, pp. 12, 189, 191. See also Anders Stephanson, *Manifest Destiny: American Expansion and the Empire of Right* (New York: Hill and Wang, 1995).
47 See Michael Sherry, *In the Shadow of War: The United States since the 1930s* (New Haven: Yale University Press, 1995); Eric Alterman, *Who Speaks for America: Why Democracy Matters in Foreign Policy* (Ithaca: Cornell University Press, 1998).
48 Novik, *That Noble Dream*, p. 7.
49 John Grey, *Isaiah Berlin* (London: HarperCollins, 1995), p. 77; Isaiah Berlin, *The Crooked Timber of Humanity: Chapters in the History of Ideas* (London: Fontana, 1991), p. 46; Ralf Dahrendorf, *Reflections on the Revolution in Europe* (London: Chatto and Windus, 1990), p. 37. See also Ngugi Wa Thiong'O, *Moving the Centre: The Struggle for Cultural Freedoms* (London: James Currey, 1993); Michael Ignatieff, *Isaiah Berlin: A Life* (London: Chatto and Windus, 1998); Ernest Gellner, *Conditions of Liberty: Civil Society and its Rivals* (Harmondsworth: Penguin, 1996 [1994]); Ben Okri, *A Way of Being Free* (London: Pheonix, 1998); Georg G. Iggers, *Historiography in the Twentieth Century: From Scientific Objectivity to the Postmodern Challenge* (Hanover: Wesleyan University Press, 1997).

Chapter 1: The empire for liberty

1 Walter LaFeber, The *American Search for Opportunity, 1865–1913* (Cambridge: Cambridge University Press, 1993), p. 237.
2 Michael Hunt, 'Traditions of American Diplomacy: From Colony to Great Power', in Gordon Martel (ed.), *American Foreign Relations Reconsidered* (London: Routledge, 1994), pp. 10–15.
3 Ibid., p. 10.
4 Marc Ferro, *Colonization: A Global History* (London: Routledge, 1997), p. 211.
5 The most recent and influential works are Theodore Draper, *A Struggle for Power: The American Revolution* (London: Abacus, 1996); Gordon S. Wood, *The Radicalism of the American Revolution* (New York: Vintage, 1991); Colin Bonwick, *The American Revolution* (London: Macmillan, 1991).
6 There is even the grammatical hurdle in the early US diplomacy. Lacking a sense of complete affinity with each other the reference to the United States

used to be made in the plural: the United States were or are The most significant point of departure, co-opting the differences came after the Civil War, when most rhetoric began to use the singular reference: the United States was or is . . . A plural unity was more pronounced after Lincoln's Gettysberg Address, a nationalism that could finally embrace the whole, at least in conceptual terms.

7 Ferro, *Colonization*, pp. 214–215.
8 Ernest Gellner, *Postmodernism, Reason and Religion* (London: Routledge, 1992), p. 52.
9 Anders Stephanson, *Manifest Destiny: American Expansion and the Empire of Right* (New York: Hill and Wang, 1995), p. 20. See also Eric Hobsbawm and Terence Ranger (eds), *The Invention of Tradition* (Cambridge: Cambridge University Press, 1983). Hobsbawm writes: 'invented tradition is taken to mean a set of practices, normally governed by overtly or tacitly accepted rules and of a ritual or symbolic nature, which seek to inculcate certain values and norms of behaviour by repetition, which automatically implies continuity with the past. In fact, where possible, they normally attempt to establish continuity with a suitable historic past.' In periods of constant social or political change it is not unusual, especially in the last two hundred years of enormous flux, to attempt to establish an aspect of life within the 'unchanging and invariant' (pp. 1–2). As Robert Hughes suggests, this may be a reason for the neo-classical architecture of the period. See also, Michael Kammen, *Mystic Chords of Memory: The Transformation of Tradition in American Culture* (New York: Vintage, 1993), esp. pp. 17–89.
10 Draper, *A Struggle for Power*; Wood, *The Radicalism of the American Revolution*.
11 Draper, *Struggle for Power*, p. 447.
12 Michael Hunt, *Ideology and U.S. Foreign Policy* (New Haven: Yale University Press, 1987), p. 20.
13 See Fernand Braudel, *Civilization and Capitalism: The Perspective of the World* (London: Fontana, 1985); Giovanni Arrighi, *The Long Twentieth Century: Money, Power, and the Origins of Our Times* (London: Verso, 1994); Andre Gunder Frank and Barry K. Gills (eds), *The World System: Five Hundred Years or Five Thousand?* (London: Routledge, 1993).
14 The Unanimous Declaration of the Thirteen United States of America, 4 July 1776, in Henry Steele Commager (ed.), *Documents of American History* (New York: Appleton-Century-Crofts, 1963), vol. I, p. 100
15 Ernest Gellner, *Postmodernism, Reason and Religion*, p. 52.
16 Seymour Martin Lipset, *American Exceptionalism: A Double-Edged Sword* (New York: W. W. Norton, 1996), pp. 77–79.
17 Stephanson, *Manifest Destiny*, p. 18.
18 Daniel Bell, *The End of Ideology: On the Exhaustion of Political Ideas in the Fifties* (New York: The Free Press, 1962); Francis Fukuyama, *The End of History and the Last Man* (Harmondsworth: Penguin, 1992).
19 Ricard, 'The Exceptionalist Syndrome', pp. 73–74.
20 Eric L. McKitrick, 'Did Jefferson Blunder?' *New York Review of Books* 37, no. 19 (6 December 1990), p. 57.
21 Edward Said, *Orientalism* (London: Penguin, 1995 edn), p. 333.
22 Hunt, *Ideology*, p. 12.
23 Novik, *That Noble Dream*, p. 4.
24 Gordon S. Wood, 'Disturbing the Peace', *New York Review of Books* 42, no. 10 (8 June 1995), pp. 19–20.

25 A. J. Ayer, *Thomas Paine*, p. 35; Bonwick, *The American Revolution*, p. 91; Rush cited by Wood, 'Disturbing the Peace', p. 19.

26 Francis Canavan, SJ, 'Thomas Paine', in Leo Strauss and Joseph Cropsey (eds), *History of Political Philosophy* (Chicago: University of Chicago Press, 1963, 1981 edn), p. 652; J. S. McClelland, *A History of Western Political Thought* (London: Routledge, 1996), p. 351.

27 Hunt, *Ideology*, pp. 19–20.

28 G. W. Hegel, translated by T. M. Knox as *Hegel's Philosophy of Right* (London: Oxford University Press, 1967), p. 219 (paragraph 351).

29 David M. Fitzsimons, 'Tom Paine's New World Order: Idealistic Internationalism in the Ideology of Early American Foreign Relations', *Diplomatic History* vol. 19, no. 4 (Fall 1995), p. 577.

30 Paine cited in ibid., p. 578.

31 Ibid., pp. 573–576.

32 Michael Foley, *American Political Ideas: Traditions and Usages* (Manchester: Manchester University Press, 1991), pp. 46–53; Walter LaFeber, 'The Tension between Democracy and Capitalism during the American Century', *Diplomatic History* vol. 23, no. 2 (Spring 1999), pp. 263–284; and response to the *Diplomatic History* Roundtable on the American Century on H-Diplo at http://www.h-net.msu.edu/logs/showlogs.cgi?list = h-diplo&file = h-diplo.log9904d/2& ent = 0, 22 April 1999.

33 John Grey, *False Dawn: The Delusions of Global Capitalism* (London: Granta, 1998), p. 2.

34 McClelland, *A History of Western Political Thought*, p. 357.

35 Ibid., p. 351.

36 Eric Alterman, *Who Speaks for America: Why Democracy Matters in Foreign Policy* (Ithaca: Cornell University Press, 1998).

37 Hofstadter (and Madison cited by) Richard Hofstadter, *The American Political Tradition and the Men Who Made It* (New York: Vintage, 1989 [1948]), pp. 16–18.

38 McClelland, *A History of Western Political Thought*, p. 361.

39 Madison, Paper 10, James Madison, Alexander Hamilton and John Jay, *The Federalist Papers*, ed. Isaac Kramnick (Harmondsworth: Penguin, 1987 [1788]), pp. 124–128.

40 Herbert Marcuse, *One-Dimensional Man* (London: Routledge, 1991, originally 1964); Francis Fukuyama, *The End of History and the Last Man* (Harmondsworth: Penguin, 1992); Noam Chomsky, *Manufacturing Consent: The Political Economy of the Mass Media* (New York: Pantheon, 1988).

41 Reinhold Niebuhr, *The Irony of American History* (New York: Charles Scribner's Sons, 1952), pp. 135–141.

42 Merrill D. Peterson, *The Jefferson Image in the American Mind* (New York: Oxford University Press, 1962).

43 Ibid., p. 269.

44 Hunt, *Ideology and US Foreign Policy*, pp. 46–91; David S. Painter, 'Explaining U.S. Relations with the Third World', *Diplomatic History* 19, no. 3 (Summer 1995), p. 527.

45 Bradford Perkins, *The Creation of a Republican Empire, 1776–1865*, pp. 111–113, 137–143; LaFeber, *The American Age*.

46 Walter LaFeber, 'Jefferson and an American Foreign Policy', in Peter S. Onuf, *Jeffersonian Legacies*, p. 370.

47 John Quincey Adams, cited in Paul A. Varg (Baltimore: Penguin, 1970), *Foreign Policies of the Founding Fathers*, p. 147.

48 Arthur Schlesinger, *The Cycles of American History* (Harmondsworth: Penguin, 1986), pp. 136–139.
49 William Appleman Williams, *Empire as a Way of Life* (New York: OUP, 1980), pp. 57–61.
50 James R. Sofka, 'The Jeffersonian Idea of National Security: Commerce, the Atlantic Balance of Power, and the Barbary War, 1786–1805', *Diplomatic History* vol. 21, no. 4 (Fall 1997), pp. 519–544.
51 Jürgen Osterhammel, *Colonialism: A Theoretical Overview* (Princeton: Markus Wiener, 1997), pp. 5–6.
52 Kammen, *Mystic Chords of Memory*, p. 13.
53 Stephanson, *Manifest Destiny*, p. 17.
54 Ricard, 'The Exceptionalist Syndrome', pp. 73–74.
55 Said, *Culture and Imperialism*, p. 7.
56 Fitzsimons, 'Tom Paine's New World Order', p. 574.
57 The White House, *A National Security Strategy of Engagement and Enlargement*, July 1994.
58 Geir Lundestad, '"Empire by Invitation" in the American Century', *Diplomatic History* vol. 23, no. 2 (Spring 1999), pp. 189–217; see also Geir Lundestad, *The American Empire* (London: Oxford University Press, 1990).
59 Perkins, *The Creation of a Republican Empire*, p. 232.
60 Kammen, *Mystic Chords of Memory*, p. 13.
61 Louis Hartz, *The Liberal Tradition in America: An Interpretation of American Political Thought since the Revolution* (New York: Harcourt, Brace and Co., 1955), pp. 189–190.

Chapter 2: Spheres of influence

1 Cecil V. Crabb, *The Doctrines of American Foreign Policy: Their Meaning, Role, and Future* (Baton Rouge: Louisiana State University, 1982), p. 10; Dexter Perkins, *Hands Off: A History of the Monroe Doctrine* (Boston: Little, Brown and Co., 1946).
2 Crabb, *Doctrines of American Foreign Policy*, p. 2.
3 President James Monroe, Seventh Annual Message to Congress, 2 December 1823, in Henry Steele Commager (ed.), *Documents of American History* (New York: Appleton-Century-Crofts, 1963), vol. 1, p. 236.
4 Perkins, *Hands Off*, pp. 17–19.
5 Richard Hofstadter, *The American Political Tradition: And the Men Who Made It* (New York: Vintage, 1989, [1948]), p. 5.
6 Hunt, *Ideology*, p. 12.
7 Novik, *That Noble Dream*, p. 4.
8 Bradford Perkins, *The Creation of a Republican Empire, 1776–1865* (Cambridge: Cambridge University Press, 1993), pp. 169, 155–156.
9 H. U. Addington to George Canning (No. 1), Washington, 5 January 1824, FO 5/185, in C. K. Webster (ed.), *Britain and the Independence of Latin America 1812–1830: Select Documents from the Foreign Office Archives* (New York: Octagon Books, 1970), p. 508.
10 Perkins, *Hands Off*, p. 57.
11 John Quincy Adams, *The Diary of John Quincy Adams, 1794–1845*, Allan Nevins (ed.) (New York: Longmans, Green and Co., 1929), p. 313.
12 Thomas Jefferson to James Monroe, 24 October 1823, in Paul Leicester Ford (ed.), *The Works of Thomas Jefferson*, vol. XI (New York: G. P. Putnam's Sons, 1905), p. 318. And Crabb, *Doctrines of American Foreign Policy*, p. 14.

13 Thomas Jefferson to James Monroe, 24 October 1823, in Ford (ed.), *The Works of Thomas Jefferson*, vol. XI, p. 318.

14 See more broadly, David Gress, *From Plato to NATO: The Idea of the West and its Opponents* (New York: The Free Press, 1998).

15 John Quincy Adams, Address, 4 July 1821, in Walter LaFeber (ed.), *John Quincy Adams and the American Continental Empire: Letters, Papers and Speeches* (Chicago: Quadrangle Books, 1965), p. 45.

16 Perkins, *Republican Empire*, pp. 160–163.

17 Monroe, 2 December 1823, in Commager, *Documents*, p. 236.

18 *Memoirs of John Quincy Adams*, in LaFeber (ed.), *John Quincy Adams*, pp. 39–41.

19 Ibid., p. 37.

20 See Joan Hoff, 'The American Century: From Sarajevo to Sarajevo', *Diplomatic History* vol. 23, no. 2 (Spring 1999), pp. 285–319.

21 Lars Schoultz, *Beneath the United States: A History of U.S. Policy toward Latin America* (Cambridge, Mass.: Harvard University Press, 1998), p. 9; William Appleman Williams, *Empire as a Way of Life* (New York: Oxford University Press, 1980), pp. 64–65.

22 George Canning cited in Perkins, *Hands Off*, p. 37.

23 Jefferson to Monroe, 24 October 1823, in Ford (ed.), *Works of Thomas Jefferson*, p. 318; James Madison to James Monroe, 30 October 1823, in Gaillard Hunt (ed.), *The Writings of James Madison, 1819–1836*, vol. 9 (New York: G. P. Putnam's Sons, 1910), pp. 157–159; Adams, *Diary*, pp. 304–313.

24 H. U. Addington to George Canning, No. 25, 1 December 1823, in Webster (ed.), *Britain and the Independence*, p. 506.

25 Robert Lansing, memorandum, 11 June 1914, *FRUS, The Lansing Papers 1914–1920*, vol. II (Washington, D.C.: Government Printing Office, 1940), p. 462; Gabriel Kolko, *Main Currents in Modern American History* (New York: Harper and Row, 1976), p. 47; Perkins, *Republican Empire*, pp. 160, 163.

26 Jefferson to Monroe, 24 October 1823, *Thomas Jefferson*, p. 320; Madison to Monroe, 30 October 1823, *James Madison*, p. 159; Adams to Nelson, 28 April 1823, in LaFeber (ed.), *John Quincy Adams*, pp. 129–130; Adams, *Diary*, p. 302. See Noam Chomsky, *Year 501: The Conquest Continues* (London: Verso, 1993), p. 143.

27 Perkins, *Hands Off*, p. 50 and ff. 51–62 for explanation of the European situation.

28 President James Monroe, Seventh Annual Message, 2 December 1823, in LaFeber, *John Quincy Adams*, p. 114.

29 Perkins, *Hands Off*, pp. 63–64.

30 LaFeber, *The American Age*, p. 85; Schoultz, *Beneath the United States*, p. 9; Dexter Perkins, *The Monroe Doctrine, 1823–1826* (Cambridge, Mass.: Harvard University Press, 1927); Dexter Perkins, 'Defense of Commerce and Ideals', in Thomas G. Paterson and Dennis Merrill (eds), *Major Problems in American Foreign Relations, to 1920*, vol. I (Lexington: D. C. Heath, 1995), pp. 185–186.

31 Perkins, *Hands Off*, pp. 55–60.

32 Gaston Nerval, *Autopsy of the Monroe Doctrine: The Strange Story of Inter-American Relations* (New York: Macmillan, 1934), pp. 127–128.

33 Attributed to Egaña, 'Project of a Declaration of Rights of the People of Chile', 1810, and Don Manuel Torres to John Quincy Adams, 1821, in Nerval, *Autopsy*, pp. 130–133.

34 Secretary of State Clay, 1826, is cited by Nerval, p. 151; his quotation is in *Autopsy*, pp. 153–154.

35 James William Park, *Latin American Underdevelopment: A History of Perspectives in the United States, 1870–1965* (Baton Rouge: Louisiana State University

Press, 1995), p. 11; Walter LaFeber, 'The Evolution of the Monroe Doctrine from Monroe to Reagan', in Lloyd C. Gardner (ed.), *Redefining the Past: Essays in Diplomatic History in Honor of William Appleman Williams* (Corvallis: Oregon State University, 1986), p. 127; Hunt, *Ideology*, p. 62.

36 LaFeber, 'The Evolution of the Monroe Doctrine', p. 124.

37 Ibid., pp. 123, 132.

Chapter 3: Imperialisms

1 Walter LaFeber, *The New Empire: An Interpretation of American Expansion 1860–1898* (Ithaca: Cornell University Press, 1963); David Healy, *US Expansionism: The Imperialist Urge in the 1890s* (Madison: University of Wisconsin Press, 1970), pp. 9–33.

2 David Ryan 'Colonialism and Hegemony in Latin America: An Introduction', *The International History Review* vol. 21, no. 2 (June 1999), pp. 287–296.

3 Edward Said, *Culture and Imperialism* (London: Chatto and Windus, 1993), p. 8; Joseph A. Fry, 'Imperialism, American Style, 1890–1916', in Gordon Martel (ed.), *American Foreign Relations Reconsidered, 1890–1993* (London: Routledge, 1994), p. 67; Jürgen Osterhammel, *Colonialism: A Theoretical Overview* (Princeton: Markus Wiener, 1997), p. 21. See also: Healy, *US Expansionism*; Ernest R. May, *Imperial Democracy: The Emergence of America as a Great Power* (New York: Harper and Row, 1961); James A. Field, 'American Imperialism: The Worst Chapter in Almost Any Book', *American Historical Review* vol. 83 (1978).

4 Stephanson, *Manifest Destiny*, p. 67.

5 Cary Fraser, 'Afterword', in Ryan and Pungong (eds), *United States and Decolonization*, pp. 230–232; see also, Bradford Perkins, *The Great Rapprochement: England and the United States, 1895–1914* (London: Victor Gollancz, 1969), pp. 3–11, 31–63.

6 Stephanson, *Manifest Destiny*, p. 67.

7 Perkins, *The Great Rapprochement*, pp. 10–11.

8 Henry Cabot Lodge cited within Hunt quotation, *Ideology*, p. 37. See also Walter LaFeber, *The American Search for Opportunity, 1865–1913*.

9 LaFeber, 'The American View of Decolonization, 1776 to 1920', in Ryan and Pungong (eds), *The United States and Decolonization*, pp. 24–40.

10 Paul Kennedy, *The Rise and Fall of the Great Powers: Economic Change and Military Conflict from 1500 to 2000* (London: Fontana, 1989), pp. 250–252, 315–318; Howard Zinn, *A People's History of the United States* (London: Longman, 1980), p. 290; Kolko, *Main Currents*, p. 35.

11 For divergent views see: Joseph A. Fry, 'From Open Door to World Systems: Economic Interpretations of Late Nineteenth Century American Foreign Relations', *Pacific Historical Review* vol. 65, no. 2 (May 1996), pp. 277–303; Arthur M. Schlesinger, *Cycles of American History* (Harmondsworth: Penguin, 1986), pp. 118–162; William Appleman Williams, *The Tragedy of American Diplomacy* (New York: Delta, 1959), pp. 16–50.

12 Ronald Steel, *Temptations of a Superpower* (Cambridge, Mass.: Harvard University Press, 1995), p. 50.

13 See Emily S. Rosenberg, *Spreading the American Dream: American Economic and Cultural Expansion, 1890–1945* (New York: Hill and Wang, 1982), pp. 38–62.

14 LaFeber, 'The American View of Decolonization', and Michael Hunt, 'The Decolonization Puzzle in US Policy', in Ryan and Pungong, *The United States and Decolonization*, pp. 207–229.

15 LaFeber, *The American Search for Opportunity, 1865–1913*; Arthur Schlesinger, *The Imperial Presidency* (New York: Houghton, 1992).

16 LaFeber, *New Empire*, p. 82.

17 José Martí, cited in Laurie Johnston, 'The Road to Our America', in Ryan and Pungong, *United States and Decolonization*, pp. 41–62.

18 Ernest R. May, *Imperial Democracy: The Emergence of America as a Great Power* (New York: Harper and Row, 1961), p. 243.

19 LaFeber, *American Search for Opportunity*, pp. 129–149.

20 Wood cited in LaFeber, *The American Age*, p. 197.

21 Tony Smith, *America's Mission: The United States and the Worldwide Struggle for Democracy in the Twentieth Century* (Princeton: Princeton University Press, 1994), pp. 37–45; Stanley Karnow, *In Our Image: America's Empire in the Philippines* (London: Century. 1990), pp. 78–138.

22 Smith, *America's Mission*, p. 42.

23 Stephanson, *Manifest Destiny*, p. 78.

24 Peterson, *The Jefferson Image*, pp. 266–267; Ryan, 'US Expansionism', p. 185.

25 Hunt, *Ideology*, p. 39; Christopher Hitchens, *Blood, Class, and Nostalgia: Anglo-American Ironies* (London: Chatto and Windus, 1990), pp. 63–66; Stephanson, *Manifest Destiny*, pp. 79–83.

26 Robert L. Beisner, 'The Anti-Imperialist Case and Failure', in Thomas G. Paterson and Stephen G. Rabe (eds), *Imperial Surge: The United States Abroad, the 1890s–Early 1900s* (Lexington: D. C. Heath, 1992), pp. 111–126.

27 LaFeber, *Opportunity*, p. 237.

28 Hunt, *Ideology*, p. 39.

29 Ryan, 'US Expansionism', p. 188. See also the various contributions on democracy and capitalism in 'The American Century: A Roundtable', *Diplomatic History* vol. 23, no. 2 (Spring 1999).

30 LaFeber, *The New Empire*, pp. 63–72; Stephanson, *Manifest Destiny*, pp. 81–82. Frederick Jackson Turner, *The Frontier in American History* (New York: Holt, Rinehart and Winston, 1920); see also Fukuyama, *The End of History and the Last Man*.

31 LaFeber, *The New Empire*, pp. 80–95.

32 Rosenberg, *Spreading the American Dream*, pp. 38–54.

33 Ibid., pp. 50–62; see also, David Healy, *US Expansionism: The Imperialist Urge in the 1890s* (Madison: University of Wisconsin Press, 1970), pp. 194–209.

34 William Appleman Williams, *Empire as a Way of Life* (New York: Oxford University Press, 1980).

35 Fry, 'Imperialism, American Style, 1890–1916', p. 63; see also, Louis A. Perez, 'Dependency', in Hogan and Paterson (eds), *Explaining*, pp. 99–110.

36 Williams, *Tragedy*, pp. 37–39; Zinn, *A People's History*, p. 294; Thomas J. McCormick, *America's Half Century: United States Foreign Policy in the Cold War* (Baltimore: Johns Hopkins University Press, 1989), p. 19.

37 Kennedy, *The Great Powers*, p. 317; Cohen cited in Crabb, *Doctrines of American Foreign Policy*, p. 72 n. 33; see also Kolko, *Main Currents*; Warren I. Cohen, *America's Response to China: A History of Sino-American Relations* (New York: Columbia University Press, 1990), pp. 26–54; Akira Iriye, *Across the Pacific: An Inner History of American–East Asian Relations* (New York: Harcourt, 1967), pp. 82–85.

38 Williams, *Tragedy*, p. 43; McCormick, *America's Half Century*, p. 18.

39 Secretary of State John Hay, Circular letters of 6 September 1899, 20 March 1900 and 3 July 1900, in Henry Steele Commager (ed.), *Documents of American*

History, vol. 2, pp. 9–11; Hunt, 'Traditions of American Diplomacy', in Martel (ed.), *Reconsidering*, pp. 7–8.

40 Hunt, 'Traditions of American Diplomacy', in Martel (ed.), *Reconsidering*, p. 8.

41 Williams, *Tragedy of American Diplomacy*, pp. 36–50.

42 Zinn, *A People's History*, p. 290; Hunt, *Ideology*, p. 20; Perkins, *Republican Empire*, p. 232.

43 LaFeber, *Opportunity*, p. 237; David Held, *Prospects for Democracy: North, South, East, West* (Cambridge: Polity Press, 1993), pp. 27–30; William Pfaff, *The Wrath of Nations: Civilization and the Furies of Nationalism* (New York: Simon and Schuster, 1993), p. 161; Ryan, 'US Expansionism', p. 188.

Chapter 4: Constructing the American Century

1 See Richard Collin, *Theodore Roosevelt, Culture, Diplomacy, and Expansion* (Baton Rouge: Louisiana State University, 1985); John Milton Cooper, *The Warrior and the Priest: Woodrow Wilson and Theodore Roosevelt* (New York: Norton, 1983); Walter LaFeber, *The American Search for Opportunity* (Cambridge: Cambridge University Press, 1993); Robert H. Ferrell, *Woodrow Wilson and World War I, 1917–1921* (New York: Harper and Row, 1985); Lloyd C. Gardner, *Safe for Democracy: The Anglo-American Response to Revolution, 1913–1923* (Oxford: Oxford University Press, 1987); Akira Iriye, *The Globalization of America, 1913–1945* (Cambridge: Cambridge University Press, 1993); Arthur S. Link, *Wilson the Diplomatist: A Look at his Major Foreign Policies* (Chicago: Quadrangle Books, 1957); idem., *The Diplomacy of World Power, the United States 1889–1920* (London: Edward Arnold, 1970); Emily Rosenberg, *Spreading the American Dream: American Economic and Cultural Expansion, 1890–1945* (New York: Hill and Wang, 1982); Tony Smith, *America's Mission* (Princeton: Princeton University Press, 1994).

2 Rosenberg, *Spreading the American Dream*, pp. 38–42.

3 Walter LaFeber, *The American Search for Opportunity, 1865–1913* (Cambridge: Cambridge University Press, 1993), p. 184.

4 In wider context see also V. G. Kiernan, *Imperialism and Its Contradictions* (New York: Routledge, 1995), pp. 121–143.

5 Joan Hoff, 'The American Century: From Sarajevo to Sarajevo', *Diplomatic History* vol. 23, no. 2 (Spring 1999), pp. 285–319.

6 Stephanson, *Manifest Destiny*, p. 106.

7 Walter LaFeber, *The Panama Canal: The Crisis in Historical Perspective* (New York: Oxford University Press, 1989), p. 45.

8 Frank Ninkovich, 'Theodore Roosevelt: Civilization as Ideology', *Diplomatic History* 10, no. 3 (Summer 1986), pp. 222–230. On the 'Imperial Presidency' see Arthur M. Schlesinger, *The Imperial Presidency* (Boston: Houghton Mifflin, 1973, 1989).

9 See Fukuyama, *The End of History and the Last Man*; and Theodore Roosevelt, *American Ideals: The Strenuous Life, Realizable Ideals* (New York: Charles Scribner's Sons, 1926). For Roosevelt, 'it was the journey rather than the destination, the unending quest for change, the restless pursuit of happiness rather than its ultimate consumption, that both limited and extended the possibilities of civilized attainment. Thus the final victory of civilization would actually be, like death, "the final defeat"' (Ninkovich, 'Theodore Roosevelt: Civilization as Ideology', p. 231).

10 Stephanson, *Manifest Destiny*, p. 106. See Bradford Perkins, *The Great Rapprochement: England and the United States 1895–1914* (London: Victor Gollancz, 1969).
11 Stephanson, *Manifest Destiny*, pp. 83–97.
12 See, for instance, Lars Schoultz, *Beneath the United States*, pp. 176–204; Perkins, *Hands Off*, pp. 228–275; Park, *Latin American Underdevelopment*, pp. 63–99.
13 Theodore Roosevelt, Annual Message, 6 December 1904, in Commager, *Documents*, p. 33.
14 Fry, 'Imperialism', pp. 53, 63.
15 Ibid.
16 Bradford Burns, 'The Continuity of the National Period', in Jan Knippers Black (ed.), *Latin America: Its Problems and Its Promise* (Boulder: Westview, 1991), pp. 67–68.
17 William E. Dodd, The Monroe Doctrine, A Brief Report, Inquiry Document no. 135, 2 February 1918, microfilm, NARA.
18 Roosevelt, *American Ideals*, p. 168.
19 Kennedy, *Great Powers*, p. 252.
20 Giovanni Arrighi, *The Long Twentieth Century: Money, Power, and the Origins of Our Times* (London: Verso, 1994), pp. 58–60.
21 Ibid., p. 61.
22 Kennedy, *Great Powers*, pp. 249–252, 312–316; Rosenberg, *Spreading the American Dream*, pp. 38–62.
23 Gabriel Kolko, *Main Currents in Modern American History* (New York: Harper and Row, 1976), pp. 34–64; Robert Lansing, 'Present Nature and Extent of the Monroe Doctrine, and its Need for Restatement', 11 June 1914, *FRUS: The Lansing Papers*, vol. 2, pp. 460–463.
24 LaFeber, *Inevitable Revolutions*, p. 52.
25 *The Messages and Papers of Woodrow Wilson* (New York: The Review of Reviews Corporation, 1924), p. 355; Woodrow Wilson, *Why We Are at War: Messages to the Congress and the American People* (New York: Harper and Brothers, 1917), p. 55; See also Walter LaFeber, 'The American View of Decolonization, 1776 to 1920: An Ironic Legacy', in David Ryan and Victor Pungong (eds), *The United States and Decolonization*.
26 Smith, *America's Mission*, pp. 84–87; Wilson's Address to Congress stating the War Aims and Peace Terms of the United States, 8 January 1918, *The Messages and Papers of Woodrow Wilson*, pp. 464–470.
27 Tony Smith, 'Making the World Safe for Democracy in the American Century', *Diplomatic History* vol. 23, no. 2 (Spring 1999), p. 178.
28 Smith, *America's Mission*, pp. 87–89.
29 Lloyd C. Gardner, *Safe for Democracy: The Anglo-American Response to Revolution, 1913–1923* (Oxford: Oxford University Press, 1987), p. 122.
30 Eric J. Hobsbawm, *Nations and Nationalism since 1780: Programme, Myth, Reality* (Cambridge: Canto, 1990), pp. 131–136.
31 Clark, *Globalization and Fragmentation*, pp. 56–57.
32 Arrighi, *The Long Twentieth Century*, p. 64.
33 Both Wilson and Lenin competed for global influence. They were both anti-imperialist, therefore challenging the European centres from the periphery; both sought to end the war; both were in favour of a particular conception of democracy; both promoted self-determination, of different varieties; and both provided ethnocentric visions of development as universalist in application (Clark, *Globalization and Fragmentation*, p. 64).

34 Lloyd C. Gardner, *Safe for Democracy: The Anglo-American Response to Revolution, 1913–1923* (Oxford: Oxford University Press, 1987), pp. 160–161; McClelland, *History of Western Political Thought*, p. 601; Mark Sandle, *A Short History of Soviet Socialism* (London: UCL, 1998), pp. 59–71.

35 Alan Cassels, *Ideology and International Relations in the Modern World* (London: Routledge, 1996), pp. 146–152.

36 Stephanson, *Manifest Destiny*, p. 118; Cassels, *Ideology*, p. 147.

37 LaFeber, *The American Age*, pp. 307–309.

38 Arrighi, *The Long Twentieth Century*, p. 65.

39 Hartz, *The Liberal Tradition*, p. 295.

40 James P. Young, *Reconsidering American Liberalism: The Troubled Odyssey of the Liberal Idea* (Boulder: Westview, 1996), pp. 152–157; Gardner, *Safe for Democracy*, pp. 38–41; Woodrow Wilson, *The New Freedom: A Call for the Emancipation of the Generous Energies of a People* (Englewood Cliffs: Prentice Hall, 1961 [1913]); Arrighi, *The Long Twentieth Century*, p. 293.

41 McCormick, *America's Half-Century*, p. 21; Woodrow Wilson, Address Before the Southern Commercial Congress at Mobile, Alabama, 27 October 1913, *The Messages and Papers of Woodrow Wilson*, pp. 35–36; see also, E. M. Hugh-Jones, *Woodrow Wilson and American Liberalism* (London: English Universities Press, 1947), pp. 180–183.

42 Cingranelli, *Ethics*, pp. 109–118.

43 Gardner, *Safe for Democracy*, pp. 114–115.

44 Clark, *Globalization and Fragmentation*, pp. 58–59.

45 LaFeber, *Inevitable Revolutions*, p. 109.

46 Kennedy, *Great Powers*, pp. 353–354.

47 Paul A. C. Koistinen, *Mobilizing for Modern War: The Political Economy of American Warfare 1865–1919* (Lawrence: University Press of Kansas, 1997), pp. 297–298; Michael S. Sherry, *in the Shadow of War: The United States since the 1930s* (New Haven: Yale University Press, 1995).

48 Clark, *Globalization and Fragmentation*, pp. 57–58; Rosenberg, *Spreading the American Dream*, pp. 63–86; Michael J. Hogan, 'Corporatism', in Hogan and Paterson (eds), *Explaining the History of American Foreign Relations*, p. 230.

49 Clark, *Globalization and Fragmentation*, p. 57; Immanuel Wallerstein, *Geopolitics and Geoculture: Essays on the Changing World-System* (Cambridge: Cambridge University Press, 1991), p. 4.

50 Rosenberg, *Spreading the American Dream*, p. 86.

Chapter 5: Arsenal for democracy and self-determination?

1 Warren F. Kimball, *The Juggler: Franklin Roosevelt as Wartime Statesman* (Princeton: Princeton University Press, 1991), pp. 8–10; Isaiah Berlin, *The Sense of Reality: Studies in Ideas and Their History* (London: Chatto and Windus, 1996), p. 47.

2 Walter LaFeber, 'The Tension between Democracy and Capitalism during the American Century', and Bruce Cumings, 'The American Century and the Third World', *Diplomatic History* vol. 23, no. 2 (Spring 1999), pp. 263–284 and 355–370.

3 Terry Eagleton, *Ideology: An Introduction* (London: Verso, 1991), pp. 18–19, 15.

4 Tony Smith, *America's Mission: The United States and the Worldwide Struggle for Democracy in the Twentieth Century* (Princeton: Princeton University Press, 1994), p. 123. Franklin Roosevelt is cited in Smith, ibid.

5 See Phil Paine, 'Democracy's Place in World History', *Journal of World History* 4, no. 1 (Spring 1993), pp. 23–45.

6 Kwame Nkrumah cited in Tony Spybey, *Social Change, Development and Dependency: Modernity, Colonialism and the Development of the West* (Cambridge: Polity Press, 1992), p. 168. A similar observation had been made much earlier by Cuban patriot and revolutionary, José Martí: 'The nation that buys, commands. The nation that sells, serves. It is necessary to balance trade in order to guarantee liberty. The nation eager to die sells to a single nation, and the one eager to save itself sells to more than one. A country's excessive influence over the commerce of another becomes political influence' (Laurie Johnston, 'The Road to Our America: The United States in Latin America and the Caribbean', in David Ryan and Victor Pungong (eds), *The United States and Decolonization*).

7 Kimball, *Juggler*, pp. 11–13; Robert A. Divine, *Second Chance: The Triumph of Internationalism in America During World War II* (New York: Atheneum, 1967), *passim*; Smith, *America's Mission*, p. 123.

8 Smith, *America's Mission*, p. 124; Norman Davies, 'The Misunderstood War', *The New York Review of Books* 41, no. 11 (9 June 1994), p. 20; Mark A. Stoler, 'A Half-Century of Conflict: Interpretations of U.S. World War II Diplomacy', in Michael J. Hogan, *America in the World: The Historiography of American Foreign Relations since 1941* (Cambridge: Cambridge University Press, 1995), p. 172.

9 Franklin Roosevelt, 'Hands off the Western Hemisphere', 14 April 1939; The 'Four Freedoms Speech', 6 January 1941, and the Atlantic Charter, 14 August 1941, in Commager, *Documents*, vol. 2, pp. 414–415, 446–449, 451.

10 George Kennan, *American Diplomacy 1900–1950* (Chicago: University of Chicago Press, 1951).

11 Hunt, *Ideology*, p. 147.

12 Declaration on Liberated Europe, included in the Protocol of Proceedings of Crimea Conference, in Commager, *Documents*, vol. 2, p. 489.

13 Lloyd C. Gardner, *Spheres of Influence: The Partition of Europe, from Munich to Yalta* (London: John Murray, 1993), p. x.

14 Lloyd C. Gardner, in Ernest R. May (ed.), *American Cold War Strategy: Interpreting NSC 68* (Boston: Bedford Books, 1993), p. 148. Given the deindustrialised state of the Soviet economy, the growth rates appear somewhat exaggerated.

15 LaFeber, *America, Russia, and the Cold War*, p. 9; Thomas J. McCormick, *America's Half-Century: United States Foreign Policy in the Cold War* (Baltimore: Johns Hopkins University Press, 1989), pp. 29–30.

16 Lloyd C. Gardner, *Spheres of Influence: The Partition of Europe, from Munich to Yalta* (London: John Murray, 1993), p. 25. See also Herbert Hoover, *American Individualism* (New York: Doubleday, 1922).

17 McCormick, *America's Half-Century*, pp. 30–32.

18 Sumner Welles, 'Commercial Policy after the War', address before the National Foreign Trade Convention, New York, 7 October 1941 in Sumner Welles, *The World of the Four Freedoms* (New York: Hutchinson and Co. 1943), pp. 16–19.

19 William Appleman Williams, *Empire as a Way of Life: An Essay on the Causes and Character of America's Present Predicament along with a Few Thoughts about an Alternative* (New York: Oxford University Press, 1980), pp. 156–162.

20 Gardner, *Spheres of Influence*, p. 18. See also Sumner Welles, *The Time for Decision* (London: Hamish Hamilton, 1944), pp. 61–118.

21 David Reynolds, 'Roosevelt, Churchill, and the Wartime Anglo-American Alliance, 1939–1945: Towards a New Synthesis', in Wm Roger Louis and Hedley Bull (eds), *The 'Special Relationship': Anglo-American Relations since 1945* (Oxford: Clarendon Press, 1989), p. 18.
22 Jürgen Osterhammel, *Colonialism: A Theoretical Overview* (Princeton: Marcus Wiener, 1997), pp. 115–116.
23 President Franklin Roosevelt, State of the Union Address (The Four Freedoms Speech), 6 January 1941, in Commager (ed.), *Documents of American History*, vol. 2, pp. 446–449.
24 The Atlantic Charter, 14 August 1941, ibid., p. 451.
25 President Roosevelt, 'The Light of Democracy Must be Kept Burning', 15 March 1941, in *Public Papers and Addresses of Franklin D. Roosevelt*, vol. 10 (1941) (New York: Russell and Russell, 1941), pp. 60–69.
26 Reynolds, 'Roosevelt, Churchill, and the Wartime Anglo-American Alliance', p. 18.
27 Kimball, *The Juggler*, p. 130.
28 Ibid., pp. 129–145.
29 Ibid., p. 144.
30 Ibid., p. 130; Paul Orders, '"Adjusting to a New Period in World History": Franklin Roosevelt and European Colonialism', in Ryan and Pungong (eds), *The United States and Decolonization*, pp. 63–84. For more on the debate see essays by Victor Pungong, Lloyd Gardner and John Kent in that volume.
31 Clark, *Globalization and Fragmentation*, p. 119.
32 Hoff, 'The American Century', *Diplomatic History*, p. 297.
33 Gardner, *Economic Aspects of New Deal Diplomacy*, p. 283.
34 Eric Hobsbawm, *The Age of Extremes* (London: Michael Joseph, 1994), pp. 200–203; Gardner, *Economic Aspects of New Deal Diplomacy*, pp. 175–176.
35 McCormick, *America's Half Century*, p. 33.
36 Lloyd C. Gardner, *Economic Aspects of New Deal Diplomacy* (Madison: University of Wisconsin Press, 1964), pp. 276–280.
37 See John Kent, 'The United States and the Decolonization of Black Africa 1945–1963', Walter LaFeber, 'The American View of Decolonization, 1776 to 1920: An Ironic Legacy', and my 'The United States, Decolonization and the World System', in Ryan and Pungong (eds), *The United States and Decolonization*, pp. 1–23.
38 Cary Fraser, 'Understanding American Policy towards the Decolonization of European Empires, 1945–64', *Diplomacy and Statecraft* vol. 3, no. 1 (1992), pp. 105–107.
39 On this point see Kent, 'The United States and the Decolonization of Black Africa 1945–1963', in Ryan and Pungong, *United States and Decolonization*, pp. 168–187; and Abbott Gleason, *Totalitarianism: The Inner History of the Cold War* (New York: Oxford University Press, 1995), pp. 72–81.
40 Policy Planning Staff (Kennan), 'Review of Current Trends U.S. Foreign Policy', PPS/23, 24 February 1948, *FRUS*, 1948, vol. 1, part 2, p. 526.
41 Robert J. McMahon, 'Towards a Post-Colonial Order: Truman Administration Policies toward South and Southeast Asia', in Michael J. Lacey (ed.), *The Truman Presidency* (Cambridge: Cambridge University Press, 1989), p. 343.
42 Lloyd Gardner, 'How We "Lost" Vietnam, 1940–1954', in Ryan and Pungong (eds), *The United States and Decolonization*, pp. 121–139
43 Summary, 'Ho Chi Minh: Asian Tito?' Pentagon Papers, in Williams *et al* (eds), *America in Vietnam: A Documentary History* (New York: W. W. Norton, 1989), pp. 93–97.

44 US Ambassador in France, Caffery, to the Secretary of State, 13 March 1945, in William Appleman Williams, Thomas McCormick, Lloyd Gardner and Walter LaFeber (eds), *America in Vietnam: A Documentary History* (New York: W. W. Norton, 1989), pp. 61–62.

45 Noam Chomsky, *On Power and Ideology* (Boston: South End Press, 1987), p. 10.

46 Dennis Merrill, 'The Ironies of History: The United States and the Decolonization of India', in Ryan and Pungong, *United States and Decolonization*, pp. 102–120.

47 McMahon, 'Towards a Post-Colonial Order', pp. 363–364.

48 David Ryan, 'Colonialism and Hegemony in Latin America: An Introduction', *The International History Review* vol. 21, no. 2 (June 1999), pp. 287–296.

49 David Reynolds, 'Beyond Bipolarity in Space and Time', in Michael J. Hogan (ed.), *The End of the Cold War: Its Meaning and Implications* (Cambridge: Cambridge University Press, 1992), pp. 252–256.

50 Ibid., p. 255.

51 David Gress, *From Plato to NATO: The Idea of the West and its Opponents* (New York: The Free Press, 1998), p. 424.

52 PPS/23, 24 February 1948, *FRUS*, 1948, vol. 1, part 2, p. 524.

53 Ibid., p. 511.

54 Robert E. Wood, 'From the Marshall Plan to the Third World', in Leffler and Painter, *Origins of the Cold War*, pp. 202–205.

55 Kolko, *Confronting the Third World*, pp. 17–19.

56 Leffler, *Preponderance of Power*, pp. 18–19.

57 Giovanni Arrighi, *The Long Twentieth Century: Money, Power, and the Origins of Our Times* (London: Verso, 1994), pp. 68–72, 274–281.

58 Emily S. Rosenberg, *Spreading the American Dream: American Economic and Cultural Expansion, 1890–1945* (New York: Hill and Wang, 1982), pp. 229–232. See also Barry Eichengreen and Peter B. Kenen, 'Managing the World Economy under the Bretton Woods System: An Overview', in Peter B. Kenen (ed.), *Managing the World Economy: Fifty Years after Bretton Woods* (Washington, D.C.: Institute for International Economics, 1994), p. 14.

59 Diane B. Kunz, *Butter and Guns: America's Cold War Economic Diplomacy* (New York: The Free Press, 1997), p. 20; Robert A. Pollard and Samuel F. Welles, 'The Era of American Economic Hegemony', in William H. Becker and Samuel F. Welles (eds), *Economics and World Power: An Assessment of American Diplomacy since 1789* (New York: Columbia University Press, 1984), p. 338; Wm. Roger Louis, 'American Anti-Colonialism and the Dissolution of the British Empire', in Wm Roger Louis and Hedley Bull (eds), *The 'Special Relationship': Anglo-American Relations since 1945* (Oxford: Clarendon Press, 1989), p. 263.

60 David Held (ed.), *Prospects for Democracy: North, South, East, West* (Cambridge: Polity Press, 1993), p. 29; Alan Milward, *The European Rescue of the Nation-State* (London: Routledge, 1992), pp. 21–46; Arrighi, *Long Twentieth Century*, p. 69.

61 National Security Council, U.S. Policy toward Africa South of the Sahara Prior to Calendar Year 1960, NSC 5719, 31 July 1957, Record Group 273, pp. 9–10.

62 Denis Judd, *Empire: The British Imperial Experience, from 1765 to the Present* (London: Harper Collins, 1996), p. 29.

63 Geoffrey Barraclough, *An Introduction to Contemporary History* (Harmondsworth: Penguin, 1967), pp. 154–156. For an overview of the historical trajectory

see a chapter on the 'implanting of Western Institutions around the world' in Spybey, *Social Change*, pp. 100–118.

64 Clark, *Globalization and Fragmentation*, p. 144.
65 Arrighi, *Long Twentieth Century*, pp. 274–275.
66 Geoffrey Hawthorn, 'Sub-Saharan Africa', in Held (ed.), *Prospects for Democracy: North, South, East, West*, p. 333.
67 David S. Landes, *The Wealth and Poverty of Nations: Why Some Are So Rich and Some So Poor* (London: Little, Brown and Co., 1998), pp. 422–439.
68 Eric Hobsbawm, *Nations and Nationalism since 1780* (Cambridge: Cambridge University Press, 1990), pp. 136–137; idem., *The Age of Extremes*, p. 201.
69 Hobsbawm, *Nations*, pp. 137, 148–150.
70 Ibid., p. 153.

Chapter 6: Containing the East; integrating the West

1 For the latest concise overview, see David S. Painter, *The Cold War: An International History* (London: Routledge, 1999), pp. 4–30.
2 Sherry, *Shadow of War*, passim.
3 Richard Immerman, 'Psychology', in Hogan and Paterson, *Explaining*, p. 160.
4 Generally on the issues of ideology in the Cold War see Hunt, *Ideology*; Rosenberg, *Spreading the American Dream*; Noam Chomsky, *On Power and Ideology* (Boston: South End Press, 1987); Frank A. Ninkovich, *The Diplomacy of Ideas: U.S. Foreign Relations and Cultural Relations, 1938–1950* (Cambridge: Cambridge University Press, 1981); Smith, *America's Mission*.
5 Thomas G. Paterson, *On Every Front: The Making and Unmaking of the Cold War*, rev. edn (New York: W. W. Norton, 1992), p. 106.
6 David Green, *The Containment of Latin America: A History of the Myths and Realities of the Good Neighbor Policy* (Chicago: Quadrangle Books, 1971), pp. 291–293; Mark T. Gilderhus, 'An Emerging Synthesis? U.S.–Latin American Relations since the Second World War', in Hogan (ed.), *America in the World*, p. 435; Geoffrey Barraclough, *An Introduction to Contemporary History* (Harmondsworth: Penguin, 1990), p. 124; Cohen, *America*, p. 21.
7 Michael H. Hunt, 'Ideology', in Hogan and Paterson, *Explaining*, pp. 193–194.
8 See for instance Feis, *From Trust to Terror*, and Gaddis, 'The Tragedy of Cold War History', *Diplomatic History* 17, no. 1 (Winter 1993); and comment on this, Michael J. Hogan, 'State of the Art', in his *America in the World*, pp. 4–9.
9 William Appleman Williams, *The Tragedy of American Diplomacy*, revised edition (New York: Delta, 1962), p. 229; Foley, *American Political Ideas*, pp. 46–49; Paterson, *On Every Front*, pp. 103–104.
10 Martin Walker, *The Cold War* (London: Fourth Estate, 1993), p. 29–31; see also, Noam Chomsky, *Necessary Illusions: Thought Control in Democratic Societies* (Boston: South End Press, 1989), pp. 21–44; Frank Kofsky, *Harry S. Truman and the War Scare of 1948* (New York: St. Martin's Press, 1993).
11 James M. McCormick, *American Foreign Policy and Process* (Itasca: Peacock Publishers, 1992), p. 79; Richard A. Melanson, *Reconstructing Consensus: American Foreign Policy since the Vietnam War* (New York: St. Martin's Press, 1991), pp. 4–8; David Ryan, 'Asserting US Power', in Philip John Davies (ed.), *An American Quarter Century: US Politics from Vietnam to Clinton* (Manchester: Manchester University Press, 1995), pp. 103–105.
12 Melanson, *Reconstructing Consensus*, p. 4.

13 LaFeber, *America, Russia*, p. 38; Lloyd Gardner, *Architects of Illusion: Men and Ideas in American Foreign Policy 1941–1949* (Chicago: Quadrangle Books, 1970), p. 315.

14 John Lewis Gaddis, *Strategies of Containment: A Critical Appraisal of Postwar American National Security Policy* (Oxford: Oxford University Press, 1982), pp. 49–50; John Lewis Gaddis, *The United States and the Origins of the Cold War 1941–1947* (New York: Columbia University Press, 1972), p. 322.

15 George Kennan, *The New Yorker* (1985).

16 Churchill's Iron Curtain speech, 5 March 1946, with commentary and Stalin's reply, 13 March 1946, reprinted in Walter LaFeber (ed.), *Eastern Europe and the Soviet Union*, vol. II, part 1, of Arthur Schlesinger (ed.), *Dynamics of World Power*, pp. 210–221.

17 Gaddis, *Origins of the Cold War*, p. 355; John Lewis Gaddis, 'The Insecurities of Victory: The United States and the Perception of the Soviet Threat after World War II', in Lacey (ed.), *The Truman Presidency*, pp. 262–264; Gaddis, *Strategies of Containment*, p. 201; Leffler, 'Interpretative Wars over the Cold War', pp. 111–112.

18 Gaddis, *Origins of the Cold War*, pp. 356–357; John Lewis Gaddis, 'The Tragedy of Cold War History', *Diplomatic History* 17, no. 1 (Winter 1993), pp. 1–16; Stephanson, 'United States', pp. 36–40.

19 Hunt, 'Ideology', pp. 194–196; Hunt, *Ideology*, pp. 152–158.

20 Stephanson, 'The United States', in Reynolds (ed.), *Origins of the Cold War in Europe*, p. 31.

21 LaFeber, *America, Russia*, pp. 10, 26.

22 Noam Chomsky, *Deterring Democracy* (London: Verso, 1991), pp. 37, 27; Chomsky, *On Power and Ideology*, pp. 7, 62, 6; Noam Chomsky, *Turning the Tide: U.S. Intervention in Central America and the Struggle for Peace* (Boston: South End Press, 1985), p. 56.

23 McCormick, *America's Half-Century*, pp. 59–63.

24 LaFeber, *America, Russia*, p. 9; Leffler, *Preponderance of Power*, pp. 17–18.

25 Hogan, 'State of the Art', in his *America in the World*, p. 14; Leffler, *Specter of Communism*, pp. 38, 62; Leffler, *Preponderance of Power*, pp. 5–7; Lynn Eden, 'The End of US Cold War History', *International Security* 18, no. 1 (Summer 1993), p. 177; Melvyn Leffler, 'National Security', in Hogan and Paterson (eds), *Explaining*, p. 211.

26 Leffler, *Preponderance*, pp. 130–131, 138.

27 Gardner, *Architects of Illusion*, p. 311; Gaddis, *Origins*, pp. 338–341; Leffler, *Preponderance*, p. 139. See also Graham White and John Maze, *Henry A. Wallace: His Search for a New World Order* (Chapel Hill: University of North Carolina Press, 1995).

28 Hunt, *Ideology*, p. 178; Saul Landau, *The Dangerous Doctrine: National Security and U.S. Foreign Policy* (Boulder: Westview Press, 1988), p. 48.

29 Crabb, *Doctrines of American Foreign Policy*, pp. 108–109.

30 Gabriel Kolko, *Century of War: Politics, Conflict, and Society since 1914* (New York: The New Press, 1994), pp. 375–385; Thomas G. Paterson and J. Garry Clifford, *America Ascendant: U.S. Foreign Relations since 1939* (Lexington: D. C. Heath, 1995), p. 71.

31 Halle, *Cold War as History*, pp. 110–112.

32 Ambrose, *Rise to Globalism*, pp. 78–83.

33 The United States had undergone rapid demobilisation after the war from 10 million people in the forces to 1.4 million by 1947; similarly, military spending had been reduced from $90 billion in 1945 to $10 billion in 1947 (LaFeber,

America, Russia, p. 50); Ambrose, *Globalism*, pp. 83–84; Gaddis, *Origins of the Cold War*, pp. 348–349; Chomsky, *Power and Ideology*, p. 32.

34 LaFeber, *America, Russia*, p. 53.
35 President Truman, Address to a Joint Session of Congress, 12 March 1947, in Raymond Dennett and Robert K. Turner, *Documents on American Foreign Relations*, vol. 9 (Princeton: Princeton University Press, 1949), p. 7; Crockatt, *Fifty Years War*, p. 75; Ambrose, *Globalism*, p. 85.
36 Kolko, *Century of War*, p. 379; Paterson and Clifford, *America Ascendent*, p. 71; Paterson, *On Every Front*, p. 100. See also Hunt, *Ideology*, pp. 46–91.
37 Cohen, *America*, p. 37.
38 Hunt, *Crises in US Foreign Policy*, p. 124; Daniel Yergin, *The Prize: The Epic Quest for Oil, Money and Power* (London: Simon and Schuster, 1991), p. 416. See also Scott Lucas, 'The Limits of Ideology: US Foreign Policy and Arab Nationalism in the Early Cold War', in Ryan and Pungong, *The United States and Decolonization*, pp. 140–167.
39 McCormick, *Half-Century*, p. 75; Leffler, *Preponderance*, p. 237.
40 Leffler, *Preponderance*, pp. 143, 149; McCormick, *Half-Century*, pp. 75–77; Chomsky, *Power and Ideology*, p. 35.
41 McCormick, *Half-Century*, p. 77; Hunt, *Crises*, p. 124.
42 Kolko, *Century of War*, p. 385.
43 Draper, *A Present of Things Past*, pp. 73–75.
44 X [George Kennan], 'The Sources of Soviet Conduct', *Foreign Affairs* 25 (July 1947), pp. 575, 581; Fred Halliday, *From Potsdam to Perestroika: Conversations with Cold Warriors* (London: BBC Radio 4, 7 April 1995), p. 9; Gaddis, *Strategies*, pp. 58–59; Walter L. Hixson, *George F. Kennan: Cold War Icono-clast* (New York: Columbia University Press, 1989), pp. 42–45. See also Anders Stephanson, *Kennan and the Art of Foreign Policy* (Cambridge, Mass.: Harvard University Press, 1989), pp. 54–109.
45 Stephanson, *Kennan*, p. 101; Walter Lippmann, *The Cold War: A Study in US Foreign Policy* (New York: Harper and Row, 1947, 1972), pp. 22–23, 50–51; Paterson and Clifford, *America Ascendent*, p. 73; Ronald Steel, *Walter Lippmann and the American Century* (London: Bodley Head, 1980), pp. 444–445; Gaddis, *Origins of the Cold War*, p. 352; Halliday, *From Perestroika*, p. 13.
46 John Lewis Gaddis, *We Now Know: Rethinking Cold War History* (Oxford: Clarendon Press, 1997), p. 193.
47 Lloyd C. Gardner, *Spheres of Influence: The Partition of Europe from Munich to Yalta* (London: John Murray, 1993), p. 263.
48 LaFeber, *America, Russia*, p. 64; George Marshall, address to the Harvard University Alumni, Cambridge, Massachusetts, 5 June 1947, in Dennet and Turner (eds), *Documents on American Foreign Relations, 1947*, pp. 9–11; Halle, *Cold War as History*, pp. 123–134.
49 Cohen, *America*, p. 41; Painter, *The Cold War*, pp. 14–23.
50 Kennan cited in Crockatt, *Fifty-Years War*, p. 78.
51 LaFeber, *America, Russia*, pp. 60–62; David Reynolds, 'The European Dimen-sion of the Cold War', in Leffler and Painter, *Origins of the Cold War*, p. 134; Crockatt, *Fifty-Years War*, p. 76. See James E. Cronin, cited in Painter, *Cold War*, p. 21.
52 LaFeber, *America, Russia*, p. 62.
53 Joyce and Gabriel Kolko, 'American Capitalist Expansion', in Thomas G. Paterson and Robert J. McMahon (eds), *The Origins of the Cold War* (Lexing-ton: D. C. Heath, 1991), pp. 14–22; see also: idem., *The Limits of Power: The*

World and United States Foreign Policy, 1945–1954 (New York: Harper and Row, 1972).

54 Reynolds, 'The European Dimension of the Cold War', p. 126 and Charles S. Maier, 'Hegemony and Autonomy within the Western Alliance', in Leffler and Painter (eds), *Origins of the Cold War*, pp. 154–174.

55 Alan S. Milward, *The Reconstruction of Western Europe, 1945–1951* (London: Methuen, 1984), pp. 462–474; Lawrence S. Kaplan, 'The Cold War and European Revisionism', *Diplomatic History* 11, no. 2 (1987), pp. 143–151. See also Milward, 'Was the Marshall Plan Really Necessary?' *Diplomatic History* 13, no. 2 (Spring 1989), pp. 231–253; Pierre-Henri Laurent, 'Reappraising the Origins of European Integration', in Hans J. Michelmann and Panayotis Soldatos (eds), *European Integration: Theories and Approaches* (Lanham: University Press of America, 1994), p. 109. Alan S. Milward, *The European Rescue of the Nation-State* (London: Routledge, 1992).

56 Michael J. Hogan, *The Marshall Plan: America, Britain, and the Reconstruction of Western Europe, 1947–1952* (Cambridge: Cambridge University Press, 1987), pp. 427–431, 443; Stephanson, 'United States', p. 42; Novik, *That Noble Dream*, pp. 298–299. See also Michael J. Hogan, 'The Search for a "Creative Peace": The United States, European Unity, and the Origins of the Marshall Plan', *Diplomatic History* vol. 6, no. 3 (Summer 1982), pp. 267–285.

57 Hogan, *Marshall Plan*, pp. 438–444.

58 McCormick, 'World Systems', p. 94.

59 Kennan cited in McCormick, *America's Half Century*, pp. 53, 73–80.

60 Melvyn Leffler, 'National Security', in Hogan and Paterson (eds), *Explaining*, p. 211; Leffler, *Preponderance*, pp. 182, 218–219.

61 Cohen, *America*, p. 37; Crockatt, *Fifty Years War*, p. 80.

62 Leffler, *Preponderance*, pp. 237, 501–502.

63 Hobsbawm, *Age of Extremes*, p. 226.

64 Emily Rosenberg, in May, *America's Cold War Strategy*, pp. 161–162.

65 X [George Kennan], 'The Sources of Soviet Conduct', *Foreign Affairs* vol. 25 (July 1947), p. 582.

66 Report by the Policy Planning Staff, PPS/13, Résumé of World Situation, 6 November 1947, *FRUS*, vol. 1, 1947, pp. 770–777.

67 Report by the Policy Planning Staff, PPS/23, Review of Current Trends in U.S. Foreign Policy, 24 February 1948, *FRUS*, vol. 1, 1948, pp. 510–529.

68 Jerald A. Combs, 'The Compromise That Never Was: George Kennan, Paul Nitze, and the Issue of Conventional Deterrence in Europe, 1949–1952', *Diplomatic History* 15, no. 3 (Summer 1991), p. 364; NSC 68: United States Objectives and Programs for National Security, 14 April 1950, reproduced in Ernest R. May, *American Cold War Strategy: Interpreting NSC 68* (Boston: Bedford Books, 1993), pp. 26–27, 79–81.

69 See commentaries on NSC 68 by William Appleman Williams, Lloyd Gardner, in May, *American Cold War Strategy*, pp. 46–48; 133–135, 147–150; Walker, *Cold War*, pp. 72–73.

70 Sherry, *Shadow of War*, p. 136.

71 Paul H. Nitze, 'Grand Strategy Then and Now: NSC 68 and its Lessons for the Future', *Strategic Review* 22, no. 1 (Winter 1994), p. 16; Leffler, *Preponderance*, p. 355.

72 Gaddis, *Strategies*, pp. 89–98.

73 Robert A. Pollard, 'The National Security State Reconsidered: Truman and Economic Containment, 1945–1950', in Lacey, *Truman Presidency*, pp. 227–231; Leffler, *Preponderance*, pp. 356–357.

74 Chomsky, *Deterring Democracy*, pp. 10, 14, 20–21; Pollard, 'National Security State Reconsidered', p. 231; Ambrose, *Rise to Globalism*, pp. 113–115; Paterson, *On Every Front*, p. 93; Chomsky, *Turning The Tide*, p. 203; Chomsky, *Necessary Illusions*, pp. 28–29.
75 The Acheson quotation is in Benjamin Schwarz, 'Why America Thinks it has to Run the World', *Atlantic Monthly* (June 1996), pp. 92–102.

Chapter 7: Revolution and development in the Cold War

1 Isaiah Berlin, *The Crooked Timber of Humanity* (London: Fontana, 1991), p. 46.
2 Alex Danchev, 'Fin de fearing the siècle', *The Times Higher Education Supplement* (2 October 1998), p. 31.
3 See Mark Sandle, *A Short History of Soviet Socialism* (London: UCL, 1998).
4 Barrie Axford, *The Global System: Economics, Politics and Culture* (Cambridge: Polity Press, 1995), p. 23.
5 Hugh De Santis, *Beyond Progress: An Interpretive Odyssey to the Future* (Chicago: University of Chicago Press, 1996).
6 Harvey J. Kaye, *"Why Do Ruling Classes Fear History?"* (London: Macmillan, 1996), p. 39.
7 Edward Said, *Culture and Imperialism* (London: Chatto and Windus, 1993), pp. 261–262. See also Dennis Merrill, 'The Ironies of History: The United States and the Decolonization of India', in Ryan and Pungong, *The United States and Decolonization*.
8 Hobsbawm, *Age of Extremes*, pp. 344–346.
9 Alan Ryan, 'Introduction', in his edited *After the End of History* (London: Collins and Brown, 1992), p. 3.
10 George C. Herring, *America's Longest War: The United States and Vietnam, 1950–1975* (New York: McGraw-Hill, 1986), p. 55; Barry Gills, Joel Rocamora and Richard Wilson, *Low Intensity Democracy: Political Power in the New World Order* (London: Pluto, 1993), *passim*.
11 Hobsbawm, *Extremes*, pp. 347–349.
12 Clark, *Globalization and Fragmentation*, pp. 142–143.
13 McCormick, 'World Systems', in Hogan and Paterson, *Explaining*, pp. 90–91.
14 Skocpol, *Social Revolutions*, p. 259.
15 James DeFronzo, *Revolutions and Revolutionary Movements* (Boulder: Westview Press, 1991), p. 314; Skocpol, *Social Revolutions*, p. 263.
16 McCormick, 'World Systems', p. 94.
17 Skocpol, *Social Revolutions*, p. 262; DeFronzo, *Revolutions*, p. 316.
18 Skocpol, *Social Revolutions*, p. 313.
19 Michael H. Hunt and Steven I. Levine, 'Revolutionary Movements in Asia and the Cold War', in Leffler and Painter, *Origins of the Cold War*, p. 258.
20 LaFeber, *Inevitable Revolutions*, p. 109; Schoultz, *Beneath the United States*, p. 333; Gabriel Kolko, *Confronting the Third World: United States Foreign Policy 1945–1980* (New York: Pantheon, 1988), pp. 37–38.
21 David S. Painter, 'Explaining U.S. Relations with the Third World', *Diplomatic History* 19, no. 3 (Summer 1995), p. 527; see also Dennis Merrill, 'The United States and the Rise of the Third World', in Martel, *American Foreign Relations Reconsidered*, pp. 166–186.
22 Lars Schoultz, *National Security and United States Policy toward Latin America* (Princeton: Princeton University Press, 1987), p. 63; David Ryan, *US–Sandinista Diplomatic Relations: Voice of Intolerance* (London: Macmillan,

1995), pp. 6, 8–10; idem., 'U.S. Ideology and Central American Revolutions in the Cold War', in Will Fowler (ed.), *Ideologues and Ideologies in Latin America* (Westport: Greenwood, 1997), pp. 105–124.

23 Hunt and Levine, 'Revolutionary Movements in Asia', p. 265.

24 Schoultz, *Beneath the United States*, p. 334.

25 Cole Blasier, *The Hovering Giant: U.S. Responses to Revolutionary Change in Latin America* (Pittsburgh: Pittsburgh University Press, 1983), pp. 211–238.

26 Marilyn B. Young, *The Vietnam Wars*, cited by LaFeber, 'An End to Which Cold War', in Michael J. Hogan (ed.), *The End of the Cold War: Its Meaning and Implications* (Cambridge: Cambridge University Press, 1992), p. 17; see also David W. Levy, *The Debate over Vietnam* (Baltimore: Johns Hopkins University Press, 1995).

27 Hobsbawm, *Nations and Nationalism*, p. 137.

28 Ibid., pp. 148–150; Leffler, *Preponderance of Power*, pp. 18–24; Chomsky, *On Power and Ideology*, p. 10.

29 Robert S. McNamara, *In Retrospect: The Tragedy and Lessons of Vietnam* (New York: Times Books, 1995), pp. 321–322.

30 The NSC Planning Board, A Report to the National Security Council on United States Policy Toward Iran, NSC 175, 21 December 1953, The National Security Archive, fiche 00375, document 93.

31 William Blum, *The CIA: A Forgotten History* (London: Zed Books, 1986), pp. 77–89.

32 Gaddis Smith, *The Last Years of the Monroe Doctrine 1945–1993* (New York: Hill and Wang, 1994), pp. 4–7.

33 Sheldon B. Liss, *Radical Thought in Central America* (Boulder: Westview Press, 1991), pp. 36–44.

34 NSC 144/1, 'United States Objectives and Courses of Action with Respect to Latin America', 18 March 1953, in *Foreign Relations of the United States 1952–1954: The American Republics*, vol. 4 (Washington, D.C.: Government Printing Office, 1983), pp. 6–7; Louis J. Halle to Bowie, 28 May 1954, Policy Planning Staff, Record Group 59, lot 65D101, box 79.

35 Ambassador John Peurifoy telegram to the Department of State, 17 December 1953, *FRUS 1952–1954*, vol. 4, p. 1093; LaFeber, *Inevitable Revolutions*, pp. 119–125.

36 Gleijeses, *Shattered Hope*, pp. 361, 366; LaFeber, *Inevitable Revolutions*, p. 125.

37 W. W. Rostow, 'Notes on Cuba Policy', 24 April 1961, in Chang and Kornbluh (eds), *The Cuban Missile Crisis 1962* (New York: The New Press, 1992), pp. 16–19.

38 Department of State, The Communist Totalitarian Government of Cuba as a Source of International Tensions in the Americas, 15 May 1961, The National Security Archive, 00664, fiche 203.

39 Hunt, *Ideology*, pp. 159–160.

40 Leffler, *Preponderance of Power*, p. 24.

41 Peter F. Klarén, 'Lost Promise: Explaining Latin American Underdevelopment', in Peter F. Klarén and Thomas J. Bossert (eds), *Promise of Development: Theories of Change in Latin America* (Boulder: Westview, 1986), pp. 8–12; W. W. Rostow, *The Stages of Economic Growth: A Non-Communist Manifesto* (Cambridge: Cambridge University Press, 1960, second edition 1971), *passim*, esp. 4–16.

42 National Security Council, Review of Basic National Security Policy: Basic Problems for U.S. Security Arising out of Changes in the World Situation, 19 February 1957, NSC 5707, National Security Archive, 00502, fiche 148;

Marion W. Boggs, Memorandum for the NSC Planning Board, Political Implications of Afro-Asian Military Takeovers, 2 April 1959, Record Group 273,
mill 206.

43 Cingranelli, *Ethics, American Foreign Policy*, pp. 142–144.

44 Klarén, 'Lost Promise', pp. 14–23; Tony Spybey, *Social Change, Development
and Dependency* (Cambridge: Polity Press, 1992), pp. 158–180; Ankie Hoogvelt,
*Globalization and the Postcolonial World: The New Political Economy of
Development* (Basingstoke: Macmillan, 1997), pp. 29–43; See also Victor
Bulmer-Thomas, *The Economic History of Latin America since Independence*
(Cambridge: Cambridge University Press, 1994), pp. 257–263; David Ryan,
'Colonialism and Hegemony in Latin America: An Introduction', *The Inter-
national History Review* 21, no. 2 (June 1999), pp. 287–296; Ian Roxborough,
Theories of Underdevelopment (Basingstoke: Macmillan, 1979).

45 Kaufman, 'Kennedy as World Leader', pp. 453, 466; Kolko, *Confronting the
Third World*, pp. 150–151; McCormick, *America's Half Century*, p. 143; Smith,
America's Mission, p. 234; James William Park, *Latin American Underdevelop-
ment: A History of Perspectives in the United States* (Baton Rouge: Louisiana
State University Press, 1995), p. 227; Chomsky, *Turning the Tide*, pp. 45–46;
idem., *On Power and Ideology*, p. 79.

46 Smith, *America's Mission*, p. 221.

47 Hunt, *Ideology*, p. 160.

48 Rosenberg, *Spreading the American Dream*, p. 234.

49 Ralf Dahrendorf, *Reflections on the Revolution in Europe* (London: Chatto and
Windus, 1990), p. 37.

Chapter 8: Confronting 'evil' and imagined empires

1 Crabb, *Doctrines*, pp. 280, 304, 323; Gaddis, *Strategies*, 298–304; Kissinger,
Diplomacy, pp. 707–709.

2 Stephen Pelz, 'Balance of Power', in Hogan and Paterson, *Explaining American
Foreign Relations*, pp. 112–113; McCormick, *American Foreign Policy and
Process*, pp. 118–120; Gordon Craig, 'Looking for Order', *The New York
Review of Books* 41, no. 9 (12 May 1994), pp. 8–14; Melanson, *Reconstructing
Consensus*, p. 68; Kissinger, *Diplomacy*, pp. 29–55.

3 Kissinger, cited in Clark, *Globalization and Fragmentation*, p. 154.

4 Saul Landau, *The Dangerous Doctrine: National Security and US Foreign Policy*
(Boulder: Westview, 1988), p. 102; Ryan, 'Asserting US Power', in Davies (ed.),
American Quarter Century, pp. 105–107; Cohen, *America in the Age of Soviet
Power*, p. 183; Crockatt, *Fifty Years War*, p. 207; Noam Chomsky, *Towards a
New Cold War: Essays on the Current Crisis and How We Got There* (New
York: Pantheon Books, 1982), p. 186.

5 Calleo cited in Kennedy, *The Rise and Fall of Great Powers*, p. 562; see also:
David P. Calleo, *The Imperious Economy* (Cambridge, Mass.: Harvard University Press, 1982); Diane B. Kunz, 'The Power of Money: The Historiography
of American Economic Diplomacy', in Hogan (ed.), *America in the World*,
p. 554.

6 McCormick, *America's Half-Century*, pp. 162–163, 167; Kemp, *Climax of
Capitalism*, pp. 177–185; Nassau Adams, *Worlds Apart: The North–South
Divide and the International System* (London: Zed Books, 1993), pp. 106–110.

7 Clark, *Globalization and Fragmentation*, p. 167. See also, Walden Bello, *Dark
Victory: The United States, Structural Adjustment, and Global Poverty* (London:
Pluto Press, 1994).

8 Noam Chomsky, *Radical Priorities*, C. P. Otero (ed.) (Montreal: Black Rose, 1981), p. 161.
9 Fred Halliday, *Cold War, Third World: An Essay on Soviet–American Relations* (London: Hutchinson Radius, 1989).
10 LaFeber, 'From Détente to the Gulf', p. 156; Walter LaFeber, 'The Reagan Administration and Revolutions in Central America', *Political Science Quarterly* 99, no. 1 (Spring 1984), p. 1; William K. Muir, Jr, 'The Primacy of Rhetoric', in Greenstein, *Modern Presidency*, pp. 261–262; Garry Wills, 'The Man Who Wasn't There', *New York Review of Books* 38, no. 11 (13 June 1991), p. 3; Cohen, *America in the Age of Soviet Power*, p. 219; Hunt, *Ideology*, pp. 186–187; Gaddis, *United States and the End of the Cold War*, pp. 123, 131.
11 LaFeber, *America, Russia and the Cold War*, p. 302; Ronald Reagan, *Speaking My Mind* (London: Hutchinson, 1989), p. 116; Francis Fukuyama, *The End of History and the Last Man* (Harmondsworth: Penguin, 1992), *passim*.
12 Paterson and Clifford, *America Ascendant*, pp. 257–259.
13 McMahon, 'Making Sense of . . . the Reagan Years', pp. 372–373.
14 Allen Hunter, 'The Limits of Vindicationist Scholarship', in his (edited) *Re-Thinking the Cold War* (Philadelphia: Temple University Press, 1998), pp. 2–8.
15 John Kenneth Galbraith, *The Culture of Contentment* (London: Sinclair-Stevenson, 1992), p. 126; LaFeber, *America, Russia, and the Cold War*, p. 303; Paterson and Clifford, *America Ascendant*, p. 258.
16 Raymond L. Garthoff, *The Great Transition: American–Soviet Relations and the End of the Cold War* (Washington, D.C.: Brookings, 1994), pp. 33–42.
17 Garthoff, *Transition*, p. 42; Galbraith, *Culture of Contentment*, pp. 122–126; Brands, *Since Vietnam*, pp. 87–89. For further discussion on the 'triumph of upper America' and wealth distribution to the élite see: Kevin Phillips, *The Politics of Rich and Poor: Wealth and the American Electorate in the Reagan Aftermath* (New York: Harper Perennial, 1990).
18 Sherry, *Shadow of War*, pp. 392–398.
19 McCormick, *America's Half Century*, pp. 216–219.
20 Ibid., pp. 219, 227–230; Dumbrell, *Carter to Clinton*, pp. 66–67; Paterson and Clifford, *America Ascendant*, pp. 264–265; Powaski, *March to Armageddon*, pp. 184–196. For background see: James Fallows, *National Defense* (New York: Vintage, 1981).
21 McCormick, *America's Half Century*, p. 216; Crockatt, *Fifty Years War*, pp. 324–326, citing Cromwell.
22 LaFeber, *America, Russia, and the Cold War*, pp. 305–307. See also Joseph Lepgold, *The Declining Hegemon: The United States and European Defense, 1960–1990* (New York: Praeger, 1990); Richard J. Payne, *The West European Allies, The Third World, and U.S. Foreign Policy: Post-Cold War Challenges* (New York: Praeger, 1991).
23 LaFeber, 'From Détente to the Gulf', p. 159; Selig S. Harrison, 'Afghanistan: Soviet Intervention, Afghan Resistance, and the American Role', in Michael T. Klare and Peter Kornbluh (eds), *Low-Intensity Warfare: How the USA Fights Wars Without Declaring Them* (London: Methuen, 1989), pp. 183–206; Ryan, 'Asserting US Power', pp. 115–116; on the CIA see: Bob Woodward, *Veil: The Secret Wars of the CIA 1981–1987* (New York: Pocket Books, 1987).
24 Halliday, *Cold War Third World*, p. 53; Holly Sklar, *Washington's War on Nicaragua* (Boston: South End Press, 1988), pp. 65–72; Haig, *Caveat*, pp. 117–140; David Ryan, *US–Sandinista Diplomatic Relations: Voice of Intolerance* (London: Macmillan, 1995), pp. 9–15; Brands, *The Devil We Knew*, p. 170.
25 Sherry, *Shadow of War*, pp. 338–339.

26 Halliday, *Cold War, Third World*, pp. 69–92; LaFeber, *Inevitable Revolutions*, p. 329; Department of State, *Revolution Beyond Our Borders: Sandinista Intervention in Central America*, Special Report no. 132 (Washington, D.C.: U.S. Department of State, 1985).

27 Christopher Hitchens, 'A Dynasty Divided', *The Independent Magazine* (London), no. 76 (17 February 1990), p. 25; Ryan, *US–Sandinista Diplomatic Relations*, pp. 2–5; Sklar, *Washington's War*, p. 38; Pastor, *Condemned to Repetition*, pp. 191–212. The literature on Nicaragua is vast. A good place to start is: Thomas W. Walker (ed.), *Revolution and Counterrevolution in Nicaragua* (Boulder: Westview Press, 1991); idem., *Reagan versus the Sandinistas: The Undeclared War on Nicaragua* (Boulder: Westview Press, 1987); Dennis Gilbert, *Sandinistas: The Party and the Revolution* (Oxford: Blackwell, 1988); James Dunkerley, *Power in the Isthmus: A Political History of Modern Central America* (London: Verso, 1988).

28 John A. Booth and Thomas W. Walker, *Understanding Central America* (Boulder: Westview Press, 1989), pp. 55–61; Ryan, *US–Sandinista Diplomatic Relations*, pp. 13–21.

29 Lars Schoultz, *National Security and United States Policy toward Latin America* (Princeton: Princeton University Press, 1987), p. 63; Carl C. Jacobsen, *Soviet Attitudes towards, Aid to, and Contacts with Central American Revolutionaries* (Washington, D.C.: Department of State, 1984), pp. 16–17, 31; Ryan, *U.S.–Sandinista Diplomatic Relations*, pp. 45, 61. More generally, on the actual rather than the imagined Soviet presence, see Nicola Miller, *Soviet Relations with Latin America, 1959–1987* (Cambridge: Cambridge University Press, 1989); Wayne S. Smith, *The Russians Aren't Coming: New Soviet Policy in Latin America* (Boulder: Lynne Reinner, 1992).

30 Background Paper for NSC meeting on Central America, 30 October 1984, copy with author. William Goodfellow and James Morrell, 'From Contadora to Esquipulas to Sapoá and Beyond', in Walker (ed.), *Revolution and Counterrevolution*, pp. 369–393; Ryan, *US Sandinista Diplomatic Relations, passim*.

31 Chamorro cited in Ryan, *US–Sandinista Diplomatic Relations*, p. 93; Barry Goldwater letter to William Casey, 9 April 1984, US Congress, *Iran-Contra Investigation*, 100th Congress, 1st sess., 100–11, 4–6 August 1987, pp. 1069–1070; International Court of Justice, *Nicaragua v. U.S.A.*, The Hague: ICJ, 1986), p. 137. The best place to start on the covert war is: Peter Kornbluh, *Nicaragua: The Price of Intervention* (Washington, D.C.: Institute for Policy Studies, 1987).

32 Truth Commission, cited in Paterson and Clifford, *America Ascendant*, p. 269; Guillermo O'Donnell, Philippe C. Schmitter and Laurence Whitehead, *Transitions from Authoritarian Rule: Latin America* (Baltimore: Johns Hopkins University Press, 1986); John A. Booth and Mitchell A. Seligson, *Elections and Democracy in Central America* (London: University of North Carolina Press, 1989); William I. Robinson, *A Faustian Bargain: U.S. Intervention in the Nicaraguan Elections and American Foreign Policy in the Post-Cold War Era* (Boulder: Westview Press, 1992); Ryan, *US–Sandinista Diplomatic Relations*, pp. 88–106, 170–188; Barry Gills, Joel Rocamora, Richard Wilson (eds), *Low Intensity Democracy: Political Power in the New World Order* (London: Pluto Press, 1993); James Dunkerley, *The Pacification of Central America: Political Change in the Isthmus, 1987–1993* (London: Verso, 1994).

33 Ronald Reagan, 'Text of Address on Central America', 27 April 1983, *Congressional Quarterly* 41, no. 17 (30 April 1983), pp. 853–856; Vladimir I. Stanchenko, 'United States–USSR–Latin America: Soviet Role in Central

America', paper delivered at Jean Donovan Conference, Cork University, Ireland, 26–27 January 1990.
34 Diana Melrose, *Nicaragua: The Threat of a Good Example?* (Oxford: Oxfam, 1985), pp. 11, *passim*; NSC cited in Ryan, *US–Sandinista Diplomatic Relations*, p. 24.
35 Chomsky, *Power and Ideology*, p. 7; idem., *Culture of Terrorism*, pp. 217–224; idem., *Deterring Democracy*, p. 300; Eduardo Galeano, *We Say No: Chronicles 1963–1991* (New York: W. W. Norton, 1992), p. 195. McCormick, *America's Half Century*, pp. 118–119.
36 Paterson, *On Every Front*, pp. 213–215; AP, '"Off Record" Kissinger Talk Isn't', *New York Times*, 20 April 1986; Smith, *Last Years of the Monroe Doctrine*, pp. 185–209; Halliday, *Cold War, Third World*, p. 87.
37 William I. Robinson, 'Nicaragua and the World: A Globalization Perspective', in Thomas W. Walker (ed.), *Nicaragua Without Illusions: Regime Transition and Structural Adjustment in the 1990s* (Wilmington: Scholarly Resources, 1997), p. 40.

Chapter 9: Concluding through contemporary dilemmas

1 Mikhail Gorbachev, address to the 43rd session of the United Nations General Assembly, 7 December 1988, http://www.rmt-website.org/russia/fpoly/articles/gorbachev-un1988.html, 17 November 1999.
2 Allen Hunter, 'The Limits of Vindicationist Scholarship', in idem (ed.), *Rethinking the Cold War* (Philadelphia: Temple University Press, 1998), p. 2.
3 Gaddis, in Hogan (ed.), *End of the Cold War*, pp. 21–38; idem, *The United States and the End of the Cold War*, pp. 193–216. See also idem, 'The Tragedy of Cold War History', *Diplomatic History* 17, no. 1 (Winter 1993), pp. 1–16.
4 Smith, *America's Mission*, pp. 311–312.
5 George Bush cited in ibid., p. 313.
6 Ibid., p. 322.
7 H. W. Brands, 'The Idea of the National Interest', *Diplomatic History* vol. 23, no. 2 (Spring 1999), p. 261.
8 Steel, *Temptations*, pp. 49–51.
9 Bush cited in Smith, *America's Mission*, p. 315.
10 President Bill Clinton, Inaugural Address, 21 January 1993.
11 David Ryan, 'Asserting US Power', in Philip Davies (ed.), *An American Quarter Century: US Politics From Vietnam to Clinton* (Manchester: Manchester University Press, 1995), pp. 120–121.
12 Anthony Lake, 'U.S. Credibility at Stake in Haiti Moves', Remarks to the Council on Foreign Relations, 14 September 1994, USIS text.
13 Tony Judt, 'What Are American Interests?' *The New York Review of Books* 42, no. 15 (5 October 1995), p. 37.
14 Steel, *Temptations*, p. 52.
15 Sherry, *Shadow of War*, pp. 431–432.
16 Ibid., pp. 439–442.
17 Patrick Tyler, 'U.S. Strategy Plan Calls for Insuring No Rivals Develop', *New York Times*, 8 March 1992; Ryan, 'Asserting US Power', pp. 117–118.
18 Chomsky, *Deterring Democracy*, p. 53.
19 Samuel P. Huntington, 'Clash of Civilizations', *Foreign Affairs*, 72, no. 3 (Summer 1993), pp. 22–49. See also, Samuel P. Huntington, *The Clash of Civilizations and the Remaking of World Order* (New York: Simon and Schuster, 1996), pp. 29–35.

20 Huntington, 'Clash of Civilizations', p. 25.
21 Richard E. Rubenstein and Jarle Crocker, 'Challenging Huntington', *Foreign Policy* 96 (1994), pp. 113–128; Said, *Orientalism*, pp. 329–354.
22 Edward Said, *The Politics of Dispossession: The Struggle for Palestinian Self-Determination 1969–1994* (London: Chatto and Windus, 1994), pp. 384–392.
23 Anthony Lake, 'Confronting Backlash States', *Foreign Affairs* 73, no. 2 (March/April 1994), p. 45.
24 Michael Klare, *Rogue States and Nuclear Outlaws: America's Search for a New Foreign Policy* (New York: Hill and Wang, 1995), pp. 3–34.
25 Lake, 'U.S. Credibility at Stake in Haiti Moves', Remarks to the Council on Foreign Relations, 14 September 1994, USIS text.
26 The White House, *A National Security Strategy of Engagement and Enlargement*, July 1994, pp. i–ii, 1–3.
27 Christopher Layne and Benjamin Schwarz, 'American Hegemony – Without an Enemy', *Foreign Policy* no. 92 (Fall 1993), pp. 12–13.
28 Ibid., p. 5.
29 See the annual UN Development Program (UNDP) reports, *Human Development Report* 1991 onwards; and Walden Bello, *Dark Victory: The United States, Structural Adjustment, and Global Poverty* (London: Pluto, 1994).
30 Benjamin Schwarz, 'Why America Thinks It Has to Run the World', *Atlantic Monthly* (June 1996), pp. 92–102.
31 Francis Fukuyama, 'The End of History?' *The National Interest* no. 16 (Summer 1989), pp. 3–18; idem, *The End of History and the Last Man* (London: Penguin, 1992). The responses are wide-ranging: Alan Ryan, *After the End of History* (London: Collins and Brown, 1992); Timothy Burns (ed.), *After History? Francis Fukuyama and His Critics* (London: Littlefield Adams, 1994); Alex Callinicos, *The Revenge of History: Marxism and the East European Revolutions* (Cambridge: Polity Press, 1991); Arthur M. Melzer *et al.* (eds), *History and the Idea of Progress* (Ithaca: Cornell University Press, 1995); Fred Halliday, *Rethinking International Relations* (London: Macmillan, 1994), pp. 216–235.
32 Ryan, *After the End of History*, pp. 2–3, building on the ideas of Herbert Marcuse, in *One-Dimensional Man* (London: Routledge, 1991 [1964]).
33 Fred Halliday, *Rethinking International Relations* (Basingstoke: Macmillan, 1994), pp. 229–231.
34 Ibid.; Fukuyama, *The End of History*, pp. 48–49. Halliday remarks that it is part of a constitutional myth that either the United States or Britain was fully democratic before the 1960s (p. 233).
35 Hunter, 'The Limits of Vindicationist Scholarship', p. 7; and Cary Fraser, 'A Requiem for the Cold War: Reviewing the History of International Relations since 1945', in Hunter, *Rethinking the Cold War*, pp. 93–115.
36 Stephanson, *Manifest Destiny*, *passim*.
37 Halliday, *Rethinking*, p. 231.
38 Fukuyama, 'Reflections on the End of History, Five Years Later', in Burns, *After History?* pp. 239–258; Fukuyama, *The End of History*, p. 338.
39 Ronald Steel, *Temptations of a Superpower* (Cambridge, Mass.: Harvard University Press, 1995), p. 47.
40 Clark, *Globalization and Fragmentation*, p. 192. See also, Alan S. Milward, *The European Rescue of the Nation-State* (London: Routledge, 1992).
41 Noam Chomsky, *Year 501: The Conquest Continues* (London: Verso, 1993), p. 10.

42 Karl Magyar, 'Classifying the International Political Economy: A Third World Proto-Theory', *Third World Quarterly* 16, no. 4 (1995), pp. 703–716.

43 David Held, *Prospects for Democracy*, pp. 26–27.

44 White House, *A National Security Strategy of Engagement and Enlargement*, pp. 18–19.

45 US Commerce Secretary Ron Brown, Address to the American Chamber of Commerce, 10 December 1993, USIS textfile 2250; President Clinton, 'US Assistance to Cenam to Shift from Aid to Trade', 30 November 1993, USIS textfile 3700; Alexander F. Watson, 'U.S. Policy toward Nicaragua', Statement before the Subcommittee on Western Hemisphere Affairs of the House Foreign Affairs Committee, 6 October 1993, *US Department of State Dispatch*, 25 October 1993, p. 755.

46 Grey, *False Dawn: The Delusions of Global Capitalism* (London: Granta, 1998), p. 2.

47 Michael Ignatieff, 'On Isaiah Berlin (1909–1997)', *The New York Review of Books* 44, no. 20 (18 December 1997), p. 10.

SELECTED BIBLIOGRAPHY

Abu-Lughod, Janet L. 'The World-System Perspective in the Construction of Economic History', *History and Theory*, Theme Issue 34, 1995.

Adams, James Truslow. *The March of Democracy: The Rise of the Union*. New York: Charles Scribner's Sons, 1932.

—— *The Living Jefferson*. New York: Charles Scribner's Sons, 1936.

Adams, John Quincy. *Memoirs of John Quincy Adams*, vol. 6, Ed. Charles Francis Adams. Philadelphia: J. B. Lippincott, 1875.

—— *The Diary of John Quincy Adams, 1794–1845*. Ed. Allan Nevins. New York: Longmans, Green and Co., 1929.

Adams, Nassau A. *Worlds Apart: The North–South Divide and the International System*. London: Zed Books, 1993.

Ade Ajayi, J. F. 'Peace, Stability, and Legitimacy in Africa: The Factor of Colonialism and Neocolonialism', in Geir Lundestad (ed.), *The Fall of Great Powers: Peace, Stability, and Legitimacy*. Oslo: Scandinavian University Press, 1994.

Adelman, Jonathan R. (ed.). *Superpowers and Revolution*. New York: Praeger, 1986.

Ambrosius, Lloyd E. 'The Orthodoxy of Revisionism: Woodrow Wilson and the New Left', *Diplomatic History* 1, no. 3 (Summer 1977).

Ammond, Harry. 'The Monroe Doctrine: Domestic Politics or National Decision', *Diplomatic History* 5, no. 1 (Winter 1981).

Appleby, Joyce, Lynn Hunt and Margaret Jacob. *Telling the Truth about History*. New York: W. W. Norton, 1994.

Arrighi, Giovanni. *The Long Twentieth Century: Money, Power, and the Origins of Our Times*. London: Verso, 1994.

Axford, Barrie. *The Global System: Economics, Politics and Culture*. Cambridge: Polity Press, 1995.

Barraclough, Geoffrey. *An Introduction to Contemporary History*. London: Penguin, 1964.

Becker, William H. and Samuel F. Wells. *Economics and World Power: An Assessment of American Diplomacy since 1789*. New York: Columbia University Press, 1984.

Beisner, Robert L. 'The Anti-Imperialist Case and Failure', in Thomas G. Paterson and Stephen G. Rabe (eds), *Imperial Surge: The United States Abroad, the 1890s–Early 1900s*. Lexington: D. C. Heath, 1992.

232

Bell, Daniel. *The End of Ideology: On the Exhaustion of Political Ideas in the Fifties*. New York: The Free Press, 1962.

Bello, Walden. *Dark Victory: The United States, Structural Adjustment, and Global Poverty*. London: Pluto, 1994.

Bemis, Samuel Flagg. *A Diplomatic History of the United States*. London: Jonathan Cape, 1937.

Berlin, Isaiah. *The Hedgehog and the Fox: An Essay on Tolstoy's View of History*. London: Weidenfeld and Nicolson, 1953.

—— *Four Essays on Liberty*. Oxford: Oxford University Press, 1969.

—— *The Crooked Timber of Humanity: Chapters in the History of Ideas*. London: Fontana, 1991.

—— 'On Political Judgement', *The New York Review of Books* 43, no. 15 (3 October 1996).

—— *The Sense of Reality: Studies in Ideas and Their History*. London: Chatto and Windus, 1996.

Blasier, Cole. *The Hovering Giant: U.S. Responses to Revolutionary Change in Latin America*. Pittsburgh: Pittsburgh University Press, 1983.

Blum, William. *The CIA: A Forgotten History*. London: Zed Books, 1986.

Bodnar, John. *Remaking America: Public Memory, Commemoration, and Patriotism in the Twentieth Century*. Princeton: Princeton University Press, 1992.

Bonwick, Colin. *The American Revolution*. London: Macmillan, 1991.

Booth, John A. and Mitchell A. Seligson, *Elections and Democracy in Central America*. London: University of North Carolina Press, 1989.

Booth, John A. and Thomas W. Walker, *Understanding Central America*. Boulder: Westview Press, 1989.

Brands, H. W. *The Devil We Knew: Americans and the Cold War*. New York: Oxford University Press, 1993.

—— 'The Idea of the National Interest', *Diplomatic History* 23, no. 2 (Spring 1999).

Braudel, Fernand. *The Perspective of the World: Civilization and Capitalism, 15th–18th Century*. London: Fontana, 1984.

Bryan, William Jennings. *Speeches*. New York: Funk and Wagnalls, 1909.

—— *Bryan on Imperialism*. New York: Arno Press, 1970.

Burns, Bradford. 'The Continuity of the National Period', in Jan Knippers Black (ed.), *Latin America: Its Problems and Its Promise*. Boulder: Westview Press, 1991.

Burns, Timothy (ed.). *After History? Francis Fukuyama and His Critics*. London: Littlefield Adams, 1994.

Calleo, David P. *The Imperious Economy*. Cambridge, Mass: Harvard University Press, 1982.

Callinicos, Alex. *The Revenge of History: Marxism and the East European Revolutions*. Cambridge: Polity Press, 1991.

—— *Theories and Narratives: Reflections on the Philosophy of History*. Cambridge: Polity Press, 1995.

Canavan, Francis. 'Thomas Paine', in Leo Strauss and Joseph Cropsey (eds), *History of Political Philosophy*. Chicago: University of Chicago Press, 1963, 1981.

Cassels, Alan. *Ideology and International Relations in the Modern World*. London: Routledge, 1996.

Chomsky, Noam. *Radical Priorities*. Ed. C. P. Otero. Montreal: Black Rose, 1981.

—— *Turning the Tide: U.S. Intervention in Central America and the Struggle for Peace*. Boston: South End Press, 1985.

—— *On Power and Ideology: The Managua Lectures*. Boston: South End Press, 1987.

—— *Necessary Illusions: Thought Control in Democratic Societies*. Boston: South End Press, 1989.

—— *Deterring Democracy*. London: Verso, 1991.

—— *Year 501: The Conquest Continues*. London: Verso, 1993.

Chomsky, Noam and Edward S. Herman. *The Political Economy of Human Rights*. Nottingham: Spokesman, 1979.

Christopher, Warren. *In the Stream of History: Shaping Foreign Policy for a New Era*. Stanford: Stanford University Press, 1998.

Cingranelli, David Louis. *Ethics, American Foreign Policy, and the Third World*. New York: St. Martin's Press, 1993.

Clark, Ian. *Globalization and Fragmentation: International Relations in the Twentieth Century*. Oxford: Oxford University Press, 1997.

Cohen, Warren I. *America's Response to China: A History of Sino-American Relations*. New York: Columbia University Press, 1990.

Collin, Richard. *Theodore Roosevelt, Culture, Diplomacy, and Expansion*. Baton Rouge: Louisiana State University, 1985.

—— 'Symbiosis versus Hegemony: New Directions in the Foreign Relations Historiography of Theodore Roosevelt and William Howard Taft', *Diplomatic History* 19, no. 3 (Summer 1995).

Combs, Jerald A. 'The Compromise That Never Was: George Kennan, Paul Nitze, and the Issue of Conventional Deterrence in Europe, 1949–1952', *Diplomatic History* 15, no. 3 (Summer 1991).

Commager, Henry Steele (ed.). *Documents of American History*. New York: Appleton-Century-Crofts, 1963.

Connerton, Paul. *How Societies Remember*. Cambridge: Cambridge University Press, 1989.

Cooper, John Milton. *The Warrior and the Priest: Woodrow Wilson and Theodore Roosevelt*. New York: Norton, 1983.

Cumings, Bruce. *The Origins of the Korean War: The Roaring of the Cataract*, vol. 2. Princeton: Princeton University Press, 1990.

—— 'The American Century and the Third World', *Diplomatic History* 23, no. 2 (Spring 1999).

Dahrendorf, Ralf. *Reflections on the Revolution in Europe*. London: Chatto and Windus, 1990.

Davies, Norman. 'The Misunderstood War', *The New York Review of Books* 41, no. 2 (9 June 1994).

Davies, Philip John (ed.). *An American Quarter Century: US Politics from Vietnam to Clinton*. Manchester: Manchester University Press, 1995.

—— *Representing and Imagining America*. Keele: Keele University Press, 1996.

DeFronzo, James. *Revolutions and Revolutionary Movements*. Boulder: Westview Press, 1991.

Dennett, Raymond and Robert K. Turner, *Documents on American Foreign Relations*, vol. 9. Princeton: Princeton University Press, 1949.

Divine, Robert A. *Second Chance: The Triumph of Internationalism in America during World War II*. New York: Atheneum, 1967.

Dobson, Alan. 'The USA, Britain and the Question of Hegemony', Paper delivered at the Norwegian Nobel Institute, Oslo, Spring 1997.

Dozer, Donald Marquand, *The Monroe Doctrine: Its Modern Significance*. Tempe: Arizona State University, 1976.

Draper, Theodore. *A Struggle for Power: The American Revolution*. London: Abacus, 1996.

Dunkerley, James. *Power in the Isthmus: A Political History of Modern Central America*. London: Verso, 1988.

—— *The Pacification of Central America: Political Change in the Isthmus, 1987–1993*. London: Verso, 1994.

Eagleton, Terry. *Ideology: An Introduction*. London: Verso, 1991.

Ellul, Jacques. *Propaganda: The Formation of Men's Attitudes*. New York: Vintage, 1973.

Etherington, Norman. *Theories of Imperialism: War, Conquest and Capital*. London: Croom Helm, 1984.

Fanon, Franz. *The Wretched of the Earth*. Harmondsworth: Penguin, 1967.

Fernandez-Armesto, Felipe. *Millennium: A History of Our Last Thousand Years*. London: Bantam Books, 1995.

Ferrell, Robert H. *Woodrow Wilson and World War I, 1917–1921*. New York: Harper and Row, 1985.

Ferro, Marc. *Colonization: A Global History*. London: Routledge, 1997.

Field, James A. 'American Imperialism: The Worst Chapter in Almost Any Book', *American Historical Review* 83 (1978).

Fischer, David Hackett. *The Great Wave: Price Revolutions and the Rhythm of History*. New York: Oxford University Press, 1996.

Fitzsimons, David M. 'Tom Paine's New World Order: Idealistic Internationalism in the Ideology of Early American Foreign Relations', *Diplomatic History* 19, no. 4 (Fall 1995).

Foley, Michael. *American Political Ideas: Traditions and Usages*. Manchester: Manchester University Press, 1991.

Forsyth, David P. *Human Rights and U.S. Foreign Policy*. Gainsville: University Presses, 1988.

Frank, Andre Gunder and Barry K. Gills (eds). *The World System: Five Hundred Years or Five Thousand?*. London: Routledge, 1993.

Fraser, Cary. 'Understanding American Policy towards the Decolonization of European Empires, 1945–64', *Diplomacy and Statecraft* 3, no. 1 (1992).

Fry, Joseph A. 'From Open Door to World Systems: Economic Interpretations of Late Nineteenth Century American Foreign Relations', *Pacific Historical Review* 65, no. 2 (May 1996).

Fukuyama, Francis. 'The End of History?' *The National Interest* no. 16 (Summer 1989).

—— *The End of History and the Last Man*. Harmondsworth: Penguin, 1992.

—— 'Reflections on the End of History, Five Years Later', *History and Theory*, Themed Issue 34, 1995.

Gaddis, John Lewis. *The United States and the Origins of the Cold War 1941–1947*. New York: Columbia University Press, 1972.

—— *Strategies of Containment: A Critical Appraisal of Postwar American National Security Policy*. Oxford: Oxford University Press, 1982.

—— *Russia, the Soviet Union, and the United States: An Interpretative History*, 2nd edn. New York: McGraw-Hill, 1990.

—— 'The Tragedy of Cold War History', *Diplomatic History* 17, no. 1 (Winter 1993).

—— *We Now Know: Rethinking Cold War History*. Oxford: Clarendon Press, 1997.

Galbraith, John Kenneth. *The Culture of Contentment*. London: Sinclair-Stevenson, 1992.

Galeano, Eduardo. *Open Veins of Latin America: Five Centuries of the Pillage of a Continent*. New York: Monthly Review Press, 1997 [1973].

—— *We Say No: Chronicles 1963–1991*. New York: W. W. Norton, 1992.

Gardner, Lloyd C. *Economic Aspects of New Deal Diplomacy*. Madison: University of Wisconsin Press, 1964.

—— *Safe for Democracy: The Anglo-American Response to Revolution, 1913–1923*. Oxford: Oxford University Press, 1987.

—— *Spheres of Influence: The Partition of Europe, from Munich to Yalta*. London: John Murray, 1993.

—— *Pay Any Price: Lyndon Johnson and the Wars for Vietnam*. Chicago: Ivan R. Dee, 1995.

Geertz, Clifford. *The Interpretation of Cultures*. London: Fontana, 1993 [1973].

Gellner, Ernest. *Postmodernism, Reason and Religion*. London: Routledge, 1992.

—— *Conditions of Liberty: Civil Society and its Rivals*. Harmondsworth: Penguin, 1994.

Gilderhus, Mark T. 'Wilson, Carranza, and the Monroe Doctrine: A Question in Regional Organization', *Diplomatic History* 7, no. 2 (Spring 1983).

Gills, Barry, Joel Rocamora and Richard Wilson (eds). *Low Intensity Democracy: Political Power in the New World Order*. London: Pluto Press, 1993.

Gleason, Abbott. *Totalitarianism: The Inner History of the Cold War*. New York: Oxford University Press, 1995.

Gleijeses, Piero. *Shattered Hope: The Guatemalan Revolution and the United States, 1944–1954*. Princeton: Princeton University Press, 1991.

Goodfellow, William and James Morrell. 'From Contadora to Esquipulas to Sapoá and Beyond', in Walker (ed.), *Revolution and Counterrevolution*. Boulder: Westview Press, 1991.

Green, David. *The Containment of Latin America: A History of the Myths and Realities of the Good Neighbor Policy*. Chicago: Quadrangle Books, 1971.

Gress, David. *From Plato to NATO: The Idea of the West and Its Opponents*. New York: Free Press, 1998.

Grey, John. *Isaiah Berlin*. London: HarperCollins, 1995.

—— *False Dawn: The Delusions of Global Capitalism*. London: Granta, 1998.

Halliday, Fred. *Cold War, Third World: An Essay on Soviet–American Relations.* London: Hutchinson Radius, 1989.

—— *Rethinking International Relations.* Basingstoke: Macmillan, 1994.

Hamilton, Paula. 'The Knife Edge: Debates about Memory and History', in Kate Daren Smith and Paula Hamilton (eds), *Memory and History in Twentieth Century Australia.* Melbourne: Oxford University Press, 1994.

Harris, Nigel. *National Liberation.* London: Penguin, 1990.

Harshé, Rajen. *Twentieth Century Imperialism: Shifting Contours and Changing Conceptions.* New Delhi: Sage, 1997.

Hartz, Louis. *The Liberal Tradition in America: An Interpretation of American Political Thought since the Revolution.* New York: Harcourt, Brace and Co., 1955.

Healy, David. *US Expansionism: The Imperialist Urge in the 1890s.* Madison: University of Wisconsin Press, 1970.

Hegel, G. W., translated by T. M. Knox as *Hegel's Philosophy of Right*, London: Oxford University Press, 1967.

Held, David (ed.). *Prospects for Democracy: North, South, East, West.* Cambridge: Cambridge University Press, 1993.

Herring, George C. *America's Longest War: The United States and Vietnam, 1950–1975.* New York: McGraw-Hill, 1986.

Hitchens, Christopher. *Blood, Class, and Nostalgia: Anglo-American Ironies.* London: Chatto and Windus, 1990.

Hixon, Walter L. *George F. Kennan: Cold War Iconoclast.* New York: Columbia University Press, 1989.

Hobsbawm, Eric. *The Age of Revolution: Europe 1789–1848.* London: Weidenfeld & Nicolson, 1995 [1975].

—— *Nations and Nationalism since 1780: Programme, Myth, Reality.* Cambridge: Cambridge University Press, 1990.

—— *Age of Extremes: The Short Twentieth Century, 1914–1991.* London: Michael Joseph, 1994.

Hobsbawm, Eric and Terence Ranger (eds). *The Invention of Tradition.* Cambridge: Cambridge University Press, 1983.

Hoff, Joan. 'The American Century: From Sarajevo to Sarajevo', *Diplomatic History* 23, no. 2 (Spring 1999).

Hofstadter, Richard. *The American Political Tradition: And the Men Who Made It.* New York: Vintage Books, 1989.

Hogan, Michael J. 'The Search for a "Creative Peace": The United States, European Unity, and the Origins of the Marshall Plan', *Diplomatic History* 6, no. 3 (Summer 1982).

—— 'Revival and Reform: America's Twentieth-Century Search for a New Economic Order Abroad', *Diplomatic History* 8, no. 4 (Fall 1984).

—— *The Marshall Plan: America, Britain, and the Reconstruction of Western Europe, 1947–1952.* Cambridge: Cambridge University Press, 1987.

—— (ed.). *The End of the Cold War: Its Meaning and Implications.* Cambridge: Cambridge University Press, 1992.

—— *America in the World: The Historiography of American Foreign Relations since 1941.* Cambridge: Cambridge University Press, 1995.

Hogan, Michael J. and Thomas G. Paterson (eds). *Explaining the History of American Foreign Relations*. Cambridge: Cambridge University Press, 1991.

Holland, R. F. *European Decolonization 1918–1981: An Introductory Survey*. London: Macmillan, 1985.

Hoogvelt, Ankie. *Globalization and the Postcolonial World: The New Political Economy of Development*. London: Macmillan, 1997.

Hoover, Herbert. *The Ordeal of Woodrow Wilson*. New York: McGraw-Hill, 1958.

—— *American Individualism*. New York: Doubleday, 1922.

Hopkins, Terence K. and Immanuel Wallerstein. *The Age of Transition: Trajectory of the World-System 1945–2025*. London: Zed Books, 1996.

Hugh-Jones, E. M. *Woodrow Wilson and American Liberalism*. London: English Universities Press, 1947.

Hull, Cordell. *Memoirs of Cordell Hull*, vol 2. London: Hodder and Stoughton, 1948.

Hunt, Michael H. *Ideology and U.S. Foreign Policy*. New Haven: Yale University Press, 1987.

—— 'Traditions of American Diplomacy: From Colony to Great Power', in Gordon Martel (ed.), *American Foreign Relations Reconsidered*. London: Routledge, 1994.

—— 'East Asia in Henry Luce's "American Century"', *Diplomatic History* 23, no. 2 (Spring 1999).

Hunter, Allen (ed.). *Rethinking the Cold War*. Philadelphia: Temple University Press, 1998.

Huntington, Samuel P. 'Clash of Civilizations', in *Foreign Affairs* 72, no. 3 (Summer 1993).

—— *The Clash of Civilizations and the Remaking of World Order*. New York: Simon and Schuster, 1996.

Hutson, James H. 'Intellectual Foundations of Early American Diplomacy', *Diplomatic History* 1, no. 1 (Winter 1977).

Hutton, Patrick H. *History as an Art of Memory*. Hanover: University of Vermont, 1993.

Iggers, Georg G. *Historiography in the Twentieth Century: From Scientific Objectivity to the Postmodern Challenge*. Hanover: Wesleyan University Press, 1997.

Ignatieff, Michael. 'On Isaiah Berlin (1909–1997)', *The New York Review of Books* 44, no. 20 (18 December 1997).

—— *Isaiah Berlin: A Life*. London: Chatto and Windus, 1998.

Immerman, Richard H. *The CIA in Guatemala: The Foreign Policy of Intervention*. Austin: University of Texas Press, 1982.

Iriye, Akira. *Across the Pacific: An Inner History of American–East Asian Relations*. New York: Harcourt, 1967.

—— *The Globalization of America, 1913–1945*. Cambridge: Cambridge University Press, 1993.

Jameson, Fredric. *Postmodernism or the Cultural Logic of Late Capitalism*. London: Verso, 1991.

Jefferson, Thomas. *The Works of Thomas Jefferson*, vol. XI. Ed. Paul Leicester Ford. New York: G. P. Putnam's Sons, 1905.

—— *The Papers of Thomas Jefferson*. Ed. Julian Boyd. Princeton: Princeton University Press, 1950.

Jervis, Robert. 'America and the Twentieth Century: Continuity and Change', *Diplomatic History* 23, no. 2 (Spring 1999).

Judd, Denis. *Empire: The British Imperial Experience, from 1765 to the Present*. London: HarperCollins, 1996.

Judt, Tony. 'What Are American Interests?' *The New York Review of Books* 42, no. 15 (5 October 1995).

Kahler, Miles. *Decolonization in Britain and France: The Domestic Consequences of International Relations*. Princeton: Princeton University Press, 1984.

Kammen, Michael. *Mystic Chords of Memory: The Transformation of Tradition in American Culture*. New York: Vintage, 1991.

Kaplan, Amy and Donald E. Pease (eds). *Cultures of United States Imperialism*. Durham: Duke University Press, 1993.

Karnow, Stanley. *In Our Image: America's Empire in the Philippines*. London: Century. 1990.

Kaye, Harvey J. *"Why Do Ruling Classes Fear History?"*. London: Macmillan, 1996.

Kemp, Tom. *The Climax of Capitalism: The US Economy in the Twentieth Century*. London: Longman, 1990.

Kenen, Peter B. (ed.). *Managing the World Economy: Fifty Years after Bretton Woods*. Washington, D.C.: Institute for International Economics, 1994.

Kennan, George. 'The Sources of Soviet Conduct', *Foreign Affairs* 25 (July 1947).

Kennedy, Paul. *The Rise and Fall of Great Powers: Economic Change and Military Conflict from 1500 to 2000*. London: Fontana, 1989.

Kiernan, V. G. *Imperialism and its Contradictions*. New York: Routledge, 1995.

Kimball, Warren F. *The Juggler: Franklin Roosevelt as Wartime Statesman*. Princeton: Princeton University Press, 1991.

Klare, Michael. *Rogue States and Nuclear Outlaws: America's Search for a New Foreign Policy*. New York: Hill and Wang, 1995.

Klarén, Peter F. 'Lost Promise: Explaining Latin American Underdevelopment', in Peter F. Klarén and Thomas J. Bossert (eds), *Promise of Development: Theories of Change in Latin America*. Boulder: Westview Press, 1986.

Kofsky, Frank. *Harry S. Truman and the War Scare of 1948*. (New York: St. Martin's Press, 1993.

Koistinen, Paul A. C. *Mobilizing for Modern War: The Political Economy of American Warfare 1865–1919*. Lawrence: University Press of Kansas, 1997.

Kolko, Gabriel. *Main Currents in Modern American History*. New York: Harper and Row, 1976.

—— *Vietnam: Anatomy of War 1940–1975*. London: Unwin, 1985.

—— *Confronting the Third World: United States Foreign Policy 1945–1980*. New York: Pantheon, 1988.

—— *Century of War: Politics, Conflict, and Society since 1914*. New York: The New Press, 1994.

Kolko, Joyce and Gabriel Kolko. *The Limits of Power: The World and United States Foreign Policy, 1945–1954*. New York: Harper and Row, 1972.

—— 'American Capitalist Expansion', in Thomas G. Paterson and Robert J. McMahon (eds), *The Origins of the Cold War*. Lexington: D. C. Heath, 1991.

Kornbluh, Peter. *Nicaragua: The Price of Intervention*. Washington, D.C.: Institute for Policy Studies, 1987.

Kundera, Milan. *The Book of Laughter and Forgetting*. Harmondsworth: Penguin, 1983.

Kunz, Diane B. *Butter and Guns: America's Cold War Economic Diplomacy*. New York: The Free Press, 1997.

Lacey, Michael J. (ed.). *The Truman Presidency*. Cambridge: Cambridge University Press, 1989.

LaFeber, Walter. *The New Empire: An Interpretation of American Expansion 1860–1898*. Ithaca: Cornell University Press, 1963.

—— *John Quincy Adams and American Continental Empire: Letters, Papers and Speeches*. Chicago: Quadrangle Books, 1965.

—— 'The Evolution of the Monroe Doctrine from Monroe to Reagan', in Lloyd C. Gardner (ed.), *Redefining the Past: Essays in Diplomatic History in Honor of William Appleman Williams*. Corvallis: Oregon State University Press, 1986.

—— *The Panama Canal: The Crisis in Historical Perspective*. New York: Oxford University Press, 1989.

—— *America, Russia and the Cold War, 1945–1990*. New York: McGraw-Hill, 1991.

—— *The American Search for Opportunity, 1865–1913*. Cambridge: Cambridge University Press, 1993.

—— 'The Tension between Democracy and Capitalism during the American Century', *Diplomatic History* 23, no. 2 (Spring 1999).

Lake, Anthony. 'Confronting Backlash States', *Foreign Affairs* 73, no. 2 (March/April 1994).

Landau, Saul. *The Dangerous Doctrine: National Security and U.S. Foreign Policy*. Boulder: Westview Press, 1988.

Landes, David. *The Wealth and Poverty of Nations: Why Some Are So Rich and Some So Poor*. London: Little, Brown and Co., 1998.

Layne, Christopher, and Benjamin Schwarz. 'American Hegemony – Without an Enemy', *Foreign Policy* no. 92 (Fall 1993).

Leffler, Melvyn P. *A Preponderance of Power: National Security, the Truman Administration, and the Cold War*. Stanford: Stanford University Press, 1992.

—— *The Specter of Communism: The United States and the Origins of the Cold War, 1917–1953*. New York: Hill and Wang, 1994.

Leffler, Melvyn P. and David S. Painter (eds). *Origins of the Cold War: An International History*. London: Routledge, 1994.

LeGoff, Jacques. *History and Memory*. New York: Columbia University Press, 1992.

Levy, David W. *The Debate over Vietnam*. Baltimore: Johns Hopkins University Press, 1995.

Link, Arthur S. *Wilson the Diplomatist: A Look at his Major Foreign Policies*. Chicago: Quadrangle Books, 1957.

—— *The Diplomacy of World Power, the United States 1889–1920*. London: Edward Arnold, 1970.

Lippmann, Walter. *U.S. War Aims*. London: Hamish Hamilton, 1944.

—— *The Cold War: A Study in US Foreign Policy*. New York: Harper and Row, 1947, 1972.

Lipset, Seymour Martin. *American Exceptionalism: A Double-Edged Sword*. New York: W. W. Norton, 1996.

Liss, Sheldon B. *Radical Thought in Central America*. Boulder: Westview Press, 1991.

Louise, Wm Roger and Hedley Bull (eds). *The 'Special Relationship': Anglo-American Relations since 1945*. Oxford: Clarendon Press, 1986.

Luce, Henry R. 'The American Century', *Life* (17 February 1941).

Lundestad, Geir. *"Empire" by Integration: The United States and European Integration, 1945–1997*. Oxford: Oxford University Press, 1998.

—— '"Empire by Invitation" in the American Century', *Diplomatic History* 23, no. 2 (Spring 1999).

McCormick, James. *American Foreign Policy and Process*. Itasca: Peacock Publishers, 1992.

McCormick, Thomas J. '"Every System Needs a Center Sometimes": An Essay on Hegemony and Modern American Foreign Policy', in Lloyd C. Gardner (ed.), *Redefining the Past: Essays in Diplomatic History in Honor of William Appleman Williams*. Corvallis: Oregon State University Press, 1986.

—— *America's Half-Century: United States Foreign Policy in the Cold War*. Baltimore: Johns Hopkins University Press, 1989

McClelland, J. S. *A History of Western Political Thought*. London: Routledge, 1996.

McKitrick, Eric L. 'Did Jefferson Blunder?' *New York Review of Books* 37, no. 19 (6 December 1990).

McNall Burns, Edward. *Ideas in Conflict: The Political Theories of The Contemporary World*. London: Methuen, 1960.

McNamara, Robert S. *In Retrospect: The Tragedy and Lessons of Vietnam*. New York: Times Books, 1995.

McNeill, William. *A World History*. New York: Oxford University Press, 1967.

—— 'The Changing Shape of World History', *History and Theory*, Theme Issue 34, 1995.

—— 'What We Mean by the West', *Orbis* 41, no. 4 (Fall 1997).

Madison, James. *The Writings of James Madison*. Ed. Gaillard Hunt. vol. 9, *1819–1836*. New York: G. P. Putnam's Sons, 1910.

—— *The Mind of the Founder: Sources of the Political Thought*. Ed. Marvin Meyers. Hanover: Brandeis University Press, 1981.

Madison, James, Alexander Hamilton and John Jay. *The Federalist Papers*. Ed. Isaac Kramnick. Harmondsworth: Penguin, 1987 [1788], pp. 124–128.

Magdoff, Harry. *Imperialism: From the Colonial Age to the Present*. New York: Monthly Review Press, 1978.

Magyar, Karl. 'Classifying the International Political Economy: A Third World Proto-Theory', *Third World Quarterly* 16, no. 4 (1995).

Marcuse, Herbert. *One Dimensional Man: Studies in the Ideology of Advanced Industrial Society*. London: Routledge, 1994 [1964].

Martel, Gordon. *American Foreign Relations Reconsidered, 1890–1993*. London: Routledge, 1994.

May, Ernest R. *Imperial Democracy: The Emergence of America as a Great Power.* New York: Harper and Row, 1961.

—— *American Cold War Strategy: Interpreting NSC 68.* Boston: Bedford Books, 1993.

Mazlish, Bruce and Ralph Buultjens (eds). *Conceptualizing Global History.* Boulder: Westview Press, 1993.

Melanson, Richard A. *Reconstructing Consensus: American Foreign Policy since the Vietnam War.* New York: St. Martin's Press, 1991.

Melrose, Diana. *Nicaragua: The Threat of a Good Example?.* Oxford: Oxfam, 1985.

Melzer, Arthur M. *et al.* (eds). *History and the Idea of Progress.* Ithaca: Cornell University Press, 1995.

Merk, Frederick. *The Monroe Doctrine and American Expansion.* New York: Vintage, 1966.

Miller, David (ed.), *Liberty.* Oxford: Oxford University Press, 1991.

Miller, Nicola. *Soviet Relations with Latin America, 1959–1987.* Cambridge: Cambridge University Press, 1989.

Milward, Alan S. *The Reconstruction of Western Europe, 1945–1951.* London: Methuen, 1984.

—— 'Was the Marshall Plan Really Necessary?' *Diplomatic History* 13, no. 2 (Spring 1989).

—— *The European Rescue of the Nation-State.* London: Routledge, 1992.

Munslow, Alun. *Deconstructing History.* London: Routledge, 1997.

Nandy, Ashis. 'History's Forgotten Doubles', *History and Theory*, Theme Issue 34, 1995.

Nerval, Gaston. *Autopsy of the Monroe Doctrine: The Strange Story of Inter-American Relations.* New York: Macmillan, 1934.

Ngugi Wa Thiong'O. *Moving the Centre: The Struggle for Cultural Freedoms.* London: James Currey, 1993.

Niebuhr, Reinhold. *The Irony of American History.* New York: Charles Scribner's Sons, 1952.

Ninkovich, Frank A. *The Diplomacy of Ideas: U.S. Foreign Policy and Cultural Relations, 1938–1950.* Cambridge: Cambridge University Press, 1981.

—— 'Theodore Roosevelt: Civilization as Ideology', *Diplomatic History* 10, no. 3 (Summer 1986).

Nitze, Paul H. 'Grand Strategy Then and Now: NSC 68 and its Lessons for the Future,' *Strategic Review* 22, no. 1 (Winter 1994).

Novik, Peter. *That Noble Dream: The 'Objectivity Question' and the American Historical Profession.* Cambridge: Cambridge University Press, 1988.

O'Brien, Conor Cruise. *The Long Affair: Thomas Jefferson and the French Revolution, 1785.* London: Pimlico, 1998.

O'Donnell, Guillermo, Philippe C. Schmitter and Laurence Whitehead. *Transitions from Authoritarian Rule: Latin America.* Baltimore: Johns Hopkins University Press, 1986.

Okri, Ben. *A Way of Being Free.* London: Pheonix, 1998.

Osterhammel, Jürgen. *Colonialism: A Theoretical Overview.* Princeton: Markus Wiener, 1997.

Pagden, Anthony. *Lords of All the World: Ideologies of Empire in Spain, Britain and France c.1500–c.1800*. New Haven: Yale University Press, 1995.

Paine, Phil. 'Democracy's Place in World History', *Journal of World History* 4, no. 1 (Spring 1993).

Paine, Thomas. *Common Sense*. Harmondsworth: Penguin, 1986 [1776].

Painter, David S. 'Explaining U.S. Relations with the Third World', *Diplomatic History* 19, no. 3 (Summer 1995).

Park, James William. *Latin American Underdevelopment: A History of Perspectives in the United States 1870–1965*. Baton Rouge: Louisiana State University Press, 1995.

Paterson, Thomas G. *On Every Front: The Making and Unmaking of the Cold War*, rev. edn. New York: W. W. Norton, 1992, p. 106.

Paterson, Thomas G. and J. Garry Clifford. *America Ascendant: U.S. Foreign Relations since 1939*. Lexington: D.C. Heath, 1995.

Paterson, Thomas G. and Dennis Merrill (eds). *Major Problems in American Foreign Relations to 1920*, vol. I. Lexington: D. C. Heath, 1995.

Perez, Louis A. '1898 and Beyond: Historiographical Variations on War and Empire', *Pacific Historical Review* 65, no. 2 (May 1996).

Perkins, Bradford. *The Great Rapprochement: England and the United States 1895–1914* London: Victor Gollancz, 1969.

—— *The Creation of a Republican Empire, 1776–1865*. Cambridge: Cambridge University Press, 1993.

Perkins, Dexter. *The Monroe Doctrine, 1823–1826*. Cambridge, Mass.: Harvard University Press, 1927.

—— *Hands Off: A History of the Monroe Doctrine*. Boston: Little, Brown and Co., 1946.

Peterson, Merrill D. *The Jefferson Image in the American Mind*. New York: Oxford University Press, 1962.

—— *Lincoln in American Memory*. Oxford: Oxford University Press, 1994.

Pfaff, William. *The Wrath of Nations: Civilization and the Furies of Nationalism*. New York: Touchstone, 1993.

Phillips, Kevin. *The Politics of Rich and Poor: Wealth and the American Electorate in the Reagan Aftermath*. New York: Harper Perennial, 1990.

Reagan, Ronald. *Speaking My Mind*. London: Hutchinson, 1989.

Ricard, Serge. 'The Exceptionalist Syndrome in U.S. Continental and Overseas Expansionism', in David K. Adams and Cornelis A. van Minnen (eds), *Reflections on American Exceptionalism*. Keele: Keele University Press, 1994.

Robinson, William I. *A Faustian Bargain: U.S. Intervention in the Nicaraguan Elections and American Foreign Policy in the Post-Cold War Era*. Boulder: Westview Press, 1992.

—— 'Nicaragua and the World: A Globalization Perspective', in Thomas W. Walker (ed.), *Nicaragua Without Illusions: Regime Transition and Structural Adjustment in the 1990s*. Wilmington: Scholarly Resources, 1997.

Roosevelt, Franklin D. *Public Papers and Addresses*. Ed. Samuel I. Rosenman. New York: Russell and Russell, [1941].

Roosevelt, Theodore. *American Ideals: The Strenuous Life, Realizable Ideals*. New York: Charles Scribner's Sons, 1926.

—— *The Letters of Theodore Roosevelt*. Ed. Elting E. Morison. Cambridge, Mass.: Harvard University Press, 1951.

—— *The Writings of Theodore Roosevelt*. Ed. William H. Harbaugh. Indianapolis: Bobbs Merrill, 1967.

Rosenberg, Emily S. *Spreading the American Dream: American Economic and Cultural Expansion 1890-1945*. New York: Hill and Wang, 1982.

—— 'Revisiting Dollar Diplomacy: Narratives of Money and Manliness', *Diplomatic History* 22, no. 2 (Spring 1998).

Rostow, W. W. *The Stages of Economic Growth: A Non-Communist Manifesto*. Cambridge: Cambridge University Press, 1960, second edition 1971.

Roxborough, Ian. *Theories of Underdevelopment*. London: Macmillan, 1979.

Rubenstein, Richard E. and Jarle Crocker, 'Challenging Huntington', *Foreign Policy* 96 (1994).

Ryan, Alan (ed.). *After the End of History*. London: Collins and Brown, 1992.

Ryan, David. *US–Sandinista Diplomatic Relations: Voice of Intolerance*. London: Macmillan, 1995.

—— 'Asserting US Power', in Philip Davies (ed.), *An American Quarter Century: Vietnam to Clinton*. Manchester: Manchester University Press, 1995.

—— 'U.S. Ideology and Central American Revolutions in the Cold War', in Will Fowler (ed.), *Ideologues and Ideologies in Latin America*. Westport: Greenwood Press, 1997.

—— 'Colonialism and Hegemony in Latin America', *The International History Review* 21, no. 2 (June 1999).

Ryan, David and Victor Pungong (eds). *The United States and Decolonization: Power and Freedom*. London: Macmillan, 2000.

Said, Edward W. *Culture and Imperialism*. London: Chatto and Windus, 1993.

—— *The Politics of Dispossession: The Struggle for Palestinian Self-Determination 1969–1994*. London: Chatto and Windus, 1994.

—— *Orientalism: Western Conceptions of the Orient*. Harmondsworth: Penguin, 1995.

Sandle, Mark. *A Short History of Soviet Socialism*. London: UCL, 1998.

Santis, Hugh De. *Beyond Progress: An Interpretive Odyssey to the Future*. Chicago: University of Chicago Press, 1996.

Schlesinger, Arthur M. *Cycles of American History*. Harmondsworth: Penguin, 1986.

—— *The Imperial Presidency*. New York: Houghton, 1992.

Schoultz, Lars. *National Security and United States Policy toward Latin America*. Princeton: Princeton University Press, 1987.

—— *Beneath the United States: A History of U.S. Policy toward Latin America*. Cambridge, Mass.: Harvard University Press, 1998.

Schurz, Carl. *Speeches, Correspondence and Political Papers*. Ed. Frederick Bancroft. New York: Negro University Press, 1969.

Schwarz, Benjamin. 'Why America Thinks It Has to Run the World', *Atlantic Monthly*. (June 1996).

Shannon, Thomas R. *An Introduction to the World-System Perspective*. Boulder: Westview Press, 1996.

Sherry, Michael S. *In the Shadow of War: The United States since the 1930s*. New Haven: Yale University Press, 1995.

Sklair, Leslie (ed.). *Capitalism and Development*. London: Routledge, 1994.

Smith, Gaddis. *The Last Years of the Monroe Doctrine, 1945–1993*. New York: Hill and Wang, 1994.

Smith, Tony. *America's Mission: The United States and the Worldwide Struggle for Democracy in the Twentieth Century*. Princeton: Princeton University Press, 1994.

—— 'Making the World Safe for Democracy in the American Century', *Diplomatic History* 23, no. 2 (Spring 1999).

Smith, Wayne S. *The Russians Aren't Coming: New Soviet Policy in Latin America*. Boulder: Lynne Reinner, 1992.

Sofka, James R. 'The Jeffersonian Idea of National Security: Commerce, the Atlantic Balance of Power, and the Barbary War, 1786–1805', *Diplomatic History* 21, no. 4 (Fall 1997).

Spybey, Tony. *Social Change, Development and Dependency: Modernity, Colonialism and the Development of the West*. Cambridge: Polity Press, 1992.

Steel, Ronald. *Temptations of a Superpower*. Cambridge, Mass.: Harvard University Press, 1995.

Stephanson, Anders. *Kennan and the Art of Foreign Policy*. Cambridge, Mass.: Harvard University Press, 1989.

—— *Manifest Destiny: American Expansionism and the Empire of Right*. New York: Hill and Wang, 1995.

Stern, Steve J. 'Feudalism, Capitalism, and the World System in the Perspective of Latin America and the Caribbean,' *American Historical Review* 93 (October 1988).

Strauss, Leo and Joseph Cropsey (eds). *History of Political Philosophy*. Chicago: University of Chicago Press, 1963.

Thelen, David. 'Introduction', *The Journal of American History* no. 4 (March 1989).

Tillapaugh, J. 'Closed Hemisphere and Open World? The Dispute Over Regional Security at the U.N. Conference, 1945', *Diplomatic History* 2, no. 1 (Winter 1978).

Turner, Frederick Jackson. *The Frontier in American History*. New York: Holt, Rinehart and Winston, 1920.

Varg, Paul A. *Foreign Policies of the Founding Fathers*. Baltimore: Penguin, 1970.

Walker, Martin. *The Cold War*. London: Fourth Estate, 1993.

Walker, Thomas W. (ed.). *Reagan versus the Sandinistas: The Undeclared War on Nicaragua*. Boulder: Westview Press, 1987.

—— *Revolution and Counterrevolution in Nicaragua*. Boulder: Westview Press, 1991.

Wallerstein, Immanuel. *Geopolitics and Geoculture: Essays on the Changing World-System*. Cambridge: Cambridge University Press, 1991.

—— *After Liberalism*. New York: The New Press, 1995.

—— *Historical Capitalism with Capitalist Civilization*. London: Verso, 1996.

Watson, Adam. *The Limits of Independence: Relations between States in the Modern World*. London: Routledge, 1997.

Webster, C. K. *Britain and the Independence of Latin America, 1812–1830: Select Documents from the Foreign Office Archives*, vol. II. New York: Octagon, 1970.

245

Weeks, William Earl. 'John Quincy Adams's "Great Gun" and the Rhetoric of American Empire', *Diplomatic History* 14, no. 1 (Winter 1990).

—— 'New Directions in the Study of Early American Foreign Relations', *Diplomatic History* 17, no. 1 (Winter 1993).

Welles, Sumner. *The World of the Four Freedoms*. London: Hutchinson, n.d.

—— *The Time for Decision*. London: Hamish Hamilton, 1944.

—— *Where Are We Heading?*. London: Hamish Hamilton, 1947.

Westwood, J. N. *Endurance and Endeavour: Russian History, 1812–1986*. Oxford: Oxford University Press, 1987.

White, Donald W. 'The "American Century" in World History', *Journal of World History* 3, no. 1 (1992).

White, Graham and John Maze. *Henry A. Wallace: His Search for a New World Order*. Chapel Hill: University of North Carolina Press, 1995.

Williams, William Appleman. *The Tragedy of American Diplomacy*. New York: Delta, 1959.

—— *Empire as a Way of Life: An Essay on the Causes and Character of America's Present Predicament along with a Few Thoughts about an Alternative*. New York: Oxford University Press, 1980.

Williams, William Appleman, Thomas McCormick, Lloyd Gardner and Walter LaFeber (eds). *America in Vietnam: A Documentary History*. New York: W. W. Norton, 1989.

Wills, Garry. *Lincoln at Gettysberg: The Words that Remade America*. New York: Touchstone, 1992.

Wilson, Woodrow. *The New Freedom: A Call for the Emancipation of the Generous Energies of a People*. Englewood Cliffs: Prentice Hall, 1961 [1913].

—— *Why We Are at War: Messages to the Congress and the American People*. New York: Harper and Brothers, 1917.

—— *The Messages and Papers of Woodrow Wilson*. New York: The Review of Reviews Corporation, 1924.

Wood, Gordon S. 'Americans and Revolutionaries', *The New York Review of Books* 37, no. 14 (27 September 1990).

—— 'Inventing American Capitalism', *The New York Review of Books* 41, no. 11 (9 June 1994).

—— 'Disturbing the Peace', *The New York Review of Books* 42, no. 10 (8 June 1995).

Woodward, Bob. *Veil: The Secret Wars of the CIA 1981–1987*. New York: Pocket Books, 1987.

Yates, Frances A. *The Art of Memory*. London: Pimlico, 1966.

Yergin, Daniel. *The Prize: The Epic Quest for Oil, Money and Power*. London: Simon and Schuster, 1991.

Young, James P. *Reconsidering American Liberalism: The Troubled Odyssey of the Liberal Idea*. Boulder: Westview Press, 1996.

Zinn, Howard. *A People's History of the United States*. London: Longman, 1980.

INDEX

DATE DUE

			Printed in USA

HIGHSMITH #45230